Searching for Subversives

Searching for Subversives

The Story of Italian Internment in Wartime America

Mary Elizabeth Basile Chopas

The University of North Carolina Press CHAPEL HILL

This book was published with the assistance of the H. Eugene and Lillian Lehman Fund of The University of North Carolina Press. A complete list of books published in the Lehman Series appears at the end of the book.

Set in Espinosa Nova by Westchester Publishing Services
Manufactured in the United States of America

The University of North Carolina Press has been a member of the
Green Press Initiative since 2003.

Library of Congress Cataloging-in-Publication Data
Names: Chopas, Mary Elizabeth Basile, author.
Title: Searching for subversives : the story of Italian internment in wartime America / Mary Elizabeth Basile Chopas.
Description: Chapel Hill : University of North Carolina Press, [2017] | Includes bibliographical references and index.
Identifiers: LCCN 2017013167 | ISBN 9781469634333 (cloth : alk. paper) | ISBN 9781469634340 (pbk : alk. paper) | ISBN 9781469634357 (ebook)
Subjects: LCSH: Italian Americans—Evacuation and relocation, 1942. | Immigrants—Government policy—United States. | Italians—Government policy—United States. | Italians—Legal status, laws, etc.—United States—History—1933–1945. | Concentration camps—United States. | World War, 1939–1945—Concentration camps—United States. | World War, 1939–1945—Italian Americans.
Classification: LCC D769.8.F7 I825 2017 | DDC 940.53/177308951—dc23
LC record available at https://lccn.loc.gov/2017013167

Cover illustration: Italian flag © istockphoto.com/powerofforever.
Stone wall © istockphoto.com.

For my parents, with love and respect.
And for my husband, Jim, with devotion.

Contents

Illustrations

Acknowledgments

The seed for this project was planted many years ago when, as a little girl, I used to hear my grandfather Joseph Carroccia tell stories about life in America as an Italian immigrant. In the 1930s, he made frequent trips back and forth between Italy and the United States, where he worked to raise enough money to build a home and arrange for the transatlantic passage of his wife and young children, including my mother. When World War II started, my grandparents had been settled permanently in Farmington, Connecticut, for a number of years and were raising a family. Since they were aliens, they were subject to nighttime visits by government officials searching for contraband items. My mother described these dreadful incidents to me on several occasions so that I might appreciate our family's history.

Many years later, when researching another project at the Harvard Law School Library, I fortuitously came across the alien enemy hearing board files of Erwin Griswold, who had served on Boston's board. I would later discover that Griswold's board records provided the sharpest lens into the process of selective internment, which would become the basis for my exploration of this topic. This finding triggered memories of my own family's stories about their wartime experiences and piqued my interest to find out more. When I moved to Chapel Hill in 2007 and began teaching at UNC Law School, I had the good fortune of working with Eric Muller who generously shared with me resources relevant to Italian internment that he had come across in his scholarship on the Japanese American internment. He encouraged me to pursue this little-researched topic and offered the most valuable guidance to me from early drafts through the finish of this project.

In the initial stage, my research assistants Lee Turbyfill and Caitlin Carson conducted invaluable legal research for me. When I had the opportunity to turn this topic conceived from a legal perspective into a broader historical project, I benefited greatly from the expert military history knowledge of Wayne Lee and Richard Kohn, who commented on multiple drafts, as well as the suggestions of Zaragosa Vargas regarding research in ethnic history, and the thoughts of Heather Williams on the social history chapter. Kathleen DuVal gave me constructive feedback on my presentation of the social profile of internees. With the help of Peter Feaver, I was able to construct an Afterword that tied the questions I asked as a historian to current issues of national security. At various stages of developing the manuscript, I received comments and suggestions from a wide circle of scholars. I would like to thank participants in the Triangle Legal History Seminar; the Triangle Institute for Security Studies New Faces Conference; the Research Triangle Seminar Series on the History of the Military, War, and Society; and the Legal History Roundtable at Boston College Law School for their contributions. In particular, I appreciate my friends and colleagues Al Brophy and Nora Doyle who inspired me with their scholarship and never tired of engaging in conversations with me about mine. In the final stage of revisions, Gary Mormino's insightful comments improved my depiction of Italian Americans and presentation of key events. At UNC Press, I am grateful to Chuck Grench for his support of this project throughout revisions and the production of the manuscript and to Rich Hendel for the cover illustration. I would also like to thank Stacey Byrd at the UNC Kathrine R. Everett Law Library for tracking down endless books for me, and Ashley Arthur for assisting me with formatting several versions of the manuscript.

During the entire course of this project, I consulted with many archivists who led me to the original sources that are the foundation of this book. Several deserve special recognition. I am indebted to Marian Smith of the Historical Research Branch of the U.S. Citizenship & Immigration Services for providing me with crucial materials and for patiently and cheerfully explaining some technical immigration issues to me. At the Harvard Law School Library's Historical & Special Collections, I am grateful to David Warrington, Lesley Schoenfeld, and Edwin Moloy for generously providing me access to Erwin Griswold's Papers and answering my inquiries. Elizabeth Gray at the National Archives at College Park helped me navigate the Italian internee files and numerous other government files during my visits there. Nicole Webb at the Historical Museum at Fort Missoula provided me with a collection of photographs from which illustrations in this book were chosen. Kendra Lightner at the FDR Presidential Library assisted me in locating some great nuggets of sources from the Roosevelt administration. Finally, when filling in gaps in citations to government documents, I relied upon Renée Bosman at UNC's Davis Library who brought to my attention sources that significantly improved my presentation of comparative population data.

Without the love and support of my family, this book would not have been possible. My most wonderful parents, Joseph and Angela Basile, who have nurtured my love of learning from a very young age, have provided me with constant support in this endeavor. I appreciate my brothers Joe and John, and especially thank Joe for enthusiastically assisting me by photographing Sand Island, Hawaii. My two sweet angels, Maria and Sophia, who have put up with Mommy's many "vacations" to the archives, have given me the best kind of distractions along the way. Finally, my greatest debt is to my loving husband, Jim Chopas, who has been a partner to me in every sense, from debating issues and helping me analyze statistical data to providing me with humor to keep my spirits strong through the finish of this marathon.

A Note on Terminology and the Subject Group

The terminology for referring to the subjects of this book follows legal definitions and usage in government documents. The designation "aliens" refers to Italians residing in the United States or brought to the United States from Latin America who had not obtained citizenship. Once the United States declared war against Italy, the aliens became, in the government's eyes, "alien enemies" or "enemy aliens," terms of legal status that I use interchangeably.[1] I refer to Italians who were born in Italy and obtained their citizenship in the United States as "naturalized" American citizens. To become a naturalized citizen, an Italian national, as was and is the case with any alien, would have to take an oath of allegiance and renunciation, effectively renouncing his or her former allegiance.[2] The term "Italian Americans" refers to American citizens of Italian descent, inclusive of naturalized citizens and citizens by birth. Reference to "Italians" means individuals of Italian descent, regardless of citizenship status.

In the early 1940s, Italians comprised approximately 14 percent of all foreign-born individuals in the United States.[3] In accordance with the Alien Registration Act of 1940, all aliens fourteen and older were required to register at a U.S. post office and carry identification cards indicating their status.[4] Delays in the processing of citizenship applications were a factor contributing to the large number of Italian aliens, approximately 700,000, at the start of World War II.[5] According to information collected by the National Council on Naturalization and Citizenship's Committee on Administration in December 1941, aliens who submitted applications for their second papers (Form N-400) had to wait fifteen to eighteen months in the New York and Boston districts and about a year in other districts before being called to file their petitions for citizenship. The average waiting time should have been about three months. Extraordinary delays also occurred between the first and final hearings.[6]

This study focuses on 343 men and women who were subjected to "selective internment" for varying lengths of time.[7] These "Italian civilian internees," as I refer to them throughout the book, came from three groups. The first are Italian aliens who had resided in the United States before the outbreak of World War II and who were apprehended in the United States based on reports of the Federal Bureau of Investigation (FBI) identifying them as suspect. These individuals were immediately detained and subsequently interned after a hearing. In the second group are a few naturalized citizens categorized as enemy aliens who experienced the same series of events despite being American citizens. The third group consists of forty-six Italian nationals who had resided in Latin America, were apprehended there, and were brought to internment camps in the United States pursuant to an agreement between the U.S. State Department and Latin American countries.[8] Excluded from the study are the approximately 1,300 merchant sailors from luxury liners in the Panama Canal and American ports suspected of sabotaging their ships, most of whom were interned beginning in March 1941 at Fort Missoula, Montana, and held through the end of the war.[9] Italian nationals who had worked at the 1939–1940 World's Fair in New York and were interned at Fort Missoula in spring 1941 are also excluded from the study.[10] Although these latter groups were interned with some of the subjects of the study beginning in December 1941, their legal status was substantially different.

I determined the subject group of 343 persons by reviewing the Provost Marshal General's files of Italian internees, identifying long-time residents of the United States and Latin Americans.[11] I then checked the list of Italian aliens who satisfied my criteria against U.S. Army camp lists, some of which indicated each internee's occupation, allowing me to verify that the subjects were not seamen or World's Fair employees.[12] Reference to Alien Registration forms filed pursuant to the 1940 Alien Registration Act confirmed the nationality and occupations of many of the subjects.[13] Demographic information on the internees and data that I compiled concerning the subjects' internment can be found in the appendices.

Introduction

> As to differentiating between different nationalities . . . there is a
> difference; that many of our old Italian people who came here
> years ago and who worked and raised families, and who have been
> law-abiding citizens, have very little, if any, respect for their native
> land and which would in no way interfere with their loyalty.
> Moreover, conditions in European countries are such that many
> Italian people here today feel that the only solution for their
> problem over there is for the United States to win this war.
> These people, naturally, are going to be loyal to us. Locally, a very
> great percent of our young men who are joining the Army are of
> Italian parentage, and before any action should be taken to move
> their parents away from their homes, I believe we should consider
> seriously the result that that may have upon them as soldiers.
>
> —JOHN P. FITZGERALD, District Attorney of Santa Clara County,
>   to Hon. Earl Warren, Attorney General, California, February 19,
>   1942

During World War II the U.S. government categorized persons within the United States from belligerent nations based on citizenship and race, making assumptions about their loyalty and the national security risk they presented. This study examines how federal agencies interacted to create and implement restrictions on nearly 700,000 Italian aliens residing in the United States, including internment for certain individuals, and how and why those policies changed during the course of the war. Federal decision-makers beginning in 1941 created policies of ethnic-based criteria in response to national security fears, resulting in the selective internment of Japanese, German, and Italian aliens identified as dangerous, and later the exclusion, removal, and detention of approximately 120,000 persons of Japanese descent, mostly American citizens, in camps.[1]

The U.S. government's evolving calculation of the danger posed by Italian nationals on American soil was strongly shaped by American policymakers' beliefs that Italy's military forces were not as formidable as those of either Germany or Japan. Regarding the safety of American shores, Italy posed no threat in comparison with Germany, whose submarines patrolled the Atlantic coast, and of course Japan, which had already attacked Pearl Harbor.[2] It appears that President Franklin Roosevelt allowed these notable differences in the strength of the three Axis powers to influence his views on how to handle enemy aliens in the United States. In discussing internment with Attorney General Francis Biddle, the president expressed his lack of concern about Italians, saying, "I don't care so much about the Italians. . . . They are a lot of opera singers, but the Germans are different, they may be dangerous."[3] Secretary of State Cordell Hull shared Roosevelt's view that a distinction should be drawn between the Italians on the one hand and the Germans and Japanese on the other. This distinction not only recognized Americans' history of friendship with the Italians, but was also part of the administration's strategic plan to bring about an earlier withdrawal of Italy from the war, which in turn might hasten the surrender of Germany and Japan.[4]

The perception of Italians as the least threatening and potentially most loyal of the alien enemy groups pervaded policy decisions at all levels of the administrative state, from decisions regarding internment of a much smaller number of Italian aliens to their earlier elimination from alien enemy status in October 1942. The significant representation of Italian Americans in the U.S. armed forces cannot be underestimated in strengthening this perception.[5]

This is a comprehensive study of the government's treatment of Italians during World War II, but comparisons with the numbers of Japanese and Germans affected by wartime policies and to statements of government officials referring specifically to those groups provide context for evaluating the policies and legal processes applied to Italians. We may have a better understanding of where Italians fit on the spectrum of experiences of the three enemy alien groups through the following comparative information on selective internment. According to the official historian for the FBI, during World War II, 3,567 Italian aliens were arrested, of which 367 were interned. Of 7,043 German aliens arrested, 1,225 were interned, and 1,532 Japanese aliens were selectively interned from a total of 5,428 arrested.[6] When comparing the respective percentages of each alien population represented by the number of internees, we realize how the government conceived the level of security threat from each group. On a proportional basis, there were eight times as many Germans as Italians selectively interned, and sixty-four times more Japanese selectively interned than Italians.[7]

Another critical component of American policy calculation was the British example. Widely perceived outside of Great Britain as a mistake, that country hastily interned at least 74,000 aliens, mostly German and Austrian Jews. Taking his cue from that lesson, Biddle strongly opposed mass internment and may have influenced Roosevelt to use selective internment for Italians and Germans.[8] With regard to Japanese and Japanese Americans, however, Roosevelt deferred to the War Department who supported the proposal of West Coast military officials for "mass internment," the terms most commonly attached to their wartime experience, overriding Biddle's opposition to the plan.[9]

Discussions about the restrictions placed upon enemy aliens during World War II center on infringement of their civil liberties as opposed to constitutional rights.[10] To date, no organized effort among Italian Americans has sought reparations for the violations of civil liberties suffered by members of their ethnic community. In fact, most Italian internees felt shame over having been considered enemies of the state, and they treated their experiences as private matters. In 1995, however, Italian Americans made efforts to raise the awareness of legislators, such as Alfonse D'Amato, former U.S. senator from New York, of the hardships faced by many Italian families during the war.[11] In 2000, Congress enacted the Wartime Violation of Italian American Civil Liberties Act, which acknowledged that the government restricted the freedom of Italian-born immigrants and their families in the United States, resulting in numerous violations of civil liberties.[12] Congress estimated that, in addition to the internment of hundreds of individuals in internment camps in the months following U.S. entry into World War II, the military evacuated more than 10,000 Italians living in coastal areas on the West Coast, placed travel restrictions, made arrests, issued curfews, and confiscated property.[13] The process of "individual exclusion" affected a smaller number of Italian aliens and naturalized citizens.[14] Under this policy, at least fifty-nine persons of Italian ancestry nationally appeared before an individual exclusion board, and most of them were ordered to move from designated areas for reasons of individual suspicion, perhaps for being a community leader, or because of the sensitivity of the area where they resided.[15] Congress concluded that the "impact of the wartime experience was devastating to Italian American communities in the United States, and its effects are still being felt."[16] However, it was not until 2001, after the Justice Department conducted investigations pursuant to the Wartime Violation of Italian American Civil Liberties Act and produced a report on its findings, that a more complete picture of the restrictions and resulting violations of civil liberties became known.[17]

Many scholars have explored the process, legal underpinnings, and consequences of the mass internment of persons of Japanese descent.[18] This book discusses the much less understood process of selective internment that had different legal structures as well as different consequences for ethnic communities and individuals. At the highest level, it traces interactions and conflicts among governmental leaders and agencies in the process of constructing policies for enemy aliens. This in-depth legal analysis of the selective internment process incorporating case files from the National Archives uncovers many layers of political repression not revealed in scholarship about the home front during World War II, namely presumptive guilt in the initial arrest, internment based on one's membership in social and political associations and expression of political ideas, and ultimately bars to citizenship.[19] The alien enemy hearing process functioned in a way that defined concepts of loyalty and allegiance to the United States and the potential for being a good American citizen.[20] This project shows the interplay among the War Department, the Department of Justice, politicians on the national, state, and local levels, hearing board members in the districts, and internees in shaping an imperfect process for determining who was loyal and who was not.

Scholarship specifically on the internment of Italians is relatively rare. During the war, the government deliberately kept information from the public concerning the various restrictions imposed on Italians.[21] The American media conveyed confusing information to the public about who the Italian internees were, alternately referring to them as prisoners of war and internees.[22] Before the declassification of internee files in the Provost Marshal General records at the National Archives in 1987, historians had to rely upon interviews of individuals who could recollect their wartime experiences, piecing together the story of the short-term and long-term effects of the restrictions on this ethnic population.

Stephen Fox is one of the earliest scholars to relate the experiences of Italians.[23] Drawing on government documents, newspapers, and interviews with surviving internees and their family members in central and northern California, Fox concludes that economics, politics, and concerns about morale drove U.S. policy with respect to enemy aliens, "with race as a reinforcing factor."[24] He suggests that the overriding explanation for why the millions of Italians and Germans living in the United States avoided mass evacuation and relocation was that their numbers, as well as the fact that they were scattered across the country, made it impractical; not only were they necessary to civilian production jobs, but relocating them would have presented logistical problems. He also recognizes the European enemy aliens' assimilation into American society as a benefit.[25] This project corroborates Fox's assessments that are supported by the government documents but presents a contrasting government rationale for the selective internment of Italians from what Fox has shown with respect to Germans. In his several studies specifically on the German experience in the United States during World War II, Fox concludes that the government believed selective internment was necessary to pacify the German American population, whose integrity and loyalty the American public still doubted, even though many years had passed since World War I.[26] The results of my study reveal a governmental fear that a relatively few Italian community leaders, such as those working in the media, could have influenced their fellow countrymen, a largely loyal and peaceful population. My methodological approach to the material also differs. Fox structures his book on Italians during World War II around personal stories reflecting the experience of Italians on the West Coast gathered from many oral histories, which he took during the mid to late 1980s, mainly concerning relocation, and he relies predominantly on sources for the Western Defense Command for his conclusions about the government's motives. This project builds upon Fox's work by taking a more comprehensive national perspective in tracing the decision-making process among the branches of government and focuses on a legal analysis of the wartime restrictions on the Italian population, particularly the process of selective internment.

Other scholars portraying the situation of Italians during World War II have emphasized racial prejudice as a motivation for government policies regarding Italians and have drawn likenesses to the treatment of persons of Japanese descent during the war, discounting theories of racial prejudice exclusively against this latter group. Lawrence DiStasi believes that the U.S. government associated Italians with Fascism, sending them the same message given to the Japanese, that their "ways were racial, genetic, indelible," when Italian immigrants were "branded enemy aliens" and some were removed from the general population.[27] Rose Scherini, who studied internees from San Francisco, suggested that all enemy aliens—Japanese, Italians, and Germans—were "scapegoats" for the attack on Pearl Harbor, as immigrants were "often the targets of fear and hatred."[28] These scholars have provided invaluable firsthand accounts of Italians affected by wartime restrictions in interviews and letters that they have brought to light. In several instances, I supplement their stories from the perspective of the Italians through reference to the government files concerning the individuals they profile and a legal analysis of the policies and programs affecting the civilian internees and Italian families. My work dispels the mystery surrounding the alien enemy hearings portrayed in the stories these scholars tell by showing the interaction between the Attorney General's Office and hearing board members in reaching decisions about internment. Another important distinction is that the work of these scholars is situated in the Western Defense Command where the belief that the Japanese posed the greatest threat resulted in a stricter interpretation of federal policy, as seen in DiStasi's thorough account of evacuation and curfews, than the application of policies in the Eastern Defense Command, where Italians and Germans primarily comprised the population of enemy aliens.[29] This circumstance may have led these scholars, who mainly cover wartime experiences in California, to view the treatment of Italians as a massive violation of civil liberties. However, the research and analysis of the treatment of Italians nationwide set forth herein against the background of constitutional guarantees afforded enemy aliens, and the sharp contrast with how the government treated Japanese Americans, supported by statistical data, reveal a different story.

An analysis of the case of the 343 Italians interned illustrates how the federal government defined race and immigrant status and its impact on eligibility for citizenship during the war. While persons of Japanese descent, aliens and American citizens alike, were subject to mass internment on the basis of race, the subjects of this study were identified on the basis of their alien status and the perceived threat that they posed to American security to undergo the process of selective internment. For some perspective on the number of Italian civilian internees, it is instructive to note that 343 represents only approximately five-hundredths of one percent of the Italian alien population living in the United States at the time. The government's perception of racial distinctions and degrees of loyalty among the alien enemy groups affected its implementation of federal policy with respect to each group.[30] Italian Americans' establishment as political players and the assimilation of the Italian community into American society were key factors in their ability to avoid mass evacuation and internment, as they were for the German Americans.[31] The race/whiteness paradigms that scholars have applied to European immigrant groups before they were all considered "white" are consistent with evidence in this book of how Italians responded well to the persistent expectation for Americanization and amalgamation.[32] Although Italians experienced racial prejudice in the nineteenth and early twentieth century, by World War II they enjoyed certain privileges of white status among ethnic groups, particularly with respect to political power.

This case study, which provides the first social profile of the Italian civilian internees, exhibits how the system of justice operated during the war, making it relevant to current debates over the balance of civil liberties and national security. The government identified some Italians as potential threats because of their professed Italian nationalist and Fascist beliefs. Italians in leadership roles in industries and social organizations were the most feared because they might have wielded enough influence over their communities to endanger the United States, or at least enough to impede the support the Roosevelt administration needed for the war effort.[33] This was particularly the case for those employed in the Italian-language media. Aliens who possessed contraband weapons or had prior arrests also caused concern since officials perceived such factors in one's background as indicating at least a propensity for sedition. Once in internment camps, those internees who could convince camp officials that they were capable of becoming loyal American citizens by expressing positive feelings about democracy or exhibiting a good work ethic had a chance at securing an earlier parole or release.

An analysis of the Justice Department's litigation files for internees and of the personal papers of alien enemy hearing board members reveals problems in how the alien enemy hearing boards functioned across the country. Indeed, in the process of examining enemy aliens, some hearing boards explored whether they were ideologically and morally opposed to the United States, and therefore, whether they would make good citizens. Other thoughtful hearing boards grappled with the meaning of due process as it pertained to enemy aliens and strove for a contextualized adjudicatory process. But as the war progressed, the Justice Department recognized the problems of a legal policy that rested on presumptive guilt as applied to all enemy aliens and made efforts to provide greater due process even though a strict interpretation of the law did not require it. Procedural defects, such as the lack of formal charges against the subjects, the failure of some hearing boards to admit testimony favorable to subjects, and a lack of transcripts from hearings and recommendations evaluating the evidence, led the Justice Department to issue a series of remedial instructions to the boards, beginning in February 1942 and continuing through 1943.[34] However, by the time the Justice Department corrected problems in the process so as to provide greater democratic procedure, it was too late for the hundreds of Italians already interned.

This project expands upon earlier portrayals of Attorney General Francis Biddle demonstrating his commitment to constitutional values in his strong opposition to political and military pressures for the mass internment of Japanese.[35] It shows how under Biddle's direction, the Justice Department oversaw alien enemy hearings when neither U.S. nor international treaty law required them, indicating a similar commitment to democracy in the midst of war with respect to enemy nationals detained for the selective internment process. After a hearing before an alien enemy hearing board, those aliens not released or paroled were interned in Immigration and Naturalization Service (INS) and army camps where many remained until the end of 1943, several months after Italy's surrender to the Allies, and some even later.

Some background on the role of immigration, assimilation, whiteness, and the acceptance of an American national identity is essential because government officials' perception of how thoroughly Italians had integrated into American society influenced wartime policies with respect to this group. Therefore, what follows in chapter 1 traces the evolution in Italians' social, political, and economic status in the United States, beginning with the effects of early twentieth-century immigration law bearing an anti-alien and racist tone. It shows that Italians' progression in the labor market coincided with their changing racial identity and white consciousness but that political involvement was more instrumental in raising the public perception of Italians.

The last two sections of chapter 1 are devoted to the simultaneous prewar intelligence activities of the FBI and the formulation of policy for alien enemy internment. Several years before U.S. involvement in World War II, the FBI built a domestic intelligence program through the collection of information about any Communist, Fascist, or subversive individuals or organizations. Government officials even trusted Italian exiles to provide invaluable intelligence information on Fascist groups and activities. A joint agreement reached in July 1941 between the War Department and the Justice Department established policy for handling suspicious persons of enemy nations residing in the United States.

Chapter 2 provides a social profile of the 343 Italian civilian internees, assessing their ages, the regions of the country where they were apprehended, their occupations, and the duration of their internment. The types of people who gave the government concern were mainly those who held leadership roles in their communities or possessed special knowledge that could be used against the United States. In contrast to the apprehension of

Italians who were permanent legal residents in the United States, expedient circumstances prompted the deportation of Latin Americans, citizens of both Italy and a Latin American country, to the United States without visas or passports.

The second section of this chapter develops arguments introduced in chapter 1 about the political influence of Italian Americans by the 1940s. It traces the debate among President Roosevelt and his advisors, the War Department, the Justice Department, and legislative committees, namely the Tolan Committee in February and March 1942, about whether to evacuate the entire population of Italian aliens from military areas. Italian American politicians and prominent members of the Italian community testified to the loyalty of their community toward the United States, best exemplified in the numbers of Italian alien families who sent their sons to fight in the armed forces. Logistical concerns about evacuating and confining the huge Italian population, the need for Italian labor in the wartime industries, racial distinctions among the alien enemies, and the significance of the country's largest immigrant population as a viable political constituency were factors in the government's decision not to conduct a mass evacuation.

The final section of chapter 2 shows distinct variation in the military defense commands' interpretation of Executive Order 9066 regarding the protection of military areas and policies of individual exclusion and restrictions upon enemy aliens. The location of wartime industries and strategic military installations, the different philosophies of the military commanders on each coast, and the varying size of the Italian population resulted in stricter restrictions in the Western Defense Command as compared to those in the Eastern Defense Command.

In examining the alien enemy hearings, chapter 3 explores the question of what process is due enemy aliens through legal constitutional theories concerning the rights of aliens. After comparing the alien enemy hearings to deportation proceedings, this chapter documents debates in the Tolan Committee over what constitutional rights under the Fifth and Fourteenth Amendments endure in wartime and their applicability to the form of procedure afforded enemy aliens. In instructing alien enemy hearing boards across the country, Attorney General Biddle made the distinction between aliens and *enemy* aliens, or citizens of countries at war with the United States. He explained that since "all alien enemies are subject to detention and internment for the duration of the war without hearing," as is the law under the Alien Enemy Act, the hearings were provided "not as a matter of right, but in order to permit them to present facts in their behalf."[36]

Through discussion of the case files of interned Italians that follows them from their arrest through their hearings and course of internment, a theme emerges of tension in the internment process between what internees felt was a just process and the legal guarantees for enemy aliens. Despite efforts by the Justice Department to provide fairer hearings, internees felt despondent over not being able to prove their innocence and their potential to be good American citizens. For most of them, the Justice Department's attempts to infuse greater due process into the system came too late to alter the hearing board's determination that they presented a national security risk.

Chapter 4 turns to the daily lives and experiences of the internees in INS and army camps to provide a comprehensive picture of their physical and emotional challenges. The greatest hardships were being frequently moved among camps and not being able to communicate freely with family and friends since their mail was censored and their visits monitored. Many developed a sense of powerlessness as requests for a reevaluation of their situation and a rehearing went unanswered. Because the United States chose to extend prisoner of war protections in the 1929 Geneva Convention to enemy aliens in internment camps, internees could refer to the convention's guarantees of safe and humane treatment and a good standard of living to redress complaints about their living conditions. Despite their frustrations, this chapter shows how the internees exercised agency by finding ways in the camp setting to prove that they could be loyal American citizens, particularly by exhibiting a good work attitude. Although the balance of power still weighed heavily in favor of the government, the personal letters of internees tell a story of resiliency in the bleak setting of internment.

The conclusion emphasizes that although Italians as a group statistically fared better than the other alien enemy groups, those who experienced injustices felt the effects long after the war. Italians were detained by the INS under the alien enemy program and interned in far fewer numbers than Germans and Japanese, despite their much greater population size, and were removed from alien enemy status sooner. Yet, as documented through personal stories in this final chapter, while World War II generally strengthened Italians' increasing identification as Americans, the wartime experiences of internees slowed their assimilation processes by narrowing job prospects and tarnishing their reputations in their former communities. Italian communities themselves had changed because of the war, becoming less homogenous and less connected to their homeland as the strength of the Italian media dwindled. Families affected by internment and other wartime restrictions did not discuss their experiences after the war because of the shame associated with the memories and confusion over what their loved ones had done wrong.

Finally, this story is more than a historical curiosity because there are specific lessons that may inform lawyers and policy-makers in addressing current national security problems. Recognizing that the lessons of this narrative may be the questions that it poses, the afterword reflects philosophically on how modern liberal democracies wage war while remaining true to democratic values and how they might guard against an overreaction to perceived threats. Questions that this case study raises continue to have relevance today to how democratic governments assess the loyalty of individuals—what role do various categories of citizenship play, what types of evidence are productive and predictive, and what form of process is to be afforded in the determination of loyalty? An examination of the form of justice that the United States government constructed during World War II in the selective internment process, as evaluated in the case of Italians, offers lessons in providing fair process and depicts the realities of a national crisis that moved too quickly for the lessons to be applied effectively to individual outcomes.

The Legal and Political History of Italian Immigrants in the United States before 1941

The history of the treatment of alien residents in the United States reveals tension between the liberty of the individual, as expressed in state and federal bills of rights, and the security of the nation. The concepts of "guilt by suspicion" and "guilt by association" pervaded statutory law concerning aliens from as early as the Alien and Sedition Acts of 1798, a series of four bills passed by the Federalists in the aftermath of the French Revolution to remove political heresy and to silence dissent that might undermine their administration.[1] These laws asserting the power of the government over the public initiated a pattern of imposing limits on civil liberties through legislation and executive action during the Civil War, the World Wars, and the Cold War.[2] In all cases, government policy was directly shaped by fears that foreigners on American soil would commit disloyal acts and threaten U.S. security. Those fears were typically heightened by a broader cultural xenophobia that has existed at various key moments in American history.

The widespread xenophobia of the late nineteenth and early twentieth century led to specific immigration laws and restrictions that also laid the groundwork for the national security programs applied to Italians during World War II. Beginning in 1875, the United States initiated immigration and deportation procedures of a summary and nonjudicial nature that were designed to keep out undesirable races, the poor, and the physically infirm.[3] Toward the end of the nineteenth century, a fear grew of aliens with radical political beliefs, despite the basic conservatism of peasant immigrants in their yearning for tradition (especially religion), status, and authority.[4] In 1893, the U.S. Supreme Court decided that deportation was not a punishment for crime but an administrative process for the return of undesirable alien residents.[5] As a consequence, immigration officials could follow procedures that guaranteed results instead of providing due process for deportees. Fearing anarchists, Congress passed a series of immigration acts beginning in 1903 that excluded certain immigrants from entry into the United States because of presumed beliefs and associations.[6] The Naturalization Act of 1906 under President Theodore Roosevelt further targeted alien radicals in requiring an oath that the alien was not opposed to organized government, supported the U.S. Constitution, and had exhibited five years of good moral character.[7]

Hysteria over the threat to security posed by resident aliens heightened with the entry of the United States into World War I. After signing the declaration of war in 1917, President Woodrow Wilson issued a proclamation invoking the 1798 Alien Enemy Act, asserting his right to apprehend and deport alien enemies, and requiring them to register. Regulations enforceable by the attorney general prohibited alien enemies from possessing, among other things, guns, explosives, and radio transmitters, from coming within a half mile of military zones, from entering and leaving the United States, and from publishing attacks or threats against the government.[8] Attorney General Thomas Gregory instructed his department that his plan was to consider each individual alien enemy separately.[9] John Lord O'Brian, head of the Justice Department's Emergency War Division, interned German and Austro-Hungarian aliens for the duration of the war whenever a government official had reasonable doubts about the alien's reliability, and he overruled clemency pleas, believing that the law required internment whenever an alien appeared to pose any measure of danger.[10] Some 2,300 Germans nationwide, including crew members and sailors of German steamships seized by the federal government when the United States declared war against Germany, were taken into custody and interned at Hot Springs, North Carolina.[11]

In addition to these activities within the executive branch, national anxiety over alien radicals also found expression in legislation. The Espionage Act of 1917 was an aggressive measure designed to ferret out disloyal elements in the population. This act made it a crime to make or convey false reports for the purpose of interfering with American military success, to cause disloyalty in the military, or to obstruct recruitment or enlistment in the armed forces.[12] Although it was intended to protect the armed forces from propaganda, the Justice Department and the judiciary used the Espionage Act of 1917 to suppress all "disloyal utterances."[13] The Immigration Act of 1918 expanded the definition of those who could be deported on political grounds, resulting in the deportation of "hundreds of alleged anarchists, Bolsheviks, and other dissidents."[14] Under this act, the government could deport any alien who was a member of an anarchist organization by an administrative process that did not afford the alien the right to counsel in the preliminary investigation nor a jury in the hearing or a subsequent right of appeal. Naturalized citizens were subject to the same process.[15] As will be seen, the hearings for enemy aliens during World War II resembled these deportation proceedings in the limited extent of due process afforded. Specifically applicable during wartime, the Sedition Act of 1918 forbade, among other things, the uttering or printing of disloyal or abusive language about the U.S. government.[16]

It was in this climate of suspicion that the General Intelligence Division within the Bureau of Investigation, under the direction of J. Edgar Hoover, gathered information on the radical activities of individuals, many of whom were deported during the first "Red Scare" of 1919 to 1920. The "Palmer Raids" were attempts by the Justice Department, under the direction of Attorney General Alexander Palmer, to arrest and deport radical individuals from the United States, including anarchists from recent European immigrant populations, who wanted to eliminate the state. Hoover's method for proceeding in deportation of alien radicals was to first obtain a ruling that an organization to which they belonged fell within the class proscribed under the Immigration Act of 1918 for advocating political violence or anarchy, and then to produce membership cards, dues books, or testimony of attendance at meetings without direct evidence of personal beliefs.[17] In late 1919, approximately 650 individuals were arrested on suspicion of radicalism, of whom 249 were deported. On January 2, 1920, 4,000 additional people suspected of radicalism were rounded up in raids in thirty-three cities.[18] Jurists criticized the Justice Department for using undercover spies and not following proper legal procedures in the arrests, detentions, and so-called trials of aliens before inspectors, which eventually led to an end to the deportations.[19]

Coinciding with the Red Scare was the conviction of Italian immigrants Ferdinando Nicola Sacco and Bartolomeo Vanzetti for the murders of two men during an armed robbery at a shoe factory in South Braintree, Massachusetts, in 1920. The public attention given to their case may account in part for the FBI's increased efforts to eradicate Italian radicals believed to pose a risk of revolution against the U.S. government. Sacco and Vanzetti were linked to the anarchist group the Galleanists, which a year earlier had sent letter bombs to prominent government officials, businessmen, and law enforcement officials. In what has frequently been called a kangaroo court, Judge Webster Thayer, outspoken about his desire to suppress Bolshevism and radicalism, allowed the introduction of circumstantial evidence, including information about Sacco and Vanzetti's radical background, to influence the outcome of the case.[20] The duo's sentencing to execution by the electric chair in 1927 had broad social and political implications as the international community claimed a miscarriage of justice because the court allowed the racism and nativism of legal authorities and the prejudices of the community to be factors in the treatment of these defendants.[21]

The racist tone of immigration legislation was best exemplified by the acts of 1917, 1921, and 1924. Laws included mandates for literacy tests aimed at excluding new immigrants from southern and eastern Europe.[22] The Quota Act of 1921 established numerical limits on immigration from Europe and quotas restricting the number of immigrants from any country annually to 3 percent of the number of residents from that country living in the United States as of the 1910 U.S. Census.[23] The Society for the Protection of Italian Immigrants, founded in New York City in 1901 to assist Italian immigrants who arrived at Ellis Island in locating relatives and finding work, kept track of the quota's effect on the Italian population.[24] According to this society's January 1922 report, the 3 percent rule effectively reduced the number of immigrant arrivals, but failed in its other intended purpose by admitting "a non-productive class of immigration, but den[ying] admittance to good productive laborious immigrants, who were not within the preferred clauses of the law."[25] The Immigration Act of 1924 set the annual quota for immigrants entering the United States at 2 percent of the residents from that country living in the continental United States as of the 1890 U.S. Census, thus further restricting Italians and other southern as well as eastern Europeans since fewer of them lived in the United States in 1890, and favoring immigrants from northern and western Europe.[26] As a result of the 1924 Act, Italy was accorded a maximum of 3,845 persons, which was a tiny percentage of the 296,000 Italians who had come over in 1914, the year World War I began.[27]

Despite this restrictive legislation, by 1930 Italian-born residents constituted a significant portion of the American population, numbering approximately 1.8 million.[28] Ten years later, in the year before the entry of the United States into World War II, there were more than four million persons in the United States of Italian descent, of whom 1.6 million had been born in Italy. Of this latter number, approximately 700,000 were aliens, the vast majority residing on the Atlantic Seaboard.[29] Before turning to specific government policies for Italians at the outset of World War II, we need to understand the evolution of Italians' place in American society from the start of their immigration to the United States. As a whole, resident Italians underwent processes of assimilation in terms of their economic status and political consciousness, affording them increasingly greater power in employment and politics, even while they retained their Italian identity through language and customs. Victims of discrimination for years in American society that classed them as undesirable aliens, the force of economic and political improvement served to diminish discrimination against them.

The progression that Italians experienced in the labor market was intertwined with their changing racial identity and white consciousness. Race was a changing concept in immigration policy across chronological periods, partly due to variations in legal definitions among state and federal policies, changes in eligibility requirements for citizenship, and varying local contexts.[30] Italians' racial status was complicated by the distinction between race and color. When Italian immigrants arrived in the United States in the late nineteenth century, color was a social category rather than a physical description, meaning that "white" Italians could have darker skin than "black" Americans, and race was a description of nationality like North and South Italians. Thus, on the federal government's naturalization papers, Italians stated their region of origin for the category of race and white as their color.[31] Unlike African Americans already resident in the United States who were prevented from enjoying the full extent of their constitutional rights, Italians could obtain citizenship and partake of all attendant rights upon their arrival. Their acceptance as whites gave them access to politics, ownership of land, and certain employment.[32] But there was a dichotomy between the legal and social treatment of Italians. Irish who had been in the United States longer dominated the hierarchy of the Catholic Church.[33] In certain regions of the Jim Crow South, Italian immigrants were stigmatized for accepting jobs marked as "black" by local custom and for living and working among blacks. In Louisiana, Mississippi, and West Virginia, Italians were lynched for alleged crimes or for fraternizing with blacks in violation of local racial codes. Italian organizations reacted to violence in New Orleans by demanding protection against racial prejudice.[34] Poor southern Italian peasants sometimes "replaced" freed black slaves in the Gulf states, working for low wages, and proved eager to work as "scabs" during strikes in factories of the Northeast.[35] Italians in the North were known to take the dirtiest, lowest-paying jobs of "digging ditches, picking rags," and "shoveling manure off the streets."[36] They were also farmers, fishermen, and laborers in the transportation industry, building roads, railroads, and the New York City subway. The more skilled opened businesses as barbers, tailors, butchers or undertakers.[37] As late as the interwar years, Italian immigrants remained overrepresented in low-paying unskilled and semiskilled jobs, limited by their poor command of the English language.[38]

In the several decades following their arrival in the United States, however, Italians' socioeconomic status improved demonstrably. Rising out of the labor class, some Italians living in rural areas became farm operators whose produce supplied cities in the Northeast, the West, and parts of the South. Italians specifically became known as growers of strawberries in Louisiana and of grapes in California. They grew cotton in Alabama and Tennessee and rice in Texas.[39] Italians living in urban centers found success in a variety of professional roles. Writing in the early 1920s about the assimilation of Italian immigrants into American society, Gino Speranza, a director of the Society for the Protection of Italian Immigrants, stated that although the "Italian colony" in New York City was among the poorest in the United States, its total estimated material value was seventy-five million dollars. His breakdown of professions was as follows: 115 physicians, sixty-three pharmacists, four dentists, twenty-one lawyers, sixteen public school teachers, nine architects, seven mechanical engineers, and four manufacturers of technical instruments. Other signs of economic and social progress by New York City Italians were their support of two hospitals, a savings bank, a trust company, and a chamber of commerce.[40] However, nationally, the Italian professional class remained small and unremarkable. From 1900 to 1920, it consisted mainly of physicians, dentists, and lawyers, most of whom had attended second-rate professional schools and did not attain any eminence in their field.[41] By the 1930s, a national survey conducted by an Italian language newspaper showed that the number of Italian Americans in professional categories had drastically increased, although there was no measure of their success in these roles.[42]

A more successful vehicle for raising the public perception of the Italian community in the United States was the involvement of Italian Americans in politics. Italian immigrants displayed an active interest in local and national politics once expectations of return migration subsided and they decided to remain permanently in the United States. Those who entered politics at the turn of the century had already achieved prominence in their communities and enjoyed the support of an Italian American political base. Examples in New York include Democrat Antonio Zucca, president of the Italian Chamber of Commerce, who was elected coroner for Greater New York in 1897, followed by Democrat Pietro Acritelli, who was elected to that same position in 1904. Also benefiting from the support of a heavily Italian district in New York City, financier James E. March (Antonio Michelino Maggio) won a seat to the Electoral College in 1904. After World War I, there was an increasing number of Italian Americans achieving political positions, most noticeably in major cities like New York, San Francisco, Baltimore, Philadelphia, and New Orleans where there were large populations of Italians.[43] During the Prohibition era in New York City, for instance, Italians made inroads into politics through the Tammany machine, but the links of some Italian American politicians, such as Al Marinelli, to illicit means of acquiring wealth eventually cost them their positions. One historian has attributed the powerful political influence of Italians in New York City by the early 1940s to Frank Costello, a former bootlegger turned real estate investor, and Generoso Pope, the owner of the two largest Italian-language dailies and a radio station. Pope controlled the channels of communication with Italian speakers in that city and became a leader in the Democratic Party.[44] He was accused of engaging in Fascist activities and authoring pro-Fascist articles, as well as maintaining close links with officials in Benito Mussolini's regime, all of which led to an examination of his character by the Dies Committee in 1941.[45] Although Pope, also the millionaire owner of Colonial Sand and Stone Company, never held an appointed or elected office, he built a status as the country's most important Italian political leader, with the exception of Fiorello H. La Guardia. Pope and La Guardia often found themselves in opposing political camps competing for the Italian American constituency. Pope developed a wide circle of friends among Italian American politicians, including many city and state judges who relied upon his endorsement.[46]

From 1916 through 1946, La Guardia was a dominant political figure both in New York and nationally. La Guardia was the first Italian American reflecting that group's political consciousness elected to Congress, where he served for several terms, and he was the first to serve as New York City's mayor, an office he held for three consecutive terms.[47] La Guardia's Italian heritage put him in an awkward position in the 1930s with a constituency largely sympathetic to Italian Fascism, causing him to hedge in his attacks on Mussolini and even attend events in support of Italy in its fight against the international coalition led by England.[48] As mayor, he secured many jobs for his Italian constituents, which proved to be an asset to him when he sought re-election.[49] But his popularity crossed ethnic lines and political parties, evidenced in the widespread support he received when the mayor came under attack from members of Congress and the media, who urged President Roosevelt to remove him as director of the Office of Civilian Defense.[50] Upon La Guardia's resignation from this position, Rabbi Isserman of Temple Israel in St. Louis, Missouri, in a radio broadcast told listeners that it was wrong to characterize La Guardia, the son of a naturalized citizen and decorated veteran of World War I, as an

Italian because to do so failed to capture his essence as the ultimate "people's candidate" who represented the true spirit of democracy.[51]

Overlapping with La Guardia's career was that of Vito Marcantonio, a seven-term congressman from east Harlem whose constituents included Italian Americans, Puerto Ricans, and African Americans. Known for his radical positions, such as his support of the Communist Party and labor unions and his initial opposition to American involvement in World War II, "Marc," as he was affectionately called, was able to retain the support of his more conservative southern Italian immigrant followers even in the face of Italian competitors. However, after his public attacks on Mussolini and Fascism cost him the 1936 election, he avoided events in protest of the Italian government, which allowed him to regain popularity and his congressional seat in the next election.[52] He did not refrain, however, from counteracting "the combined forces of reaction in [his] district, composed of Tammany, Hearst and Fascists" through the publication of *The People's Voice*, dedicated to local issues such as unemployment relief and slum clearance, as well as the campaign against war and Fascism.[53] In addition to helping to build a Farmer Labor Party, the goal of the weekly newspaper was to send Marcantonio back to Congress and to promote other "liberal and progressive legislators who will fight for the rights and civil liberties of the people," such as stronger trade unions and better working conditions.[54]

Marcantonio was very close to his constituents, many of whom contacted him—often writing in Italian—for help in obtaining jobs, food stamps, assistance in housing, and to deal with discrimination issues.[55] He received appeals from numerous Italian organizations such as the Italian Welfare Association, the Italian-American World War Veterans, the Harlem Italian Defense League, and the Sons of Italy Grand Lodge.[56] In many instances, he served as a sponsor before the Immigration Bureau for Italians seeking to obtain their American citizenship and contacted the Justice Department on behalf of aliens who failed to register.[57] Although there appeared to be no evidence of appeals to Marcantonio specific to internment, upon America's entry into the war, the congressman was called upon to aid an Italian naturalized citizen whose position as the director of the Italian War Veterans in New York led to the blocking of his personal account and later the accounts for his food import business.[58] That an organization incorporated under the laws of New York with a mission of aiding "unfortunate, disabled and impoverished Italian veterans of the first World War" became targeted as a promoter of Fascism is merely one example of how the hysteria of the times caused the government to forego thorough investigations into the activities of Italian organizations as well as those of their members.[59]

Other Italian Americans held prominent political positions on the East Coast during wartime. Charles Poletti, a son of Italian immigrants, who had been lieutenant governor of New York, succeeded to the governorship in December 1942, becoming the first Italian American to serve in that position. After his brief time as governor, Poletti was special assistant to War Secretary Henry Stimson, and three months later received an army commission to serve in the reconstruction of Italy after the fall of Fascism.[60] In Rhode Island, John Pastore, the son of an Italian immigrant tailor, became the first Italian American elected to a governorship, serving as that state's governor from 1945 to 1950.[61] On the West Coast, Angelo Joseph Rossi, a florist by trade, held several offices in San Francisco before being elected that city's mayor in 1931, a position he held until 1944. Subpoenaed in May 1942 by the Assembly Fact Finding Committee on Un-American Activities in California to answer to allegations that he supported Fascism, Rossi pledged his complete loyalty to the United States. The following year his bid to be reelected mayor failed.[62] Like other Italian American politicians, Rossi enjoyed the benefits of a political base from his ethnic community but had to navigate a tricky course between establishing his own political profile and retaining the support of an Italian population with strong ties to its homeland. Having political leaders from their own community helped to solidify Italians' identification with the United States and their adoption of its democratic ideals, which in turn accelerated their acceptance as fellow citizens.

Although this history of immigration, assimilation, and government fears of radicals and anarchists laid a crucial foundation for the government policies of the 1940s, a more immediate context was the shifting attitudes of Americans toward Mussolini and Fascism in the 1920s and 1930s, alongside the parallel vicissitudes in Italian Americans' nationalistic sentiment for their homeland. Understanding the political identity of Italians in the decades leading up to World War II helps explain the power that they had as a voting bloc in elections. As will be revealed, the power reflected in that bloc translated into influence among Italian American politicians during congressional hearings to prevent the Italian population from undergoing mass internment and to save some individual Italians from a decision of internment by alien enemy hearing boards.

In the 1920s, Americans were not attracted to Fascism as a political ideology but rationalized it as acceptable or even laudable on grounds of "efficiency," "discipline," and "progress."[63] The middle class and business community admired the leadership qualities of Mussolini whose rationality and willpower seemed to model American values.[64] Historian John Diggins described the progression in the American businessmen's opinion of Fascism: suspicion of Fascist violence and lawlessness; optimism and even enthusiasm after the 1922 March on Rome and the takeover by the seemingly antiradical Mussolini and his Fascist Party; skepticism about the announcement of corporatism involving state intervention in private business in 1926; positive feelings about Italy's centralized economy during the early years of the Depression; and repudiation of the Fascist "experiment" after 1934.[65]

Once Mussolini came into power in Italy in October 1922, *Il Duce* fostered Italian Americans' pride in their homeland, especially when he appeared to be revitalizing Italy. Perhaps in response to anti-alien sentiment culminating in the discriminatory immigration laws of the 1920s, which gave immigrants a sense of inferiority, Italian Americans looked to Italy for self-esteem.[66] Italians in the United States took pride in how Mussolini's political and economic accomplishments raised Italy's international status and hoped his achievements would raise their own status in American society, but these sentiments did not translate into a desire to import Fascism into the United States.[67] Historian Oscar Handlin noted that "among some Italians in the New World, admiration for Mussolini implied not so much approval of Fascism as gratitude for the achievement of having earned the respect and fear of the great powers of the earth."[68] The middle and working classes were united in endorsing Il Duce for dealing with homeland problems of church-state relations, the Mafia, and radicalism, and hoped that their glorification of Italy would defend against American contempt for new immigrant groups.[69] Jerre Mangione, a journalist and the director of the public relations program of the INS during World War II, recalls that his relatives believed Mussolini "would bring increasing glory to Italy and respect to all Italians, even to those in the United States."[70]

When Franklin D. Roosevelt became president in 1933, he had to be aware that his relations with Mussolini were under close scrutiny by Italian Americans. By his own admission, President Roosevelt miscalculated the course that Mussolini and Fascism would take. In 1939, he reflected: "During the early Mussolini period up through 1932, I very clearly analyzed it as a phenomenon somewhat parallel to the Communist experiment in Russia. I had a good many contacts during those years both with the Mussolini Italians and with Italian exiles who were driven out of Italy by Mussolini. It should be remembered that during those years Mussolini still maintained a semblance of parliamentary government, and there were many, including myself, who hoped that having restored order and morale in Italy he would, of his own accord, work toward a restoration of democratic processes."[71] Roosevelt's initial regard for Mussolini affected the reputation that Italians enjoyed in the United States. Even the majority of non-Italian American citizens admired Mussolini for his charisma and plans for Italy. During the early 1930s, accounts reached Americans of "trains running on time, of vast public enterprises, of the 'tremendous' building projects," as well as the elimination of slums and beggars from Italy's streets.[72] Mussolini's appeal crossed religious lines in the United States; Catholics credited Mussolini with the "resurrection" of Italy, while Protestants liked his anticlericalism.[73]

President Roosevelt and his party could not forget that Mussolini had widespread support in Italian American urban districts on which they depended for the Italian vote. After Roosevelt's private appeals failed to persuade Mussolini to halt the invasion of Ethiopia and submit to arbitration, the president in 1936 persuaded oil shippers to restrict their trade with Italy. Italian Americans vociferously opposed Roosevelt's shift from neutrality to a moral embargo and consideration of economic sanctions. During the election that fall, hostility toward Roosevelt lingered in Italian neighborhoods in the face of the government's refusal to recognize Italy's annexation of Ethiopia.[74] For example, Chicago's Italian American community generally supported Italy's effort in Ethiopia, identifying with the Fascist campaign in terms of the Italian race and national identity.[75] However, other Italians came to realize the full significance of Fascism. Writing soon after these events, Professor Constantine Panunzio observed that the American reaction to the Ethiopian War accelerated a movement by Italian Americans of withdrawing from Fascist groups. He wrote: "Many Italians took out their naturalization papers and brought over their families. They knew where they stood."[76]

The United States persisted in refusing to recognize Italy's African conquest, although it followed a pattern of diplomatic leniency toward Mussolini and Fascism.[77] Roosevelt continued corresponding with Mussolini, urging armament reduction and eventually a reduction of trade barriers. Addressing Mussolini as "my dear Duce," the president expressed his confidence that Mussolini shared his "fear that the trend of the present international situation is ominous to peace" and "the desire to turn the course of the world toward stabilizing peace."[78] After 1937, Roosevelt did not allow his press secretary to publicize his relationship with Il Duce.[79] This behavior was in keeping with Roosevelt's "evasive and political cautious" style, as seen in his later partnership with British Prime Minister Winston Churchill.[80] In March 1938, the German annexation of Austria and the Nazi occupation of the Brenner Pass met with "tacit acceptance" from the Fascists, and in May, Adolf Hitler marched into Italy at the invitation of the Fascists.[81] Roosevelt's administration also was deeply troubled by Italy's anti-Semitism, and would not defer to Mussolini's policies. In January 1939, after Roosevelt learned of the uprooting of Jewish refugees in central and southern Europe, he proposed to Mussolini that they be resettled in Ethiopia, a plan Mussolini rejected.[82]

By 1940, Roosevelt was convinced that Mussolini would bring Italy into the war on Hitler's side. Angered by Italy's decision to enter the war with the Axis powers even as France fell, Roosevelt added the famous line to his University of Virginia commencement speech about "the hand that held the dagger striking its neighbor in the back." He ignored objections from the State Department that adding this phrase would complicate the relations of the United States with Italy and instead followed his conscience. Believing that the two countries were "long past the stage of diplomacy when we could curry favor with any of the Nazi nations," Secretary of War Henry Stimson told Roosevelt that he had no objection to the phrase because "the only language that they understood was force."[83] Roosevelt boldly risked offending Italian American communities but stood firm in America's posture with respect to Italy.

The number of Italian Americans who actively supported and participated in Fascist activities in the United States in the years leading up to World War II has been the subject of wide debate. While Italy's aggressive military activities in Ethiopia during 1935 and 1936 turned American public opinion against Italy, Italian American support for Mussolini remained strong as tens of thousands turned out for mass rallies in New York, Chicago, Philadelphia, and Boston, and communities collected gold wedding rings, watches, and other items to help finance the war effort.[84] Gaetano Salvemini, a political exile from Mussolini's Fascist dictatorship and Harvard lecturer, estimated that in 1940, 5 percent of Italian Americans were "out and out Fascists."[85] In 1943, California state senator Jack B. Tenney estimated that 10 percent of the Italian American population at that time were under the influence of Fascism.[86]

In pure isolationist rhetoric, U.S. Congressman Martin Dies from Texas wrote: "We invited the evils of the old world's social, political and economic disorders by offering our fertile lands and priceless resources, which our fathers designed as a heritage for their children's children, as a refuge for the problems and malcontents of Europe."[87] Included in his list of undesirable aliens were Italians, many of whom he believed were Fascist. In evaluating testimony before the House Un-American Activities Committee (HUAC) in 1940, Dies, the chairman of the committee, estimated that there were approximately 10,000 members of the Italian Blackshirts in the United States, and that approximately 100,000 people of Italian descent participated in meetings of Fascist organizations.[88] Dies's greatest concern with the Italian community was that Fascist ideology and support for Mussolini were "concealed behind the barrier of the Italian language."[89] Even though Dies admitted that this factor cast an air of mystery over meetings of Italian societies at which Italian consular officials addressed members, he maintained that "Italian consular officials and secret Fascist agents are spreading Fascist propaganda throughout the ranks of many Italian-American organizations in the United States."[90] He also believed that the seven dailies published in the Italian language in the United States were "Fascist publications under direct guidance from Rome."[91] Additionally, radio stations and the film industry were supposedly promoting Fascist propaganda.[92] Dies was convinced that danger lurked in the younger generation of Italians after testimony before HUAC that American children of Italian extraction were indoctrinated in Fascist ideology under the guise of education both in the United States through the Dante Alighieri Society and in Italy during vacations at Fascist camps.[93]

Despite these "findings," the Dies committee was harshly criticized for not broadening its investigation of Fascism and Nazism to include homegrown elements of these movements.[94] Like its counterpart in the 1930s, the Special Committee to Investigate Communist Activity in the United States headed by Congressman Hamilton Fish Jr., the Dies committee's focus was Communism.[95] Finding fault with its "un-American" methods of relying upon rumors and encouraging character assassination and libel without providing fair hearings, attorneys of the American Civil Liberties Union (ACLU) argued that the Dies Committee spent most of its efforts on exposing Communism, condemning every progressive cause as such, and relatively little time on uncovering the operations of native organizations that took on a fascist character.[96] The ACLU believed that "vigilante" groups, such as the Silver Shirts, the Black Legion, and the Ku Klux Klan, were "vastly more active in the United States than other movements aimed at our democratic liberties" since they "arose in almost every strike to serve the interests of employers against the interests of law and order."[97] Still another fascist organization with considerable influence in the Southwest and Midwest during the late 1930s and early 1940s that threatened the U.S. government was the *Union Nacional Sinarquista* (the National Union of Sinarchistas), which exploited the racial discrimination suffered by Mexican Americans to advance the fascist cause.[98]

United States senator Huey P. Long from Louisiana, who embodied the politics of economic protest and was a champion of the common man, and Father Coughlin, the Detroit priest who rose to national popularity through his radio sermons denouncing concentrated wealth in the hands of the few, may be understood as representing early forms of American fascism. During the 1930s, when the United States was recuperating from the Great Depression in the latter part of its transformation from a rural, fragmented society to an urban, industrial one accompanied by a new mass culture, the charismatic personalities of Long and Coughlin appealed to a population seeking social justice.[99] As historian Alan Brinkley explains, "there is nothing to suggest that either man ever communicated with or even thought much about Hitler, Mussolini, or any other European fascist leader."[100] Indeed, those fascists in the United States who tried to organize popular movements on the German and Italian models did not follow Long and Coughlin. But there was a group of intelligent and well-educated men who believed that these popular leaders could be vehicles for their ideas. Coughlin did begin to discuss fascism in 1938, but neither he nor Long openly approved of fascism or showed interest in connecting with fascist movements or thinkers.[101] In his exploration of whether Long and Coughlin were implicitly counterparts to the movements of Hitler and Mussolini, Brinkley draws similarities in their appeal to the traditional community and "hostility toward 'internationalism' in politics and economics."[102] There were sharp contrasts in the openly racial and religious hatred and "commitment to a belligerent super-nationalism" of European Fascists as compared to the less defined social philosophies of Long and Coughlin, who espoused greater sharing of wealth, power, and influence.[103] Despite contradictions in both movements, the sway that leaders had over their followers in homegrown groups with roots in American populism and Italian Fascist organizations in the United States are comparable.

Until the summer of 1940 when Italy attacked France, "there was no question that Italian-Americans in general were solidly behind Mussolini," although the basis of that support seemed driven by love for their homeland rather than a belief in Fascist ideology.[104] The critical problem that immigrant admirers of Mussolini faced was that they believed they could be ardent Fascists *and* good Americans.[105] The great majority of them were moved by social status, desiring to fit into American society, rather than by theories about political liberties.[106] After Italy's invasion, however, they found it essential to their acceptance into American society to abandon patriotic nostalgia for Italy for loyalty to their adopted homeland. There were 122 Italian organizations in New York alone that pledged allegiance to the United States in approval of President Roosevelt's resolutions condemning the invasion and of his characterization of Mussolini as a "back-stabber."[107] At the Supreme Convention of the Order of the Sons of Italy in America in August 1941, members unanimously adopted a resolution pledging the organization's loyalty and resources to America and its unity, which Roosevelt warmly acknowledged.[108] In the year and a half between Italy's attack on France and the Japanese attack on Pearl Harbor, Italian American sentiment appeared to be "hung suspended between hope and fear"; hope that the United States would not enter the war and fear that if it entered, Italian Americans would be forced to fight against their homeland.[109]

The Italian community was aware of how the American population perceived them. The association of aliens generally with criminal activity was unmistakable in 1941. That year Congress debated the Hobbs Bill concerning the detention and deportation of alien criminals and proven Nazis, Communists, and Fascists. One editorial cited a Justice Department estimate of "at least 100,000 aliens illegally in this country," a number which included "Nazis and Fascists sent here to swell the fifth column."[110] The author traced the "alien-criminal situation" to the practice of the INS, when it was under the Department of Labor led by the "misplaced sympathy" of Secretary Frances Perkins, to free deportable aliens and make them legal residents. According to testimony at a Senate hearing in 1939, "nearly 6,000 *mandatory* deportations were suspended by Secretary Perkins in six years." The editorial also cited the failure of the Justice Department to impose an immigration statute making re-entry of deported aliens a felony, punishable by five years of prison.[111] Thus, the author argued that a lax INS in the 1930s set the stage for the presence of law-breaking and potentially subversive aliens in the United States at the start of the war.

Anti-alien sentiment varied by regions of the country. A government report issued in April 1942 indicates that nationally, discrimination against Italians and Germans was felt in employment opportunities. The attitude toward Italians as reported by state directors varied by state. In Massachusetts, skepticism toward the alien population was "directed especially toward Italians, those naturalized as well as those of alien status." In this respect, Massachusetts differed from other states in the Northeast such as Rhode Island where "no real feeling exist[ed] against Italians, a substantial portion of [the] State's population." In New York, the average citizen thought "every precaution" should be taken with respect to the alien situation, but that "we should try to avoid hurting innocent aliens," and labor groups felt that aliens should not be set aside as a class. Pennsylvania reported few instances of discrimination against Italians and Germans.[112]

In some communities, employers adopted blanket policies of not hiring persons of Italian, German, and Japanese extraction, and government departments and war industry contractors made efforts to weed out potentially dangerous persons from their workforces pursuant to army and navy regulations on the employment of aliens in defense production.[113] Noncitizens already employed in a defense or related industry could lose their jobs unless their employer submitted an affidavit to the naval or army authorities stating a belief in the enemy alien's loyalty to the United States. If an employer was not willing to do this, the only recourse for an alien was to write to the President's Committee on Fair Employment Practices and claim discrimination on the basis of ancestry.[114] One Italian-language newspaper decried employers who discriminated against aliens, saying that the United States needed the skill of every able and loyal person, citizens and foreigners, to participate in the war effort.[115]

In order to combat "fear, hysteria and rumor-mongering—three weapons of the enemy that are as deadly as bombs, or tanks or guns," James Rowe Jr., Assistant to Francis Biddle, spoke on the radio, urging listeners to leave the handling of suspects to the government, particularly agents of the FBI who were trained in matters of espionage and sabotage. To assure the public of its safety in the able hands of the Justice Department, Rowe claimed that it was "significant that approximately half of the alien enemies that have been apprehended by the Federal Bureau of Investigation since the war began were taken into custody within 48 hours after the start of the war." The public's job, then, was to stay "level-headed" and not to take matters into their own hands, thereby "engendering a spirit of national unity which no one can ever break."[116]

Sensing the discrimination and anti-alien sentiment in Boston prompted some organizations to urge tolerance of aliens and American-born citizens of Italian, Japanese, and German descent. At the annual dinner of the

International Institute in Boston, the executive secretary told members that citizens should leave it to the FBI to handle the subversive individuals and to be sympathetic and tolerant of the rest. A consul of Czecho-Slovakia and lecturer from the Tufts School of Law and Diplomacy said that the "only solution for international cooperation is cultural pluralism," an acceptance that this is "a world of the many."[117]

Tolerance was also the message of Attorney General Biddle's address on "Democracy and Racial Minorities," before the Jewish Theological Seminary of America in New York City. Biddle reminded attendees that "our sons today are fighting side by side with the sons of Italians, of Germans and of Japanese . . . . For this is the essence of our democracy in practice."[118] Ultimately, the war solidified Italians' loyalty to the United States, as many families sent their sons to fight in the U.S. armed forces and many Italians worked in the war industries. Some families with one or more members of alien status sent several sons to war, such as the Massaglis of the Humboldt Bay area in California who had four sons in different divisions of the armed services. Gino Massagli described "a little flag, a little banner with four stars" on his parents' front door while he and his brothers were serving. He recalled that his Italian heritage did not divide his loyalty when he encountered Italian soldiers overseas.[119]

The war also strengthened Italians' appreciation of democracy, which in turn caused more Americans to accept them as fellow citizens. Don Rafaelli's parents were not alone in their disapproval of Mussolini's building of a military state and their decision to sever their ties with the old country. Rafaelli remembered how his father spoke out against Mussolini, which was a reason why "he tried to assimilate so readily into the American community."[120] Another example of political assimilation was the transformation experienced by Joseph Maniscalco's father in San Francisco. Mr. Mansicalco idolized Mussolini until he saw "that the Italian people were very deeply offended by Mussolini's actions," and realized that "Mussolini did make a big mistake," causing him to feel "very pro-American, even more pro-American than before."[121]

The absence of Italian American disloyalty during the war and the Italian American newspapers' swift repudiation of Mussolini and Fascism after the Japanese attack on Pearl Harbor suggest that pro-Fascist sentiment among the majority of Italian immigrants, regionally concentrated in northeastern metropolitan areas, resulted from pride in Italy, rather than ideology. Yet the dangers of Italian American Fascism could not be discounted even if its appeal was predominantly social or economic rather than political.[122] Government suspicion of Italian aliens with ties to Fascist organizations and fears of their sway over their community led to plans to remove them from their neighborhoods, some for the entire duration of the war. Those plans took root well before the formal U.S. declaration of war in 1941.

The Government's Identification of Italian Fascists

Building an extensive domestic intelligence operation requires balancing the need for secrecy in national security plans with the right of citizens in a democratic society to know what their government is doing. Several years prior to the restrictive wartime programs imposed on the Italian population, plans were already under way for security measures against particular alien groups. In 1936, the FBI began collecting information about any Communist, Fascist, or subversive individuals or organizations.[123]

When President Roosevelt in 1936 asked the FBI for "a broad picture" of the effects of Communism and Fascism on "the economic and political life of the country as a whole," he did not appear much concerned with public accountability.[124] Since his request went beyond investigations of violations of law, he resorted to the Appropriation Act as a legal basis for the type of intelligence activity that he wanted the FBI to undertake. The act allowed the FBI to investigate matters referred to it by the State Department. Thus, Secretary of State Cordell Hull asked that such investigations be conducted.[125] Although there was no evidence that Congress or the attorney general had intended the appropriations statute to authorize the type of permanent domestic intelligence structure that FBI Director J. Edgar Hoover envisioned, that is, broadly sweeping activities from the steel and coal industries to Fascism and Nazism, organized labor, and the activities of African Americans, Roosevelt approved Hoover's plan in 1938 for a joint FBI–military domestic intelligence program.[126] One analyst suggests that the relationship of trust and loyalty between Roosevelt and Hoover "erased any limit set by custom or law to the requests the president might make of the FBI director, or to the favors the director might do for the president."[127] The fact that Roosevelt gave Hoover assignments directly maintained their covert nature, giving Hoover the ability to direct investigations of Communist and Fascist activities without Roosevelt formally notifying Congress.[128]

In 1939, the FBI's domestic intelligence program had the dual purposes of supplying Roosevelt and his executive officers information for decision-making and developing governmental policies, and of gathering "preventive intelligence" to be used in the case of an emergency or war.[129] FBI field offices were tasked with obtaining information on a variety of categories of people: "persons of German, Italian, and Communist sympathies," including subscribers of German- and Italian-language newspapers and officers of these newspapers in the United States and newspapers published by the Communist Party or its affiliates, as well as members of German and Italian societies and other organizations "whether they be of a fraternal character or of some other nature" and other organizations with "pronounced Nationalistic tendencies."[130] The sources for the list of individuals, described as a "custodial detention" list, were "public and private records, confidential sources of information, newspaper morgues, public libraries, employment records, school records, et cetera."[131] Those persons in "Class 1" were to be apprehended and interned immediately, while "Class 2" persons were to be carefully watched. The primary subjects in mid-1940 were active Communists, the German-American Bund, Italian Fascist organizations, and American Fascist groups.[132] Pro-Fascist activities of the late 1920s and early 1930s had been confined largely to propaganda, but analysts believed that espionage agents had joined propagandists in the following decades.[133]

The need for referrals from the State Department for FBI investigations ended in June 1939 when Roosevelt issued a directive that "investigation of all espionage, counterespionage, and sabotage matters be controlled and handled by the Federal Bureau of Investigation of the Department of Justice, the Military Intelligence Division of the War Department, and the Office of Naval Intelligence in the Navy Department."[134] The domestic intelligence program became public in September 1939 when war broke out in Europe.[135] In January 1940, Hoover announced to a House subcommittee that the FBI had revived the General Intelligence Division of the Palmer Days and that it was operating a general index in the case of an emergency.[136]

In early 1941, the army's list of suspect enemy aliens was combined with those of the Office of Naval Intelligence and the FBI, resulting in a comprehensive list, called the "ABC list," of individuals (Japanese, German, and Italian aliens) to be arrested in case of war.[137] The list categorized an individual's level of security risk in the following way: A, the most dangerous category, was comprised of "aliens who led cultural or assistance organizations"; B was for "slightly less suspicious aliens"; and Category C "were members of, or those who donated to, ethnic groups, Japanese language teachers and Buddhist clergy."[138] All those on the ABC list were promptly arrested in early December 1941.[139] This list became the framework of the Custodial Detention Program utilized by the FBI to classify suspect persons.

The FBI had lists of Italians organized both alphabetically and geographically. In clarifying instructions, Hoover requested his offices across the country to submit names of "members of all definitely identified Italian Fascist organizations," as well as persons reported as "pro-Italian, or pronouncedly disloyal or hostile to the United States, or loyal or sympathetic to any foreign country."[140] Investigations of such individuals were to focus on the nature of their occupations and activities, whether they held leadership positions in subversive organizations, their military and criminal background, and information on whether they had relatives in the armed forces of a foreign country.[141]

The aim of the Custodial Detention Program was to allow the government to make individual decisions about the threat posed by individual aliens or U.S. citizens instead of basing internment decisions on race or ethnicity alone so as to avoid the discrimination of a race-based policy of internment. The primary problem with the program's classification system for suspect individuals was that it created a risk that mere affiliation with an organization for social purposes or otherwise harmless reasons like ethnic solidarity could be used as proxies for disloyalty, a weak justification for detention and further violations of civil liberties. Perhaps those Italians who had become naturalized American citizens before the war experienced the gravest violations because they were interned as if enemy aliens. Although the United States Senate 1976 Report on Intelligence Activities states "the plans for internment of potentially dangerous American citizens were never carried out," the internee files from the Office of the Provost Marshal General confirm that a number of American citizens were actually interned in different locations.[142] Biddle informed Hoover that the lists generated through this program lacked legal justification, that the FBI's classification system was flawed, and that the lists should not be used; yet Hoover persisted in using it, calling the project a "Security Matter" instead of "Custodial Detention." Hoover directed his agents to continue researching and maintaining lists.[143]

There in fact existed Italian Fascist organizations and individuals within the United States, many of which were identified by the FBI with the help of Gaetano Salvemini who consulted with government officials.[144] In 1942 Professor Constantine Panunzio reported that Fascists had worked from the early 1930s through organizations already established in this country, chiefly the Italian Embassy, Italian consulates, the Dante Alighieri Society, Fasci Abroad, and the Sons of Italy.[145] Other Italian organizations that appeared in intelligence files, some considered inherently dangerous and others seemingly innocuous in character, included Casa Coloniale, Cenacalo Club, Combattenti (Italian War Veterans), Council of Marconi, Italian American Chamber of Commerce, Italian Language Schools, Mario Morgantini Circle, Italian Fascists, and the Italian National Tourist Information Bureau.[146] The FBI targeted members of certain Italian social groups believed to be fronts for Fascist organizers.

In addition to concern about these organizations, the government feared that the foreign-language media had the potential to sway Italian communities toward allegiance to Italy. On the FBI's list of suspicious Italian publications, distributors, and bookstores were: *L'Italia*, L'Italia Press Company, Italian Chamber of Commerce, *Il Grido della Stirpe* (newspaper published by the Italian Lictor Society), *Fair Play* (magazine published by the Lictor Society), Sons of Italy, and *La Voce Del Popolo*.[147] Assistant Secretary of War John McCloy recommended that Italian publications not be prohibited categorically but rather reviewed individually. Publications considered subversive were to be reported to the postmaster general for investigation by a committee that included the attorney general and secretary of war.[148] Also on the FBI's radar were Italian radio stations and their announcers who broadcast Fascist propaganda directed at Italian neighborhoods in New York and Boston, where an unassimilated and mostly illiterate audience listened to broadcasts on their shortwave radios, particularly to maintain contact with the "old country."[149]

Along with Gaetano Salvemini, the Italian statesman Count Carlo Sforza, who had taken up residence in the United States after the outbreak of World War II, was among the political exiles from Italy (*fuorusciti*) who gained the respect of Roosevelt's administration. Sforza began working in the Italian diplomatic service in 1896, most notably saving Italy from conflict with Yugoslavia after World War I in his role as Italian Foreign Minister. He became a leader of anti-Fascism within Italy and outside it, and in the wake of World War II sought to purge high-ranking Fascists and contain Italian Communism, without disqualifying either movement.[150] As early as the 1920s, he was an advocate of European unity and, after the war, felt it was dangerous to cling to nationalism.[151] With Salvemini and several liberal journalists and academicians, Count Sforza was a leader of the Mazzini Society.[152] Named after Giuseppe Mazzini, a nineteenth-century politician who espoused republican nationalism, the Mazzini Society was founded in 1940 by Italian exiles dedicated to the principles of the *Risorgimento*. Composed of groups in fifty American cities, the Mazzini Society operated as an elite organization of no more than 900 members who worked to mobilize the American public, its political leaders, and Italian American communities toward supporting the establishment of a secular democracy in postwar Italy.[153] Like Salvemini, Sforza brought "intellectual respectability" to the resistance effort in the United States.[154]

At the outset of World War II, "a promising rapport developed between the fuorusciti and the administration."[155] In March 1941, at the urging of Count Sforza, Harold Ickes, Secretary of the Interior, raised the issue to the Cabinet of supporting anti-Fascist Italian newspapers.[156] When government attention focused on Generoso Pope, as discussed below, Sforza, who had entered the president's confidence, informed Roosevelt that Pope's daily Italian language newspaper *Il Progresso* pretended to be patriotic but in fact was deceiving Italian Americans, leading to the president's discussions with Pope. Sforza also advised the president to establish an anti-Fascist daily.[157]

What began as a mutually beneficial relationship between the administration and anti-Fascists, with the Office of War Information (OWI) receiving intelligence from anti-Fascists, and anti-Fascists utilizing the Office of Strategic Services to send funds to the underground, eventually turned course.[158] As the United States' war with Italy came to a close, anti-Fascists became disillusioned with the State Department's changing position on King Vittorio Emmanuel and with the Allies' failure to effect the type of political change in Italy that they hoped for, namely liberty and social justice. In its response to America's foreign diplomacy in late 1943, the Mazzini Society broke into two factions; Sforza's group sided with the administration, preferring to oppose policy from within, while many others attacked the government's policy that allowed ex-Fascists to assume important positions on liberation committees.[159] Upon his return to Italy in September 1943, Sforza assumed a position as a minister in the Pietro Badoglio government during the transition period, opposing the retention of the monarchy and the continuance of the Badoglio government despite the pledge of support he gave to Assistant Secretary of State Adolf Berle to secure his return to his homeland.[160] This seeming hypocrisy gained him the distrust of Prime Minister Churchill, particularly when the Badoglio government fell in June 1944 and was succeeded by Ivanoe Bonomi, whom Sforza supported. Yet Sforza continued to receive American support, as his influence through the Mazzini Society assisted Roosevelt in the 1944 election, in which New York was a critical state. In Italy he advanced the cause of the Allies in his role as the minister charged with purging Fascists, removing scores of senators and generals from the administration.[161]

Although the anti-Fascists were not able to influence the Allies to set up the type of political system they envisioned for Italy, the opposition did have the ears of members of the Roosevelt administration who appreciated the insight and intelligence that this group provided about Italy and subversive forces in this country for a significant period of the war years. Carlo Tresca, who from his arrival in America in 1904 had built a reputation as a newspaper editor and labor organizer, was particularly valuable to the FBI for his extensive knowledge about Italian American Fascism. While a leader of the Industrial Workers of the World in the 1910s, Tresca had led a string of strikes across the United States, beginning with the strike of textile workers in Lawrence, Massachusetts. By the 1930s, he had become outspoken against both Fascism and Communism and never tired of his fight for individual freedom.[162] Tresca's primary objective was to eradicate Fascism within the Italian American community in the United States and Canada, which he exposed through his writings and shared with FBI agents investigating potential subversive followers of Mussolini. Tresca led the FBI to Fascist agents in the Italian Consulate in New York and other Fascist individuals and organizations.[163]

Tresca focused on exposing Generoso Pope, claiming that Pope was still a devoted Fascist when Italy entered the war and hypocritical in his commitment to democracy in the United States because his only motive was to gain political and economic benefits from Tammany Hall. Well before the United States entered the war, the political leanings of Pope and the pro-Fascist articles in *Il Progresso* had come to the attention of the Justice and State Departments through complaints of the Mazzini Society. Even La Guardia urged Roosevelt to ask the FBI to conduct an investigation of Pope out of concern that Pope's newspaper could be damaging in the event of war.[164] Roosevelt was keenly aware that aggression with Pope could cost him the Italian American vote, as only a few years earlier the president had relied upon Pope, as chairman of the Democratic National Committee's Italian Division, to help secure the ethnic vote for Roosevelt's election to a second term.[165] Pope pledged Roosevelt his support in an intensive campaign in English and Italian in *Il Progresso* and his other newspaper, *Corriere D'America*.[166] Pope's influence in Washington over foreign policy was also undeniable; during Italy's Ethiopian campaign, Pope successfully led an effort among Italian American clubs and societies to pressure Washington to maintain neutrality toward Italy. The strength of the Italian American voting bloc appeared to influence Roosevelt to ignore anti-Fascist charges against Pope.[167]

Further proof of Pope's special influence on the administration can be found in a meeting between Roosevelt and Pope at the White House in April 1941 that resulted in Pope merely substituting pro-Fascist articles in the English-language section with pledges of loyalty to Roosevelt, while continuing to praise Mussolini in Italian-language articles. A second meeting in July 1941 ended in Pope's removal of the most vocal Fascists from his staff, and Pope continued to receive the support of Roosevelt and other politicians in Washington and New York.[168] It was not until September 1941, after rival New York biweekly *Il Mondo* described Pope as insincere in his conversion to anti-Fascism, that Pope's papers denounced Mussolini in both English and Italian articles.[169] Pope's shift toward a public anti-Fascist stance came slowly in 1941 when many other Italian Americans experienced insecurity and fear of Italy's alliance with Germany.[170]

In late 1942, when the OWI, through its Foreign Language Branch, sought to enlist trustworthy Italians to rally behind the war against the Axis powers and to help the government gain support among Italian American communities for America's intended policies for postwar Italy, it turned to Carlo Tresca for help. Through the establishment of Italian American Victory Councils, the OWI intended to relay news releases and promote educational programs and other forms of American propaganda.[171] However, Tresca and other anti-Fascists, feeling that war and capitalism were the real causes of Fascism, disputed an agenda that blamed Mussolini for all of Italy's woes. They opposed America's strategy for gaining Italian popular support since it was based on Churchill's plan of preserving Italy's monarchy and the papacy through a new Fascist regime, without Mussolini, that would resist Communism.[172] Although Tresca attended a preparatory meeting concerning the council in January 1943, just before his assassination, he opposed the OWI's efforts to include both ex-Fascists and Communists.[173] Controversy over Tresca's position, particularly concerning the participation of Generoso Pope and the International Workers Order in the council, continued after his death. Ultimately, amid intense intra-Italian quarrels, no Italian American Victory Council was ever established in New York.[174] Although a branch had been established in Chicago earlier, the members were not united ideologically, making it "an uneasy alliance of former fascists, communists, socialists, and liberals."[175]

The OWI was more successful in securing the help of maestro Arturo Toscanini in the war effort. Like many fellow Italians, Toscanini initially saw hope in Mussolini's programs for delivering Italy from its economic troubles in the 1920s, but became quickly disillusioned when Mussolini's policies suppressed civil liberties in a one-party state.[176] On several occasions Toscanini made it clear that he was not afraid of angering the Fascists. In 1926 on the premier of Toscanini's conducting Puccini's *Turandot* at La Scala Opera House in Milan, the conductor refused orders from Mussolini to play the Fascist anthem, *La Giovinezza*, in honor of Italy's celebration of Empire Day. Several years later, in May 1931, when Toscanini again refused to play the royal hymn and Fascist anthem in honor of official guests at a concert in Bologna, a Fascist gang physically attacked him and his family.[177] Such defiance of Mussolini and Fascism won him great respect in New York, where audiences in Carnegie Hall's balcony tossed paper slips with the messages "Down with Fascism" and "Long Live Toscanini."[178]

Toscanini garnered great admiration from President Roosevelt. Upon his departure for Italy in 1936, after eleven seasons with the New York Philharmonic-Symphony Orchestra, Toscanini was personally thanked by Roosevelt for his contributions to music in the United States.[179] The very next year, Toscanini was lured back to the United States by an offer from the Radio Corporation of America to conduct the N.B.C. Symphony in concerts broadcast to millions of radio listeners.[180] Eager to assist in the war effort, Toscanini readily agreed to N.B.C.'s proposal that he conduct a series of benefit concerts on behalf of the United States Treasury's bond drives. He also conducted concerts to raise money for the Red Cross and other charities, again receiving commendation from Roosevelt for his humanitarianism and commitment to liberty.[181] Ironically, since Toscanini had not obtained American citizenship out of concern that abandoning his tie to Italy while his countrymen suffered under Fascist rule would seem like desertion of their cause, he reportedly was treated like all other enemy aliens in the United States and was forced to relinquish his shortwave radio set until the ban was lifted.[182] Due to Toscanini's special relationship with the United States, Roosevelt considered asking Congress to make him a citizen.[183] Regardless of his citizenship status, the fine reputation that Toscanini built as a friend to America and a champion of democratic ideals made him the perfect spokesperson for a propaganda film produced by the OWI in early 1944. Designed for distribution abroad, the film featured Toscanini conducting "The Hymn of Nations," which he hoped would reach the people of Italy.[184]

Managing Italian Seamen in Domestic Waters and the Establishment of Enemy Alien Internment Policy

Simultaneous to the FBI's prewar intelligence collection of information on persons of Italian descent suspected of Fascist ties was the establishment of internment policies and programs that were first applied to Italian merchant seamen in American waters. In March 1941, the U.S. government's anxiety over the threat Italians posed domestically was heightened when intelligence reports reached the secretary of war's office indicating that a large Italian liner anchored in the Panama Canal since June 1940 would be sunk if Congress passed the Lease and Lend Bill for aid to the Allied forces.[185] There was a plan by the Italians to sabotage vessels in U.S. harbors, including two ships at Panama, and to obstruct the channel. The large Italian liner in the canal was the *Conte Biancamano*, a luxury liner of some 23,000 tons, which the army seized before it could be damaged.[186] In early 1941, President Roosevelt ordered the Coast Guard to impound all Axis ships stranded in U.S. ports upon the suspicion that the crewmen were sabotaging their own ships, setting fires and jamming the ships' gears, on the orders of Axis governments who feared the United States was going to take control of the vessels and use them against the Axis powers. The *Conte Biancamano* had been stranded in the Panama Canal Zone for many months.[187] The United States issued warrants to more than 1,200 Italian seamen in 1941, but since most of their ships were damaged and could not be used to deport them, the seamen were turned over to the INS for detention at Ellis Island and eventual internment at Fort Missoula in Montana.[188] The seamen were charged with numerous violations of immigration law at hearings before the Board of Special Inquiry on Ellis Island.[189] The INS operated Fort Missoula, a former army post, as well as internment camps at Fort Stanton, New Mexico, and Fort Lincoln in Bismarck, North Dakota, both of which were utilized for German seamen taken from vessels in American ports and the Panama Canal.[190]

The legal status as enemy aliens and the form of hearings afforded the seamen set the precedent for the treatment of resident Italian aliens who were arrested after the United States declared war on Italy, some of whom were interned alongside the seamen at Fort Missoula. In contrast to the seamen, most of the resident Italian aliens were permanent legal residents, with the exception of those who failed to register under the 1940 Alien Registration Act. Secretary of State Cordell Hull advised Secretary of War Stimson that reference should be made to Articles XIII and XV of the Hague Convention X of 1907 when classifying shipwrecked individuals who were citizens of enemy nations. He stated that "such persons should be treated as interned aliens rather than as prisoners of war."[191] Although Italy was not a party to the convention, Hull explained that "the provisions referred to may be regarded as a criterion as to the action that may be taken in such circumstances."[192] The International Committee of the Red Cross had proposed to belligerent states on September 4, 1939, that there be a general statute applicable to enemy civilians to afford them protections at least comparable to those given to prisoners of war under the Geneva Convention of July 27, 1929.[193] Thus the terms of the 1929 treaty, signed by the United States and forty-six other countries, including Italy and Germany but not Japan, were applied to civilian internees by states who chose to do so, but there was no formal mandate.[194] Although a majority of the state governments agreed to grant legal status and treaty guarantees to enemy civilians residing in the territory of a belligerent at the outbreak of war, the terms unfortunately did not apply to civilian nationals in an enemy-occupied country.[195] The treaty permitted "Protecting Powers" or neutral powers, on behalf of the warring states, to inspect internment camps and to report to the governments the extent to which the Detaining Power was abiding by the treaty's terms.[196] A typical inspection report commented on the ethnic and gender composition of the camp, the physical structure, medical care, food services, and activities of the internees.[197] The United States decided to apply prisoner of war provisions to internees and instructed its internment camp commanders accordingly.[198]

The INS records of the Italian seamen interned at Fort Missoula, beginning in March 1941 and continuing until 1944, indicate the type of risk that the government perceived this group of Italians presented.[199] Shortly after being taken into custody at ports such as Ellis Island in New York Harbor or Savannah, Georgia, they were required to complete an Alien Enemy Questionnaire which sought information such as names of family members, dates of entrances into the United States, criminal background, residences, property ownership, years of schooling, employment history, military service, financial portfolio, outstanding applications for U.S. naturalization, languages spoken, readership of any foreign-language newspapers, and memberships in organizations whose purpose was to overthrow the United

States government.[200] Those seamen who were not deported were transported to Fort Missoula. After a period at the camp, they underwent an evaluation before an alien enemy hearing board to assess their "appearance, testimony and demeanor." The Justice Department asked the board to give "as full a description of the man as possible together with your evaluation of his potential danger to the internal security."[201] The board's recommendation of parole or continued internment had to go before the attorney general for his approval.

During this period before the United States entered World War II, domestic plans were in place to handle persons of enemy nations residing in the United States. On July 18, 1941, Acting Secretary of War Robert Patterson and Acting Attorney General Francis Biddle entered a joint agreement concerning the internment of all alien enemies within the United States or its territories in the event of war. Pledging to make efforts to avoid "(a) Over-internment, . . . (c) Interference with labor through reckless internment, and (d) The internment of persons solely for careless statements made prior to the outbreak of war," the joint agreement anticipated cooperation between Army Corps area commanders and U.S. Attorneys in the transferring of alien enemies into the custody of the military for permanent detention.[202] The attorney general was to issue warrants for the apprehension of persons "believed to be dangerous to the public safety" based on information submitted to the U.S. Attorney's Office by an FBI agent or other informant.[203] The joint agreement called for a report from the U.S. Attorney concerning information on the alien enemy's "citizenship, immigration, alien registration, and selective service status, his age, loyalty, and acitivities [sic]" to be forwarded to the attorney general with his recommendations for either internment, parole (with or without bond), or conditional or unconditional release.[204] Alien enemies assigned to permanent detention would be required to fill out a questionnaire about their life, activities, and associations and to obtain affidavits from persons who have known them before review of their case before a review board.[205] Provision for a committee consisting of two representatives from the War Department and two representatives from the Justice Department indicated a plan to coordinate the handling of alien enemies.[206]

As will be seen, however, the course of relations between these departments throughout the war was characterized by power struggles. In particular, they disagreed over the implementation of President Roosevelt's Executive Order 9066 regarding the exclusion of persons of Japanese,

German, and Italian descent from military zones. While the Justice Department insisted on a policy of considering each case on an individual basis, the War Department believed that the exigencies of the national security crisis demanded a more practical and more sweeping approach by the military to ensuring the safety of the nation.[207]

CHAPTER TWO

The Face of Selective Internment and the Impact of Other Wartime Restrictions

On the night of December 7, 1941, the very day of the attack on Pearl Harbor, Attorney General Biddle authorized the FBI to take several hundred persons into custody without warrants due to the emergency.[1] J. Edgar Hoover ordered the arrest of all German and Italian aliens classified in Groups A, B, and C in the FBI Custodial Detention Program and those not previously classified in the above categories whose arrest was "necessary for the internal security of this country," and their delivery to the nearest INS office.[2] Newspaper headlines announced the "roundup of Axis aliens" as federal agents moved quickly through neighborhoods to make arrests, relying on local police officers for assistance.[3] Japanese individuals who had been identified in the program were also arrested and detained. Most individuals were not told the specific reason for their arrest and subsequent detention or where they were going, only that President Roosevelt had ordered their arrest.[4] Filippo Molinari, a forty-eight-year-old agent for the daily newspaper *L'Italia* in San Jose, California, described the abruptness and mystery of his capture:

> I was the first one arrested in San Jose the night of the attack on Pearl
> Harbor. At 11 P.M. three policemen came to the front door and two
> at the back. They told me that, by order of President Roosevelt, I
> must go with them. They didn't even give me time to go to my room
> and put on my shoes. I was wearing slippers. They took me to
> prison . . . and finally to Missoula, Montana, on the train, over the
> snow, still with slippers on my feet, the temperature at seventeen
> below and no coat or heavy clothes![5]

Thus, four days before the United States declared war on Italy, government agents began arresting Italian aliens and detaining them at INS facilities for processing before internment. On December 8, President Roosevelt, pursuant to authority under the Alien Enemy Act of 1798, issued Presidential Proclamation No. 2527, declaring the approximately 700,000 Italian immigrants without American citizenship "alien enemies," and making them subject to regulations and immediate apprehension or deportation

Italians are arriving at Fort Missoula after appearing in front of an alien enemy hearing board in their home district and receiving an order for internment from Attorney General Biddle. Most were transported to Missoula by train during the night. Due to the immediacy under which they were arrested, many came to the internment camp with few belongings. They arrived in the greatest numbers within the first six months after December 7, 1941, without any idea of how long they would be separated from their loved ones. (*Detainees Arriving at Fort Missoula, 1941–1942.* Peter Fortune Collection [2001.048.220]. Courtesy of the Historical Museum at Fort Missoula.)

if determined dangerous by the attorney general or the secretary of war. Similar to the regulations in the presidential proclamations against the Japanese and Germans, the status of alien enemy made Italians subject to restraints and multiple regulations, including those pertaining to geographical location, the possession of contraband articles, travel, and membership in certain organizations.[6] Alien enemies did not enjoy constitutional rights and privileges such as freedom from home invasions and seizure of one's possessions without probable cause, according to the guidelines of the INS.[7] Under the proclamations, duties and authority in executing the regulations rested with both the attorney general and the secretary of war.

By all accounts, there was a flurry of arrests in the days and weeks following the Japanese attack on Pearl Harbor. By 11:00 A.M. on December 9, approximately eighty-three Italian aliens were in custody.[8] On December 10, 1941, Attorney General Biddle promised that the government would make every effort to protect aliens from "discrimination or abuse" and would not "engage in wholesale condemnation of any alien group."[9] The *New York Times* reported 222 Italians arrested as of December 12.[10] This number is significantly higher than the 169 Italian aliens cited by Biddle in his press release the next day[11] Many Italians arrested had no chance to speak with family members before being taken away from their homes for several years. For example, Carmelo Ilacqua, a forty-six year-old alien employed by a poultry company who also served as a local officer of the Italian consulate, was arrested at his home in San Francisco on the evening of December 17, 1941, and forced to leave without saying good-bye to his family. As was customary when apprehending Italian aliens, FBI agents searched Ilacqua's home for contraband items such as guns and ammunition. Although the agents found nothing incriminating, they still arrested him and took him to a local INS facility for detainment. His wife and six-year-old daughter did not know what had happened to him until he could telephone them before boarding a train to Fort Missoula with other Italians and Japanese under armed guard.[12] Angelina Farese was likewise kept in the dark about the circumstances of her husband's arrest, believing it was a mistake that would quickly be straightened out and that he would return home the day after his arrest.[13]

Although Presidential Proclamation 2527 covered only alien enemies, American citizens of Italian extraction also were included in the FBI arrest lists.[14] In fact, arrests of Italians including American citizens were reported in New York and California.[15] In an effort to resolve the confusion over suspect American citizens of Axis origin, Hoover instructed officers to provide to FBI headquarters a list of such persons, emphasizing that "each recommendation must be justified by substantial evidence or information indicating actual danger to our internal security during present war effort."[16]

The following chronology, beginning on December 7, 1941, when government agents began arresting individual Italian aliens, provides a framework for understanding how the government policies affected Italian families. By mid-December 1941, with commercial traffic in and out of the San Francisco harbor already suspended, the U.S. Navy requisitioned dozens of fishing boats of Italians on the West Coast, to be followed by similar requisitions in the following months. The commercial fishing industry felt an acute blow in early 1942 when fishing restrictions prohibited Italian aliens from taking their boats out and denied them access to wharfs and piers out of concern over threats of sabotage and invasion by the enemies.[17] On January 29, the attorney general issued the first of several orders establishing prohibited zones on the West Coast that all enemy aliens had to evacuate by February 24.[18] Evacuation of more than 10,000 Italians from prohibited zones on the West Coast and relocation to areas outside these zones began in February 1942 and continued until June 1942, when Lieutenant General John DeWitt, commander of the Western Defense Command, allowed them to return to their homes.[19] In that February, the attorney general also announced restricted areas on the West Coast where more than fifty thousand Italian aliens had to observe curfews and travel restrictions.[20] In April, Lieutenant General Hugh A. Drum, head of the Eastern Defense Command, proposed the classification of prohibited and restricted areas for the Eastern Defense Command along the Atlantic Seaboard and inland, but no mass evacuation.[21] In the summer of 1942, the military instituted the process of "individual exclusion" for suspicious Italian aliens and naturalized citizens resulting in their removal from military areas.[22] Restrictions other than selective internment and individual exclusion ended with the termination of alien enemy status for persons of Italian descent on October 12, 1942.[23] Arrests of individual Italian aliens continued through mid-October 1944.[24]

The Social Profile of Italian Civilian Internees

Although Attorney General Biddle was uncomfortable about internment, he believed that Roosevelt simply felt it must be done to defend the country.[25] Biddle was determined to avoid mass internment, keenly aware of the situation in Great Britain where their initial policy of selective internment yielded to panic by August 1940. Approximately 74,000 aliens, mostly German and Austrian Jews, were taken into custody and quickly placed into camps in Great Britain.[26] In his memoir, Jerre Mangione, recalling his role as the director of the public relations program of the INS, which had initial custody of all enemy aliens and ran several internment camps, suggested that Biddle convinced Roosevelt to institute selective internment of German and Austrian nationals rather than wholesale internment. Mangione also pointed to the likely role of correspondence from several notable refugees in influencing the president.[27] Six well-known refugees, including Albert Einstein, Thomas Mann, and Arturo Toscanini, wrote to Roosevelt on behalf of "a large group of natives of Germany and Italy who by present regulations are, erroneously, characterized and treated as 'Enemy Aliens.'" They asked him to draw "a clear and practical line . . . between the potential enemies of American democracy on the one hand, and the victims and sworn foes of totalitarian evil on the other."[28] In response to Thomas Mann's plea to Biddle to give consideration to "an official announcement that the victims of Nazi and Fascist oppression are not enemy aliens," Biddle expressed his great interest but said that it was "a question of policy for the President and the State Department."[29]

Undoubtedly Biddle was troubled by the prospects of interning an entire population, including the difficulties of evaluating the loyalties of each individual and affording procedural due process even though the law did not require it with respect to enemy aliens. It is important to keep in mind that many more Italians passed through the alien enemy control program of the INS than were actually interned. Some were released before a hearing, some after a hearing, while others were paroled. By the end of the war, the total number of Italians "received by the Immigration and Naturalization Service under the alien enemy program," meaning those detained for some form of investigation, was 3,278. This number was less than one-third of the number of Germans (10,905) and about one-fifth of the Japanese in this program (16,849), although the Japanese were, of course, interned in much greater numbers.[30] Based on an estimate of 700,000 Italian aliens living in the United States during World War II, the number of Italians processed through the INS was a very small segment of the Italian population. Comparatively, the Japanese population experienced a much more severe deprivation of their civil liberties. The significant difference in the number of Germans processed through the alien enemy program may be due to the American public's skepticism about their integrity, loyalty, and place in American society, a holdover from the hysteria that accompanied World War I.[31] In contrast, Italians as a group were viewed far more favorably as a largely loyal and peaceful population.

The social profile of the Italian internees reveals the aims of the Justice Department's selective internment process. Most of the 343 Italians were aliens who had resided in the United States for many years before the outbreak of World War II and who were apprehended in the United States based on FBI reports identifying them as suspect. They were immediately detained and subsequently interned after a hearing. This group of 343 includes forty-six Italian nationals residing in Latin America and apprehended there. They were the subjects of an agreement, entered into by the State Department of the United States and Latin American countries, which provided for their internment in exchange for Americans held by Axis powers, as will be discussed in more depth. Not included in this study are the approximately 1,300 seamen introduced in the previous chapter—merchant sailors working aboard luxury liners in the Panama Canal and American ports who were suspected of sabotaging their ships. Also not part of the study are Italian nationals employed at the 1939–1940 World's Fair in New York who were interned beginning in March 1941 at Fort Missoula. The seamen were legally in a similar position to those long-term resident aliens apprehended beginning on December 7 in that they were also classified as enemy aliens, interned, and eventually appeared before alien enemy hearing boards. However, they were charged with violations of immigration law that provided the grounds to hold them in custody since the war prevented their deportation. In contrast, most of the resident aliens apprehended once the United States entered World War II had permanent legal residence status and were arrested based on criteria established by the FBI in coordination with the Justice Department.

Among the 343 long-term U.S. residents and Latin Americans interned, the average age in 1941 was forty-three. There were 330 men and thirteen females, of whom two were interned on their own account, meaning they were not accompanying a male family member. The group included six naturalized American citizens, although three of them were denaturalized or had an uncertain legal status at the time of internment. Of the 268 subjects for whom marital status was recorded, 165 were married. Of the 254 internees from the United States and its territories with known home residences, approximately 82 percent hailed from the East and West Coasts, consistent with data on geographical regions where the Italian population was most dense and with the government's perception of where the greatest dangers were. The breakdown of regions was East, 112; West, 97; South, 11; Midwest, 24; Southwest, 4; Hawaii, 3; Alaska, 2; Puerto Rico, 1 (see Appendix 2). Of this group of U.S. residents, thirty-three internees or approximately 13 percent reported having lived in the United States for ten or more years before internment, although not continuously in some cases. Of the forty-six internees from Latin America, five were children.

An important factor in comparing internment and restrictions on the East Coast with those on the West Coast was the much larger Italian population on the East Coast, making any large-scale evacuation and restrictions there more problematic. In 1940, the Middle Atlantic states had 390,068 Italian aliens, with New York having the highest number at 247,837; New England had 106,658 Italian aliens, with Massachusetts having the most at

53,531; the East North Central states had 84,431, with Illinois having the most at 34,678; and the Pacific states had 57,797, with California having 51,923.[32] The FBI field offices reported the following cities as having the highest number of Italian aliens and naturalized citizens arrested: San Francisco (453 aliens, 5 citizens); New York City (401 aliens, 5 citizens); New Orleans (233 aliens); Miami (212 aliens); and Los Angeles (141 aliens, 1 citizen). A comparison of cities in states on the East and West Coasts indicates that there were 57 percent more arrests on the East Coast than on the West Coast although the population of Italian aliens on the East Coast was almost nine times greater.[33] The number of subject internees in the study from states on the East Coast was only 15 percent greater than those from states on the West Coast.[34] According to this data, Italian internees from the West Coast represented a greater percentage of that region's population of Italian aliens than the representation of East Coast internees among their region's Italian alien population.

For the 259 internees for whom there is a date of apprehension recorded, about 77 percent of them were taken in the first six months of the war, tracking the initial anxiety over enemy nationals in the United States and the decreasing tension as the war progressed. There were sixty-five subject internees detained in both the United States and Latin America in advance of the United States' declaration of war on Italy on December 11, 1941. An additional seventeen subjects were apprehended before December 31, 1941, and eventually interned. By the end of February 1942, the total was 135, and by the end of May, 182. The greatest spike in numbers of subjects ordered interned occurred in December 1941.

An examination of occupations reveals a broad range of skills and educational levels. In the study, there were twenty-nine persons, or approximately 8.5 percent, employed in the media, some exclusively and others as a second job either as newspaper editors or radio announcers.[35] Based on the type of testimony elicited in the HUAC hearings and the Tenney Committee hearings in California, the national and state governments were concerned with how members of the media could potentially influence Italian communities whose ties to their motherland were strong and whose loyalties to the United States were just developing.

In addition to the 8.5 percent of subjects employed in the media, the subject group included the following occupational categories and approximate percentages of representation: unskilled, 31 percent; professional, 23 percent; skilled, 13.4 percent; business owner, 5 percent; student, 2.9 percent; homemaker, 2.6 percent; unemployed, 1.5 percent; and unknown, 12 percent. The two largest categories were unskilled laborers (107), such as fishermen and farm laborers, and professionals (79). Subject internees categorized as professionals included two lawyers, two medical doctors, eight teachers/professors (including some in the Italian language), seven engineers, five business executives, three accountants, and four employees of the Italian government. Persons who worked in the financial industry in roles such as accountants or credit managers in banks were of particular concern since the FBI believed they were in positions where they could assist the Italian government in raising money for the war.[36] Perhaps most noteworthy in this subcategory is Prince Boncompagno Boncompagni-Ludovisi, an export broker residing in New York City who was allegedly involved in an illegal exchange of Italian currency.[37] The government was also concerned with intellectuals who might possess special knowledge that could be used against the United States. For example, Dr. Vincent Anthony Lapenta, a surgeon and chemist who invented synthetic plasma to treat shock, was of particular interest although he reportedly shared his invention with the U.S. Army.[38] The government also feared persons employed in positions where they might have access to U.S. military information, such as Pericle Chieri, a mechanical engineer employed by the Italian Embassy who is profiled in future pages, believing they might share confidential information with the Italian government.

The types of people the FBI identified as suspicious aliens among the German population were not dissimilar to the group of Italian internees, except there were many more of them. Leaders of political, social, and cultural organizations suspected of supporting Hitler's government as well as men with business skill and those considered social problems were among the German internees. And as with the Italian population, German aliens were ordered interned based on unreliable FBI reports consisting of un-corroborated hearsay and rumors.[39]

That unskilled laborers made up almost one-third of the Italian subject group is somewhat baffling since it is difficult to imagine that the U.S. government had reason to believe that such persons could influence fellow workers or members of their Italian communities. Given that they were in a lower income bracket, such persons might have been willing to engage in subversive political activity against the United States because they had little to lose, except of course their ability to remain in this country. But a more plausible explanation for their significant representation among the subject group is that the government perceived them as undesirables who were likely to become public charges, even if they were unlikely to pose a national security threat. Since the number of unskilled Italian laborers in the United States was sizable, this segment of the subject group fairly represents the Italian community's demographics at the time.[40]

Only twelve of the subjects appear to have had prior arrests or convictions, either in the United States or Italy, and three more were undergoing criminal proceedings during internment. Most of those with a criminal record had committed minor offenses such as petty larceny or public drunkenness and disorderly conduct. One internee had been implicated in a murder in Italy, one arrested in Rome for political reasons, and one brought up on two charges of suspicion in the United States in the 1930s, meaning that the arrest was for no specific offense and the suspect was released without formal charges. Another internee had eighteen prior arrests for narcotics violations. One of the two women interned on their own account was arrested multiple times for keeping a house of prostitution. Given the existence of organized crime in the decades preceding World War II, some of the subjects may have been members of mobs, particularly those who owned their own businesses and sought protection of their property, but they were not identified as such in the records, meaning it was not necessarily a factor in their arrest.[41] At least ten had undergone deportation proceedings by the time they were interned or been labeled a "criminal deportable alien enemy." The government may have perceived prior criminals as more likely to turn to treason simply because they were inclined to commit crimes.

The selective internment process was also influenced by local loyalties and vendettas, informants, and suspicions that had more to do with an individual's personal and professional associations than with national security concerns. Some Italian aliens felt the greatest betrayal by people in their own communities where neighbors acted on jealousies and old grudges by reporting friends and even family members who violated curfews and other government restrictions. The tattlers were usually so frightened by the curfews that they stayed home all the time and became vigilantes, creating a very hostile environment in some communities.[42] Thus the singling out of certain people for investigation was somewhat circumstantial.

There were five possible outcomes after internment: outright release by the Alien Enemy Control Unit after a hearing at the internment camp; parole with release or internment again later; repatriation on the basis of exchange for American citizens held abroad; voluntary repatriation; and involuntary repatriation after a determination that the internee was deportable under immigration law.[43] The average duration of internment, calculated from the date of apprehension until the date of release, based on 155 internees for whom both dates were recorded, was two years and four months. For these 155 internees, nine were released by June 30, 1943; forty-four more by December 30, 1943; twenty-five more by June 30, 1944; twelve more by December 30, 1944; fifty-nine more by June 30, 1945; and six more were released by February 21, 1946.[44] Although most of the group of 155 internees was released after Italy surrendered in September 1943, the majority of all Italian internees were released by the end of 1943. Two internees entered the U.S. Army upon their release. The average age of internees was above that allowed for registration with the armed forces, which may account for the low number who chose to enter the military. At least fifty-one internees in the subject group were repatriated. Eight men among those studied were diagnosed with psychosis and committed to mental institutions during internment, and at least seven died in camp.

As indicated above, included in the study are forty-six individuals from Latin America. The countries of origin were Peru, Costa Rica, Honduras, Colombia, Guatemala, Panama, Ecuador, Nicaragua, and Mexico. They came from all socioeconomic backgrounds, ranging from laborers to a few professional businessmen and academics. Historian Max Friedman notes that there were "few suspected Fascists" among the Italian group from Latin America, composed primarily of merchant sailors and repatriated diplomats. The largely working-class Italian expatriates who had easily assimilated into Latin American society were more sympathetic to anarchist movements than fascism.[45] Most of the male deportees had been born in Italy and were Italian citizens; some were accompanied by women and children, called "voluntary detainees," who chose internment with their husbands, sons, or fathers. In addition to being Italian citizens, they were all citizens of the Latin American countries from which they were sent.[46] Local Latin American police apprehended a majority of this group of internees in December 1941 or January 1942 and subsequently turned them over to INS officials.[47]

These individuals were the subjects of a resolution for the deportation of dangerous Axis nationals drafted by the U.S. State Department and the Justice Department and adopted by a Conference of Foreign Ministers of the American Republics in January 1942 in Rio de Janeiro. A justification for the program was the absence of adequate local detention facilities. This group of foreign ministers, called the Emergency Committee for Political Defense, was an inter-American agency tasked with organizing "hemispheric security measures" in light of the perceived threats to continental security. The State Department offered to include in this arrangement any official and civilian nationals of participating republics in exchange for the return of Americans held by Axis powers.[48] Although the committee did not approve Resolution XX, entitled "Detention and Expulsion of Dangerous Axis Nationals," until May 21, 1943, and did not transmit it to the governments until June 4, 1943, the United States and Peru engaged in a deportation-internment program in 1942.[49] In general, in most Latin American countries, the chief executive had sole authority to expel an alien, which could be done summarily and in the absence of an individual's right to judicial proceedings. This executive control allowed Latin American countries to enter a deportation-internment program with the United States outside of legislative oversight or public awareness.[50]

Scholarship in the past two decades has challenged the generally accepted rationale for the Latin American deportation program, uncovering economic reasons for it, particularly with respect to the German deportees, rather than concerns for security, as originally understood in the several decades following World War II. Finding evidence in correspondence of the American vice consul in Peru, Stephen Fox shows that the official U.S. national security scheme was meant to mask its true objective of replacing competitive German interests in the region with those of the United States and cooperative republics. He explains how many of the Germans selected for deportation owned or managed property and businesses considered threats by local governments and the State Department.[51] Corroborating this theory, Max Friedman points out that even as the threat of a military attack on the Western Hemisphere receded, the Latin American deportation program focused more upon "individuals who could in no way be tied to Nazi activity, but had acquired significant economic positions."[52] Although the explanations offered by Fox and Friedman seem pertinent to the wealthy German businessmen in the expatriate community in Latin America, their rationale does not describe the largely working class that made up the Italian labor force in Latin America at the time. With respect to the smaller Italian deportee group, I could find no evidence that the State Department had the same interest of removing economic competition.

The first vessel to sail from South America, the *Etolin*, left from Callou, Peru, on April 5, 1942, with 173 Germans, 141 Japanese, and 11 Italians, and proceeded up the western coast to pick up additional passengers.[53] By late August 1942, there were 3,300 American citizens in China, 3,000 in the Philippines, and 700 in Japan seeking return to the United States, prompting Secretary of State Cordell Hull to call for continued efforts to remove all the Japanese and dangerous Germans and Italians, with their families, for internment in the United States.[54] Deportees from Latin America under this agreement came to the United States by plane or ship into the Gulf Coast with no legal status, that is, illegally, since deportees held no visa or passport, putting them at the mercy of American authorities.[55] This program violated U.S. and international law, which recognized humanitarian rights even before the codification of international human rights law after World War II.[56] As Jerre Mangione pointed out, once the Latin Americans were brought over the U.S. border, they ironically were charged with illegal entry.[57]

The government did not afford any of the Latin Americans a hearing prior to internment.[58] Attorney General Biddle maintained his department's right to review cases even though Latin American internees, while held under the Alien Enemy Act, did not undergo proceedings before alien enemy hearing boards.[59] Biddle's challenge to the State Department's criterion of "dangerousness" eventually led to on-the-spot reviews of pending deportee cases by Raymond W. Ickes of the Central and South American division of the Alien Enemy Control Unit. Ickes was able to halt deportation of individuals where evidence failed to support claims that they threatened security.[60]

The INS used camps at Kenedy, Seagoville, and Crystal City in Texas for the internment of these Latin Americans and their families pending repatriation. The *Etolin* arrived with passengers in San Francisco on April 20, 1942.[61] The first Latin American internee group at Kenedy was comprised of 456 Germans, 156 Japanese, and 14 Italians. Over 2,600 more individuals were received from Latin America later in 1942.[62] The disposition of these cases could be one of the following: repatriation to Italy; return to their Latin American country; detention until arrangements were made for return to Latin America; liberty in the United States but subject to the jurisdiction of the INS until a final decision on their case was reached; and "internment-at-large," which, similar to the parole procedure, required periodic reports to the internee's sponsor and the INS.[63] Being "interned-at-large" meant that the internee met INS standards for parole but could not officially be paroled because of agreements between the Department of State and the aliens' countries of origin.[64] According to State Department records, as of July 1, 1945, seventeen Italians were interned in camps; thirty-two were "interned at large"; and four were voluntary internees.[65]

Even as hundreds of resident Italian aliens were hastily detained and sent to internment camps and the first groups of Latin Americans arrived at INS camps, federal and state legislative committees debated how to handle the perceived threat presented by the large population of Italian aliens. The main policy for consideration was the evacuation of Italians from military areas.

Government Debates Regarding Treatment of Enemy Alien Populations

President Roosevelt's issuance of Executive Order 9066 on February 19, 1942, marked a shift in the delegation of power from the attorney general to the secretary of war, with a resulting change in the execution of government policies.[66] Many of the regulations in Presidential Proclamation 2527 were incorporated by reference into the order's military proclamations. Under 9066, President Roosevelt authorized Secretary of War Stimson and military commanders to exclude "any or all persons" from designated military areas, and he declared "the right of any persons to enter, remain in, or leave shall be subject to whatever restrictions the Secretary of War or the appropriate military commanders may impose in their discretion."[67] The order did not distinguish either alien from citizen or among ethnic groups, and thus could potentially have applied to all Japanese, Germans, and Italians regardless of their citizenship, although it is doubtful that this policy was ever intended to apply indiscriminately to all groups.[68] Although the Western Defense Command imposed evacuation orders from the military zones only on aliens in the Italian and German populations, family members who were citizens often accompanied them. In contrast, both Japanese aliens and Japanese American citizens were forced to leave their homes.

Only days after President Roosevelt issued Executive Order 9066, the House of Representatives Select Committee Investigating National Defense Migration formed for the purpose of conducting public hearings on the situation of European aliens and for issuing periodic reports of its findings and recommendations.[69] Unlike the case of the Japanese, there was no proposal before the committee "that the millions of second generation Germans and Italians, born in this country be treated differently from other American citizens."[70] In its preliminary report, the "Tolan Committee," named for Chairman John H. Tolan of Oakland, California, determined that the numbers would be much larger than the Japanese exodus "if we generalize the current treatment of the Japanese to apply to all Axis aliens and their immediate families."[71] The Tolan Committee debated the strain that "tax[ing] the facilities of public agencies" for the duration of the war would put on the federal budget and resources.[72] Certainly the prospect of relocating this large population, which was widely dispersed across the country, was a logistical nightmare and therefore something to be avoided. The further prospect of confining them was even more dreadful. Because the Japanese population was concentrated in identifiable communities on the West Coast, relocation was much more feasible.[73]

The National Defense Migration hearings regarding the evacuation of enemy aliens and others prohibited from military zones were held in February and March 1942 in San Francisco, Portland, Seattle, and Los Angeles.[74] Since Congressman Tolan was sensitive to the plight of the Italian community, he set a positive tone in the hearings. Personally familiar with leaders of the community who appeared before the panel, he elicited testimony from them designed to evoke sympathy for the Italians from committee members and the War Department.[75] At the start of the hearings held in San Francisco on February 21, 1942, Chairman Tolan described the purpose of the hearings as a fact-finding mission to assess how the evacuation orders affected the economic life of various communities, what labor evacuees should undertake, where they should be located, and whether any exceptions should be made to a wholesale evacuation order.[76] San Francisco Mayor Angelo Rossi captured public sentiment in testifying: "It is the well-considered opinion of many that most of these people are entirely loyal to this Nation; are in accord with its form of government, believe in its ideals and have an affection for its traditions and that under no circumstances would they engage in any subversive activities or conduct." Rossi expressed a particular concern for persons essential to the community—"fishermen, janitors, garbage collectors, produce and vegetable workers in markets" and suggested they be given special permits to engage in their activities after the 9 P.M. curfew. Rossi advised the committee that "in order to avoid injustice being done, the investigation of each individual case of German and Italian aliens is absolutely necessary." The mayor specifically suggested that federal authorities establish a system of appeals in tribunals where aliens and citizens could petition to have their loyalty verified, enabling their return to civilian occupations.[77]

Another persuasive spokesperson for the Italian community was Ottorino Ronchi, a former professor of Italian at the University of California and an editor of *La Voce Del Popolo*, a newspaper that appeared on the FBI's list of suspicious publications. Ronchi testified about interviews he conducted of alien families in northern California whose sons were serving in the armed forces to impress upon the committee that Italians were loyal to the United States and should not be considered dangerous. He retold a conversation that he had with a sixty-year-old widow facing evacuation from

Monterey whose son died in the attack on Pearl Harbor and whose second son enlisted the next day. She told Ronchi: "I wish I had a couple of more children. I will send them to fight. My interest is in America."[78] In 1942, there were some 400,000 men of Italian parents in the U.S. armed forces as well as thousands of Italians employed in defense industries.[79]

The effect of such policies on American society generally was also a concern for the committee. As historian John Diggins noted, "The determination of loyalty was often less a matter of evidence than influence."[80] The prospect in 1942 of evacuating all Italian aliens from military zones on the West Coast, especially when that would have included the parents of three popular Italian American baseball players, would not have gone over well with the American public. Italian aliens Giuseppe DiMaggio and his wife were the parents not only of New York Yankee Joe DiMaggio, who was the leading hitter in baseball for 1939 and 1940, but also of Dominic, who was with the Boston Red Sox, and of Vincent, who played for Pittsburgh. Testimony about the "splendid" DiMaggio family before the Tolan Committee in 1942 underscored the unpopularity of any policy that would remove all aliens in the name of security. On their behalf, an Italian American attorney asserted that "The senior DiMaggios, though noncitizens, are as loyal as anyone could be."[81] Although the DiMaggios were ultimately not forced to relocate from their home, Giuseppe DiMaggio was subject to a ban on fishermen that prevented him from fishing out of Fisherman's Wharf in San Francisco.[82]

Fearing that all non-American citizens of Italian descent were unfairly classed as enemy aliens regardless of their loyalties, the Secretary of the San Francisco Chapter of the Mazzini Society submitted a report to the Tolan Committee explaining the distinct factions among Italian society.[83] He identified three groups: (1) the "Fascist Italian" devoted to Hitler and Mussolini who is interned or will be placed on bail or parole and "knows very well that he has received exactly what he deserves"; (2) the "decent Italian, who out of ignorance, stupidity or misguided feeling of loyalty to the old country" hoped for a Fascist victory, although this person did not commit any unlawful action against the United States, but who realizes this country has to guard against the potential risk he presents; and (3) the "Italian anti-Fascists" devoted to the struggle against Fascism who abandoned Italy only to face the injustice in the United States of bearing the label of enemy aliens, which carried restrictions in their movement and exclusion from the armed forces.[84] The report from the Mazzini Society's secretary raised the irony that "champions of nazi-ism and fascism" could produce naturalization papers and "wrap themselves in the American flag" while they continued their subversive activities.[85]

The committee elicited testimony from longtime resident aliens of San Francisco concerning illiteracy as a bar to citizenship. For example, Luciano Maniscalo, mother of twelve children, four of whom were serving in the armed services, testified to financial difficulties as her husband's alien status barred him from fishing after December 7. He had no education in Italy and could not even write his name. Mrs. Maniscalo said that his illiteracy was the only thing preventing him from becoming a citizen.[86] Later testimony from the assistant district director of the INS in March 1942 revealed that in the San Francisco area alone about 2,000 people were classified as alien enemies because the government had not gotten around to processing their petitions. His testimony further emphasized to the committee that the legal status of citizen was not solely determinative of loyalty.[87]

Demographic reality was one reason why the military and the general public considered Italians potentially less of a national security threat than Japanese and Germans. As a general rule, the committee concluded, Italians who had not become U.S. citizens were those who were illiterate and were often "elderly people, 50 to 60 years old" who had "raised large families, and frequently one or more of their children [were] in the armed services of the United States."[88] Months into U.S. involvement in the war, military officials received information that the younger generation of Italians, citizenship notwithstanding, particularly those born shortly after World War I, were the most dangerous.[89] Carmelo Zito who was the editor of *Corriere del Popolo*, an anti-Fascist newspaper, informed the government that the leaders of the Italian Fascists in the United States were American citizens and that young Italian aliens might be dangerous.[90] By this time, General DeWitt agreed with other military leaders that "the older Italians and the refugees were harmless as a group."[91]

Zito testified in May 1942 before the Assembly Fact Finding Committee on Un-American Activities in California, chaired by Jack B. Tenney (the Tenney Committee) about Italian newspapers, radio stations, and fund-raising prior to the U.S. entry into World War II. In contrast to the atmosphere of the Tolan Committee hearings, the tone of the hearings before the Tenney Committee, which had begun in January 1941, was one of fear and suspicion.[92] In this respect, they were similar to the hearings of HUAC before Congressman Martin Dies that were discussed in chapter 1. In scathing testimony before the Tenney Committee, Zito described the pro-Fascist element in San Francisco from the early 1920s as "instrumental to drug the public opinion among the Italian Americans to the point they are not capable any more to understand the benefits of democracy and the blessings of the land in the country of their adoption."[93] He identified Fascist sympathizers among radio announcers and newspaper editors, most of whom the FBI had already apprehended for internment, and claimed that San Francisco Mayor Angelo Rossi rendered the Fascist salute in public demonstrations. Zito claimed that the Italian Chamber of Commerce received subsidies from the Italian government and promoted Fascism through its newspaper, *La Rassegna Commerciale*, while Italian language "Fascistic" schools, opened in 1932, indoctrinated young people into Fascism through textbooks filled with propaganda.[94] While much of what Zito described as occurring during the 1920s and early 1930s may have had veracity, changes in Italy's political position by the early 1940s had altered Italian Americans' public support for their homeland.

Mayor Rossi called his summons to testify before the Tenney Committee "political assassination" and the result of "religious and racial bigotry" against him. Claiming ignorance of the curriculum of the Italian language schools and propaganda promulgated by the Italian Chamber of Commerce, Rossi affirmed his complete loyalty to the United States, evidenced by his decision to remove a signed photo of Mussolini from his office prior to the declaration of war against Italy.[95] Both Mayor Rossi and New York City Mayor La Guardia had received decorations from Italy's King Emmanuel, a gesture the Tenney Committee understood to be sanctioned by Mussolini, but only La Guardia decided to destroy the decoration by melting it into bullets.[96] Testimony of pro-Fascist sentiment among San Francisco's Italian community may explain Mayor Rossi's acceptance of multiple Italian decorations in the 1930s and his failure to recollect ever publicly denouncing Mussolini.[97] It is likely that he did not want to risk offending his supporters and destroying the bond he had cultivated with the Italian community who identified with his Italian heritage. Zito pointed out that even after the start of war when public sentiment had changed, as reflected in the pledge of loyalty to the United States by formerly Fascist-oriented newspapers, outright condemnation of Mussolini seems to have remained taboo.[98]

While California was investigating suspicious individuals in its state, the legislative and executive branches of the national government reached a consensus on how to handle German and Italian aliens. In May 1942, when the Tolan Committee released its Fourth Interim Report reiterating that any mass evacuation of German and Italian aliens was "out of the question if we intend to win this war," Roosevelt, in consultation with the War Department, finalized his recommendation on the Germans and Italians.[99] The repercussions a full-scale program of evacuation would have on these populations concerned the executive office. On May 5, 1942, Roosevelt wrote to Secretary of War Stimson, expressing concern that General Drum's plans for creating a "military area" on the East Coast caused a "state of confusion" among German and Italian people who worried that they would face evacuation like what those in the prohibited zone on the West Coast had experienced beginning in February. Roosevelt said that he was "inclined to think [evacuation of German and Italian aliens] may have a bad effect on morale."[100] Certainly the president had to be concerned about losing a political base, as Italian Americans gravitated toward the Republican Party. About a month earlier, Attorney General Biddle had advised the president that any German or Italian evacuation on the East Coast, even if it involved only aliens, would cause "dislocation of our economic structure" as well as "a bitter shock to the national morale."[101] The president understood the intention of Executive Order 9066 as "primarily to give General Drum authority over the dimming of lights along the Eastern seaboard and not over alien enemies."[102] His perception that the Justice Department maintained authority over aliens from European enemy countries is evident in his statement to Stimson that "the control of alien enemies seems to me to be primarily a civilian matter except of course in the case of the Japanese mass evacuation on the Pacific Coast."[103]

However, months earlier, in February 1942, the military had treated the evacuation of Italian families from prohibited zones on the West Coast and limitations upon enemy aliens in restricted areas as matters within its command. Executive Order 9066 had placed authority in the hands of the War Department to determine military areas and policies of exclusion and restrictions upon all enemy aliens in these areas. But it was decided that in expansive military areas, European aliens would be treated differently from the Japanese population. Stimson informed the president that "the problem of the Germans and the Italians was arranged . . . to handle those in a different way from the Japanese and to do it individually with reference to the danger to key positions rather than by any block evacuations on a ratio basis."[104] The War Department secretaries agreed that defense commanders would be authorized to issue individual exclusion orders concerning aliens and naturalized citizens pursuant to Executive Order 9066.[105] The president was satisfied with this federal policy.

With respect to the mass evacuation of persons of Japanese descent, there was much disagreement between Biddle and the War Department. However, Stimson was certain that Biddle should have no "hopes of getting a change made in the powers which the President had given to me."[106] The influence of public opinion in decisions calling for disparate treatment of persons of Japanese descent cannot be underestimated. Like selective internment of Italians and Germans, the Japanese who were perceived to present the greatest danger, comprising the political, social, cultural, and business leaders of Japanese American communities ranging from Buddhist priests and martial arts instructors to leaders of nationalistic organizations, had been apprehended within days after the attack on Pearl Harbor.[107] But public sentiment about the special dangers of the Japanese population as a whole and fear of economic competition resulted in mass evacuation of this group alone.[108] Agricultural groups such as the Western Growers Protective Association, the California Farm Bureau, and the White American Nurserymen of Los Angeles, who resented the domination of the fresh-produce market by ethnic Japanese farmers, lobbied for their removal from the state.[109] There was no comparable anti-German or anti-Italian agitation among the public that would have persuaded the War Department to press President Roosevelt to treat these ethnic groups similarly to the Japanese.[110] As historian Martin Grodzins pointed out in the late 1940s, charges leveled against the Japanese as indicators of "a low degree of Americanization," such as a low rate of naturalization, frequent trips to the homeland, and separate language schools and churches, could equally have been raised against the larger foreign-born population of Italians. Likewise, there was a strong case for evacuation of Germans on the East Coast who, in the state of New York alone, outnumbered persons of Japanese descent on the entire West Coast.[111] Writing more than half a century later, historian Joseph Persico remarks that what distinguished the treatment of Germans and Italians from that of Japanese was that there had to be some basis in law for declaring an individual potentially dangerous, while the Japanese and Japanese Americans were relocated en masse because of the color of their skin, regardless of the status of their loyalty.[112] As documents cited in the following section reveal, racial prejudice is among several factors explaining the disparate treatment of the Japanese as opposed to Italians and Germans.

Regional Differences in Implementation of Enemy Alien Restrictions

Military policy with respect to the various government restrictions differed in the Eastern and Western Defense Commands. The most important factor was the location of important wartime industries that could have been targeted by enemy forces. Four days after the attack on Pearl Harbor, the adjutant general declared the Western Defense Command a "theatre of operations" and gave the commanding general special instructions for facilitating the transfer of personnel and materiel to accommodate the creation of new air units for dispatch to Panama and Hawaii.[113] By January 1942, the commanders of each defense command were assigned distinct missions. General Drum of the Eastern Defense Command was "charged with the defense against hostile attack by land, sea, or air, of United States bases in Newfoundland, the North Atlantic Coastal Frontier, that portion of the Southern Coastal Frontier east of the rear boundary of the command, and all facilities and installations within the limits of his command."[114] The concern on the Atlantic and Gulf Coasts was submarine, surface, or air attacks by the Germans, although the latter two appeared improbable by the end of December 1942.[115]

In addition to responsibility for protecting the Pacific Coastal Frontier, including Alaska, General DeWitt of the Western Defense Command was "further charged with the protection against sabotage or other internal threat of the Boeing, Douglas, and Consolidated aircraft factories, since these critical installations are so intimately associated with his coastal defense mission."[116] The United States considered the 1,300 miles along the West Coast vulnerable to Japanese attack by air until June 1942. Of greatest concern were the military aircraft factories in Los Angeles and San Diego in the south and in Seattle in the north. Naval yards and ship terminals in the Puget Sound, Portland, San Francisco Bay, Los Angeles, and San Diego areas, as well as the California oil industry, were also crucial to the war effort.[117] Secretary of War Stimson noted DeWitt's anxiety about these areas where "some of the most important airplane factories and naval shipyards" were located.[118] As revealed below, the different levels of perceived security threats on the two coasts help explain the stricter restrictions in the Western Defense Command as compared to those in the Eastern Defense Command.[119]

In a succession of press releases from the end of January 1942 until early February that year, Attorney General Biddle, on recommendations from the War Department, announced the designation of prohibited areas in the western United States from which all enemy aliens were to vacate by February 24 for the purpose of aiding the national defense and protecting the aliens.[120] After announcing the first two prohibited areas—one on the San Francisco waterfront and one that included the Municipal Airport of Los Angeles, Attorney General Biddle announced 135 additional prohibited areas in California, Washington, Oregon, and Arizona "in the vicinity of airports, hydroelectric dams and power plants, gas and electric works, airfields, pumping stations, harbor areas, and military installations."[121]

The perception of greater danger on the West Coast because of its relative proximity to Hawaii, as compared to the rest of the country, and the probability that it would be the location for the Japanese navy to attack the continental United States contributed to General DeWitt's imposition of stricter restrictions.[122] However, the likelihood of such an invasion was doubtful and not anticipated by top army and navy officials.[123] From the United States' entry into World War II in December 1941, General DeWitt intended to remove all enemy aliens from the area known as the Pacific Slope, stretching from the Pacific Ocean to the Sierra Nevada Mountains.[124] In January 1942, DeWitt considered a program under which all aliens of the Japanese, German, and Italian populations and Japanese Americans would be subject equally to evacuation from prohibited areas and resettlement outside these zones, limited access to restricted areas, and internment.[125] He also believed that the assets of all alien enemies should be taken over by the federal government and liquidated, while the aliens, including persons of Japanese and Italian descent who held dual citizenship in their native country and the United States, would work in internment camps "to earn their own keep."[126]

Beginning in February 1942, the implementation of the evacuation program in the Western Defense Command resulted in the departure of more than 10,000 Italians from their homes. Businesses were forced to relocate to areas outside the prohibited coastal zones as well.[127] Germans residing in prohibited zones were also moved inland during the war.[128] DeWitt seemed much more concerned with carrying out the evacuation plans for these most sensitive zones as efficiently as possible than with determining whether any one individual actually posed a security threat to the country. He was adamant that there be no exceptions to this evacuation program. In the case of Joe DiMaggio's father, about whom DeWitt was questioned by an editor of the *New York Sun*, the general stood firm. He warned that should the media "get soft and sentimental about this thing because a baseball player's father who has been in this country 45 or 50 years, and as a young man didn't feel that he had to study English or become a citizen, and has lost his opportunity and is caught in this particular thing, and they want to let him get from under, then they begin preferential treatment that destroys everything that we have done in the past and have been working so hard to accomplish."[129]

On March 2, 1942, DeWitt issued Public Proclamation No. 1, which designated Military Area No. 1—the southern half of Arizona and a coastal strip of land running through western California, Oregon, and Washington. If the Western Defense Command had followed through with its original plan of a mass evacuation of Italian aliens in this much wider area than the prohibited coastal zones from which 10,000 had already been evacuated, all 52,000 Italian aliens would have had to evacuate. However, under the Western Defense Command's "Individual Exclusion Program of Non-Japanese," only particular German and Italian aliens and naturalized citizens found to be potentially dangerous could be excluded from critical areas in Military Area No. 1.[130] In contrast, persons of Japanese descent were evacuated en masse; about 107,500 lived in Military Area No. 1, approximately 5,000 of whom left this area under a "voluntary" program.[131] Eventually, the rest were removed from this area.[132] Also pursuant to Public Proclamation No. 1, any Japanese, German, or Italian alien or person of Japanese lineage changing residence had to register the change.[133]

Unlike the February evacuation from prohibited zones, which indiscriminately affected all Italian aliens living and working there until June, the purpose of the individual exclusion program was to identify individuals, regardless of citizenship status, whom the government deemed suspicious and require them to undergo a process to determine whether they should be prohibited from entering any military areas in the country. The program was also meant to exclude individuals who resided in specific militarily sensitive areas.[134] The hearings were held in major West Coast cities before an individual exclusion hearing board of three military officers of field grade. Subjects had to first fill out lengthy questionnaires before they learned the general nature of the evidence against them and were questioned about matters contained in intelligence reports. Confidential sources and names of informants were not disclosed. The hearing boards made recommendations that were sent for approval to the Civil Affairs Division of the army. These, along with recommendations from U.S. Attorneys in the subjects' district, were sent to the commanding general of the defense command for his final decision. Subjects of exclusion orders were given a date by which they had to depart the specified area.[135]

As we will see was also the case with respect to alien enemy hearings, subjects complained of due process violations at exclusion hearings. Attorneys for the subject were not to speak to the hearing board nor examine government witnesses.[136] Retired U.S. Army Col. Angelo de Guttadauro recalled that his father, Nino, had short notice of the hearing and was not allowed an attorney to represent him at the hearing.[137] Nino Guttadauro, a naturalized American citizen who often worked as an accountant for the Italian consulate and was the president of the San Francisco branch of the Federation of Italian World War Veterans, was excluded from military areas in thirty states. Like many persons removed from their homes in San Francisco, Guttadauro went first to Reno, Nevada, with his family but was unable to secure work in his profession due to his legal status, which branded him as untrustworthy to potential employers. His exclusion lasted from October 1942 until mid-March 1944.[138] There were a number of legal challenges to the individual exclusion program by Japanese and Germans where the courts' decisions considered whether there was military necessity under the particular circumstances of each case.[139]

Considerable inconsistency exists in the reporting of the number of aliens and naturalized citizens who underwent the individual exclusion process. In a 1945 federal case regarding the individual exclusion of a Japanese American from military areas, the federal district court stated the number of exclusions in the Western Defense Command alone as in the thousands.[140] This estimate is far greater than the figures cited by the Justice Department in its 2001 report, where it says that between September 1942 and April 1943, the Western Defense Command heard 335 exclusion cases. The result of the hearings was the exclusion of 174 individuals, 24 of whom were of Italian descent, most from northern California with a few cases from Los Angeles and San Diego.[141] The Justice Department also reports that at least forty-seven persons of Italian ancestry nationwide were ordered to move from designated areas, and another twelve persons appeared before individual exclusion boards, although the outcomes are unknown.[142] The Congressional Research Service reported a slightly different timetable for the Western Defense Command, saying that from August 1942 to July 1943, 174 citizens and enemy aliens received exclusion orders, many of whom were German-born or Italian-born American citizens. With respect to the Eastern Defense Command, this latter report states that fifty-nine individuals received exclusion orders, as did twenty-one in the Southern Defense Command.[143] According to the Justice Department, by August 1943, there were a total of 417 exclusion cases reviewed or in process nationwide.[144] Stephen Fox, referring to "a wartime report," indicates that the government excluded higher numbers of Italians. According to Fox, there were approximately eighty-eight naturalized Italians and an unknown number of Italian aliens excluded from the West Coast. Italians were also included in the sixty-nine East Coast exclusions, as they were in the sixteen exclusions from the Southern Defense

Command.[145] Of course, even the highest estimates of Italians who were issued exclusion orders represent a minute number of the entire Italian population of 1.6 million in the United States, according to the 1940 census.

The vast inconsistency in reporting of exclusions may be explained by disparities in enforcement of the orders. The exclusion cases caused much controversy between the Justice Department and the War Department concerning which cases to prosecute. Attorney General Biddle decided not to prosecute numerous exclusion cases of individuals who, after being sent away from their residences and jobs in military areas, returned in violation of military orders. Biddle claimed discretionary power in determining whether to enforce exclusion orders, often finding "no overt acts of disloyalty" to warrant prosecution.[146] Thus, without knowledge of the context in which a subject made a statement or participated in activities giving rise to suspicion, the Justice Department could not make well-informed decisions.[147]

There was a shared perception among federal and California state officials, General DeWitt, and his staff from the Western Defense Command that each enemy alien group posed varying levels of danger, which called for varying applications of exclusion policy. A memorandum from a joint meeting of these government and military officials expressed a discriminatory attitude toward persons of Japanese descent based upon their physical appearance and public animosity toward them:

> All Japanese look alike and those charged with the enforcement of
> the regulation of excluding alien enemies from restricted areas will
> not be able to distinguish between them. The same applies in practi-
> cally the same way to alien Germans and alien Italians but due to the
> large number of Japanese in the State of California . . . and the very
> definite war consciousness of the people of California, as far as
> pertains to the Japanese participation in the war, the question of the
> alien Japanese and all Japanese presents a problem in control, separate
> and distinct from that of the German or Italian.[148]

Correspondence between General DeWitt and the War Department indicates that Secretary of War Stimson believed persons of Italian descent presented far less danger to national security than did the Japanese or Germans. Stimson requested that DeWitt "not disturb, for the time being at least, Italian aliens and persons of Italian lineage except where they are, in your judgment, undesirable or constitute a definite danger to the performance of your mission to defend the West Coast." The reasoning was that

Italians were "potentially less dangerous, as a whole, than those of other enemy nationalities."[149]

Exemptions from evacuation orders applied only to certain classes of the European aliens. German and Italian aliens seventy years of age or over would not be required to move, unless they were individually suspected. Parents, wives, and children of Germans and Italians in the U.S. armed forces would not have to move unless a special reason existed.[150] There were also exemptions for Germans and Italians based on illness and disability and for those whose American citizenship had been held up by the backlog in the offices of the INS.[151] However, as we will see in testimony from aliens and their families, government officials in charge of evacuations did not always adhere to these exemptions.

The government also showed preference for Italians and Germans with respect to letting alien enemies back into prohibited zones. In discussing who had access to prohibited zones around military installations, Assistant Secretary of War McCloy suggested letting some persons, particularly Italians, back into the zone if there was certainty that they were free of suspicion. DeWitt agreed that Germans and Italians could be allowed back into the zone "because you don't have to worry about them as a group" but "purely as certain individuals," while "a Jap is a Jap to these people now."[152] Apparently DeWitt believed that the public would be much more receptive to returning Germans and Italians whom the government determined were not dangerous than it would be to any returning Japanese. In late February, the Joint Evacuation Board echoed DeWitt's racial distinctions in the enemy alien groups. The board reported that "the normal Caucasian countenances of such persons [European stock] enable the average American to recognize particular individuals by distinguishing minor facial characteristics," leaving prevention of disloyal acts by Germans and Italians to usual police methods, while the "Japanese problem" called for a "special remedy."[153]

California politicians and publishers and editors of the state's leading newspapers shared DeWitt's feelings about the greater threat posed by the Japanese and the need for full-scale evacuation and relocation.[154] In a radio address in early February 1942, California Governor Culbert Olson said that identification of the loyalty or disloyalty among Italians and Germans was "much easier" than that of Japanese and Japanese Americans.[155] California Attorney General Earl Warren believed the inclusion of Italians and Germans in evacuation would be "disruptive of the national unity" and "cruel" because in his opinion, first-generation Italians and Germans were "no different from anybody else, regardless of what the German government or the Italian government may think about their citizenship."[156]

Logistics also figured into the plan for dealing with enemy aliens. Secretary of War Stimson stated that due to practical considerations "of the size of the Italian population and the number of troops and facilities which would have to be employed to deal with them, their inclusion in the general plan would greatly overtax our strength."[157] It was General DeWitt's plan for the Italians to be the last group to leave the military strip along the western coast, after the Japanese and Germans.[158] On the question of whether the military legally had the power to prohibit entry into military areas by any particular class of persons or citizens, the Joint Evacuation Board determined that such power existed. No infringement of constitutional guaranty would occur as long as the "classification of persons or citizens is reasonably related to a genuine war need and does not under the guise of national defense discriminate against any class of citizens for a purpose unrelated to the national defense." The board justified the disparate treatment among the alien enemy groups by stating that "it would . . . present an insuperable problem of administration, not to mention the consequent disruption of defense production, to bar the millions of persons of German or Italian stock from either seacoast area."[159]

Thus, in addition to logistical concerns about moving and housing such large populations, such a proposition would potentially harm the economy. The California Department of Agriculture felt that Italian and German aliens were more essential than the Japanese to agriculture in Area A along the coast, particularly in the grape, dairy, and deciduous fruit industries that supplied produce for the military and produced by-products and medicinal commodities needed by the armed forces. Director W. J. Cecil felt an exception from alien evacuation for Italian and German fruit laborers was justified because "the grouping of all Japanese without respect to American citizenship seems to dispel any particular consistency in the program."[160]

Italian Americans in government positions made great efforts to spare Italian communities the disruption of evacuation. John Molinari, who had served as an assistant district attorney in California during World War II, was personally familiar with many of the Italians affected by wartime restrictions. Molinari, as a member of Citizens' Committee to Aid Italians Loyal to the United States, a group created to forestall any efforts to evacuate the Italians, met with a subordinate of General DeWitt at the Presidio in San Francisco to argue that the movement of the Italian population would create a much greater logistical problem than that posed by the Japanese. Molinari recalled:

> We reminded the general that, particularly in this area, up through northern California, the Italians were very active in many industries and commercial endeavors: the garbage collection, the farmers. We talked about A.P. Giannini being the president of the Bank of America. And we impressed upon the general that if you moved all of these people, . . . it would have included people of Italian descent who were born in this country. And we impressed upon him strongly that it certainly would disrupt the productive industrial and commercial endeavors in the community. We had already had some indication of disruption of commercial activities.[161]

The arguments of Attorney Molinari, however, did not delay the evacuation of approximately 10,000 Italians from their homes and businesses from February through June 1942.[162] Some, like Celestina Stagnaro Loero, were given only forty-eight hours to leave their homes. Loero, a seventy-six year-old woman who spoke little English, had lived in the coastal community of Santa Cruz for over forty-one years when Justice Department agents came to her door in late February 1942 to tell her she must move inland of Highway 1 or face arrest. She had no choice but to leave her clapboard home to live in a room on the other side of Highway 1, where she stayed for the remainder of the year.[163] Often the evacuation orders resulted in the separation of one or more family members from the rest of the family. A resident of Arcata, California, related both the hardship and illogic of this program: "My mother, who lived here, too, was born in France, so she was able to stay in her house, even though she was Italian. I was able to stay because I was born here. But my dad and husband had to go across the street. They both lost their jobs . . . . My dad had been here since 1902; nobody ever bothered you, so you didn't become a citizen."[164]

Italian families who moved as a unit went to cramped, makeshift homes. Alien residents from Pittsburg, California, moved to Oakley, a town fifteen miles inland, where they lived in little shacks built for migrant laborers who harvested fruit in the summers. The community of about twelve "little huts" resembled an army camp. In recalling the difficulties of uprooted families in Oakley, such as the lack of transportation to shop for groceries and unfamiliar schools for their children, Frank Buccellato particularly remembered the confusion experienced by Italian aliens who had married American citizens and sent their sons to war to fight for the United States.[165]

These experiences on the West Coast reflected the harsher interpretation of threat and resulting stricter implementation of what was an open-ended proclamation in Executive Order 9066. The language of 9066 gave military commanders great discretion to determine the extent of the military zones and who were to be excluded or restricted within those zones. As a result, the East Coast produced different wartime programs. In contrast to General DeWitt, whose original intentions to remove all German and Italian aliens indicated a belief that nationality alone was the appropriate measure of a threat to national security, General Drum stated that his implementation of the government's plan would be based on evidence of disloyalty or dangerousness. Drum never contemplated the type of mass evacuation that DeWitt considered for the Western Defense Command. In late April 1942, General Drum publicly announced his intention for the East Coast to establish prohibited and restricted areas along the entire Atlantic Seaboard and inland. However, he defined military areas so as to avoid displacing people or disrupting the economy in the area.[166] Drum thought in terms of individual action against dangerous aliens and citizens, rather than actions against groups.[167] In announcing his intention to establish the Eastern Military Area, he stated: "The fundamental policy embodied in the plan is not to interfere in any manner whatever with the lives of the great mass of loyal Americans in the States included in the military areas, or with the economic life of the area, but it does express the determination of the military authorities to prevent any enemy sympathizer, whether alien enemy, alien of other nationality, or disloyal American, if any exist, from committing any act detrimental to the national security. Those persons whose conduct reflects their patriotic motives will not be affected by this administration."[168]

Drum's approach of separating the potentially dangerous from the "mass of loyal Americans," based on an individual's conduct rather than citizenship or ethnicity, stood in stark contrast to General DeWitt's policy of associating a particular heritage with suspicion, which resulted in the evacuation of thousands of Italians from their homes for approximately four months. Unique to the East Coast was General Drum's order to dim lights at night.[169] Drum believed it was necessary to control lights in such places as Coney Island and the Florida coast.[170]

Secretary of War Stimson confirmed the adoption of separate coastal policies in discussing Attorney General Biddle's concern over a rumor about "various drastic steps in the eastern seaboard for mass evacuation of aliens—Germans and Italians." Stimson allayed Biddle's fears by assuring him, as well as the president, that "we are not going to have any mass evacuations on the east coast but are going to do it very carefully with very small numbers."[171] As shown above, the application of an individual exclusion plan was also far less extensive in the Eastern Defense Command than in the Western Defense Command, both in terms of the total number of persons and the percentage of the ethnic population affected in those regions.

In addition to creating zones designated prohibited to alien enemies, in February 1942, the attorney general announced restricted areas on the West Coast where more than 50,000 Italians had to observe travel restrictions and curfews from 9 P.M. until 6 A.M. Unlike prohibited zones, where enemy aliens were barred, the government allowed them to remain in restricted areas.[172] FBI agents searched the homes of aliens and confiscated contraband items, such as firearms, shortwave radios, cameras, and other items deemed possible instruments of espionage.[173] The Justice Department reported that searches were conducted in approximately 2,900 Italian homes nationwide; approximately two-thirds of these searches occurred in New York, Pennsylvania, California, and Louisiana.[174] Many Italians were promised their possessions would be returned at the end of the war but were sorely disappointed when the government did not return items.[175] Benito Vanni, whose father turned over two shotguns, two rifles, a handgun, a saber, and a pair of binoculars before he was sent to an internment camp, recalled his father's futile efforts to reclaim the property after his release since he did not have a receipt, leading him to believe that the arresting officers took them.[176] Harry Massagli's father, who lost his radio, three rifles, and a shotgun during a search at his house, was particularly offended that the government made no exception since Massagli's children were American citizens.[177] Confiscations from Italian homes on the East Coast occurred in a similar fashion— police confiscated items by subpoena and did not provide the aliens a receipt to reclaim the items later. Joseph Carroccia, an Italian immigrant living in Farmington, Connecticut, never saw the return of the short-wave radio taken from his home during the war.[178]

Restrictions placed upon fishermen appear to have been equally damaging to Italian aliens from Boston and Gloucester, Massachusetts, to Eureka, California, and down the West Coast to San Diego, and in New Orleans as well. Although the exact terms varied from port to port, restrictions were placed on where and when fishermen could fish, and they were not allowed to take their boats out or given access to wharfs and piers, which were operated by armed guards in some locations.[179] A good number of fishermen affected by the restrictions had been in the United States for many years, but they had not become naturalized because they were too busy working or were afraid of the examination since they were illiterate and could speak very little English.[180] More importantly, in the fishing community, there was little or no pressure to obtain American citizenship. The Italian fishermen worked with *paesani* or fellow townspeople who spoke Italian and followed the same lifestyle.[181] In such insular communities, the Italians did not need to speak English or acculturate to American ways.

The effect of wartime restrictions on the fishermen's livelihood was dramatic, as was the impact on the commercial fishing industry as a whole. Many fishermen lost their boats for the duration of the war through purchase by the government or a lease arrangement.[182] Here too, "the most severe application of these restrictions occurred in the Western Defense Command and represented, at times, a conflict between the services" because the navy was concerned with minimizing the impact on the fishing industry, while the army was intent on ensuring security.[183] According to Salvatore Ferrante, a naturalized citizen, the army and navy requisitioned the best fishing boats in Monterey and San Pedro for patrolling along the Pacific coast down to Latin America and along the Atlantic coast as well. The navy requisitioned his canning plant in Port Hueneme, California, along with the entire harbor to use as "an assembly port to ship war material and men to strategic places." Ferrante was given three months to remove everything the government did not want. He was compensated for his property and equipment, but since getting the payment took a long time, he was forced to borrow money for a new plant. He did not believe the armed forces took boats because the fishermen were Italian. Rather, "they just had to have boats, and they wanted the best ones that were in the fleet. It didn't matter whether a man was a citizen."[184]

While Ferrante seemed satisfied with the government's compensation for his plant, other fishermen felt that the government did not treat them fairly. Giuseppe Spadaro, also a U.S. citizen, lost his boat for two years while the government used it for patrolling. The government paid him $600 a month and covered the expenses of insurance and taxes. Along with other fishermen, Spadaro went to Seattle to charter boats in order to earn a living. When the government returned his boat, it was in such bad shape that he had to continue fishing with the rented boat. Spadaro ended up selling it to the shipyard for $4,000, considerably less than its original value, because he could not fix it himself.[185] Compliance with the government's requests for their boats did not win the fishermen favor with respect to other government restrictions. Neither the fact that John Russo's brother had been drafted into the navy nor the requisition of his purse seiner by the navy on

February 23, 1942, prevented the evacuation of his parents from their home in Monterey the very next day.[186] As was the case with the Italians evacuated from the West Coast, the government made no exceptions to requisitions for families who had contributed significantly to the war effort.

Strategically, on Columbus Day, October 12, 1942, a holiday commemorating an Italian explorer and celebrated with parades and great fanfare in Little Italies across the United States, Attorney General Biddle announced the removal of Italians from the category of alien enemies in New York. As of this date, 653 Italians had been brought before alien enemy hearing boards, and 232 of these had been ordered interned. The proclamation removing alien enemy status set forth the following terms: Italians could travel without restriction throughout the United States; they could change their employment or residence without first obtaining permission; alien enemy certificates of identification were no longer required to be carried; and the prohibition against the use of cameras, shortwave radios, and signaling devices was lifted. However, there would be no change in the status of Italian aliens who had already been interned or paroled by the attorney general.[187] The motives for the change in policy for Italian aliens appear to have been political, as pressure was mounting from Italian American politicians and trade union leaders. The government sought the Italian community's support and hoped they might influence relatives in Italy to resist the war effort in their country.[188] One historian has suggested that congressional elections were to be held the following month, and candidates relied upon the voting bloc of the largest immigrant population.[189] The attorney general's office explained that "official recognition of the loyalty of Italian aliens" in the removal of alien enemy status for persons of Italian nationality was "an act of justice," as well as "an important weapon in the field of psychological warfare," which was shown in later military operations in Italy.[190]

The reclassification of Italian aliens was the idea of Edward Ennis, but Francis Biddle seized it enthusiastically, and Roosevelt immediately agreed.[191] The influence of Italian Americans working within Roosevelt's administration also cannot be underestimated.[192] Francis Biddle acknowledged the help that he received in writing his monumental speech at Carnegie Hall from Ugo Carusi, an Italian immigrant who served as his executive assistant, and who shared with him "the outlook of the Italian American, torn between the shoddy glories of the fascist regime and the uncertain assurances of the democratic resistance."[193] Equipped with this understanding of the plight of Italians, Biddle expressed in his speech the confidence he had in the people of Italian origin when the United States entered the war. He believed that "when war broke . . . and they were declared 'alien enemies' . . . time would tell the story of these loyalties better than any words of mine, any assurance or predictions that I could make."[194] The attorney general commended Italians for meeting the test of loyalty for which they received the government's trust, but warned that they "must prov[e] worthy of that trust, so that it may never be said hereafter that there are disloyal groups among American Italians."[195] The media reported that Biddle's announcement ending the injustice imposed upon the Italian population met with widespread approval from the American public.[196]

WE HAVE SEEN the immediacy with which the FBI arrested Italian aliens deemed the greatest security risks and detained them for the internment process, after which debates ensued among the three branches of government about what to do with each population of enemy aliens. Ultimately, Italian aliens were saved from mass evacuation and internment. Instead, the military imposed short-term evacuations of approximately 10,000 Italians from prohibited zones along the West Coast and instituted individual exclusion of aliens and naturalized citizens from military areas across the country. In implementing policies and affording exceptions to restrictions, the perception of threat, the philosophies of military commanders, and racial distinctions among the enemy aliens were all decisive factors. Now we will see how the U.S. government assessed the threat posed by aliens and naturalized citizens of Italian descent in the context of the hearings before alien enemy hearing boards in the selective internment process. Despite no legal mandate to do so, Attorney General Biddle upheld a policy throughout the war of affording hearings to enemy aliens before internment, yet he struggled to maintain consistency in the initial hearings across districts of the country and in rehearings during the aliens' internment at the camps.

CHAPTER THREE

The Struggle for Justice in the Internment Process

The most common sentiments expressed by Italian internees in letters home and in appeals to government officials were disillusionment with the U.S. government over their internment and the feeling that the hearings process was unjust.[1] Since the aliens were not notified of specific charges of misconduct, disloyalty, or even of suspicious activity, they did not know what they had done wrong.[2] The absence of formal charges did not afford them an opportunity to defend themselves at hearings before alien enemy hearing boards by presenting evidence that might have explained the activity that came under suspicion, possibly saving themselves from internment. The Justice Department's litigation files reveal the types of behavior that would convince a hearing board that a subject deserved internment, specifically reports of proclamations of loyalty to the Fascist cause or, worse, statements to that effect during the actual hearing. But it is far more difficult to discern a pattern in the types of favorable information that would result in a subject's parole or release. Avowing entire sympathy with the United States could work to one's favor.[3] Yet many civilian internees' efforts to prove their loyalty to the United States in alien enemy hearings were unsuccessful in convincing officials that they had the potential to be good American citizens. Often they could not overcome FBI reports of Fascist sympathies and anti-American dispositions. Tribunals had considerable discretion to credit certain aspects of an investigative record and to discredit others in reaching a decision on a subject. Thus, alien enemy hearings in the selective internment process served to define concepts of loyalty and allegiance to the United States and what it means to be a good American citizen.

The following examination of the Justice Department's litigation files of specific alien enemies—chosen for factors such as the internee's legal status, profession, age, or gender—and of the files of hearing board members in Boston and New York City reveals both the efforts of the Justice Department to provide fair hearings and the despondency of internees who felt they had no opportunity to prove their innocence. Complaints about the process from internees and even hearing board members who were confused about whether they were making final decisions or recommendations impacted the extent of evidence required by the attorney general.

Eventually the Justice Department issued a series of remedial instructions to the hearing boards, beginning in February 1942 and continuing through 1943. Those instructions are in many ways the best evidence that the alien enemy hearings could have been uniformly fairer. Unfortunately for the majority of Italian internees who were interned within the first six months of the alien enemy hearing program, attempts to inject greater due process into the hearings did not affect earlier determinations of internment.

Some of the case studies below illustrate the types of defective process that the Justice Department addressed, such as the lack of formal charges against the subjects, while others exhibit the failure of the board to admit testimony favorable to the subject. In other instances, cultural biases of board members and the political influence of witnesses compromised institutional standards and prevailed over objectively measurable threats, sometimes serving to disadvantage a subject and at other times positively affecting outcomes, such as in cases where Italian American hearing board members or government attorneys were involved. Still other cases offer narratives of hearing boards grappling with the meaning of due process as it pertained to enemy aliens and striving for a contextualized adjudicatory process, and of the Justice Department carefully reviewing board recommendations. Cases where multiple hearings were held, particularly when individuals were interned longer, not only gave subjects the opportunity eventually to address the government's concerns, but also allowed boards to examine more thoroughly the behavior and mind-set of the subjects.

In addition to setting forth discrepancies between what the Justice Department expected hearing boards to do and how those boards actually functioned, this chapter reveals the tension between legal guarantees for enemy aliens and what internees felt would be a just process for deciding whether they posed a danger to society. The fact that hearings were provided at all—when neither U.S. nor international treaty law required them for nationals of countries at war with the United States—indicates a commitment, even in the atmosphere of war, to the democratic ideals of justice.

For Italian aliens who had been residents on the U.S. mainland, the wartime detention plans envisioned entirely civilian proceedings from the arrest, as authorized by presidential proclamation, to the issuance of warrants by the attorney general for searches of aliens' homes, through the alien enemy hearings. The Justice Department could also consider prosecution under the Smith Act of 1940 or denaturalization proceedings for naturalized American citizens not subject to internment who were suspected of subversive activities, specifically those urging military insubordination or the violent overthrow of the government.[4]

As discussed earlier, the INS based its entire internment program on various articles of the 1929 Geneva Convention, and its camp commanders interpreted the convention's provisions to apply to civilian internees. Thus, internees who had grievances would have relied upon the convention in making arguments for their cases.[5] Part III of chapter 3 of the 1929 Convention, titled "Penal sanctions with regard to prisoners of war," concerns judicial proceedings that followed the laws, regulations, and orders of the armed forces and were to be applied if a prisoner violated such a law and regulation and was brought up for punishment. Unfortunately for the internees, these provisions, akin to procedural protections for criminal defendants, were not interpreted to have any applicability to the alien enemy hearings.[6] The provisions of Article 60, paragraph (c), requiring that prisoners of war receive a "statement of the charge or charges, and of the legal provisions applicable," were not construed to apply to interned enemy aliens who had not been charged with any criminal offenses. Not surprisingly, internees habitually complained that they were not notified of any charges against them and that the government did not explain the legal ramifications of its statements in the hearings. Unlike prisoners of war, who had the right to an attorney in proceedings and the right of appeal, alien enemies were not afforded the same procedural guarantees.[7]

The hearings before the alien enemy hearing boards during World War II more nearly modeled deportation hearings of the same time period. Characterized by the retroactivity of decisions and the lack of proportionality between an offense and its outcome, deportation proceedings can be distinguished from criminal proceedings in terms of the constitutional protections afforded, particularly the statute of limitations.[8] By 1940, the Board of Immigration Appeals that heard deportation cases was an administrative body within the Department of Justice but separate from the INS.[9] The deportation process consisted of both a preliminary hearing and a formal hearing. In the preliminary hearing, an inspector conducted an examination of the alien to obtain information in order to make out a prima facie case, and the application for a warrant of arrest was based on this information.[10] At such preliminary hearings, the alien was rarely represented by counsel and usually was not acquainted with the charges in his case because the purpose of the hearing was to discover evidence to be used against him.[11]

The more formal hearing in the second stage of deportation proceedings better comported with due process in a court of law. For instance, the aliens had a right to counsel and to hear the charges against them before the inspector's questions about their background and the particular circumstances of each case, although in actuality, few immigrants facing deportation could afford counsel.[12] Additionally, the aliens or their counsel had the opportunity to cross-examine government witnesses. Inspectors admitted hearsay evidence since they did not follow any formal rules of evidence or procedure. Finally, there was a record of the hearing, often prepared by the inspectors themselves.[13]

The hearings before the alien enemy boards resembled the informality of the preliminary hearings in deportation proceedings, and the minimal protection of the alien's rights were also comparable. The hearings lasted approximately twenty minutes to half an hour and were conducted without adherence to the rules of evidence. Circumstances such as the use of translators and the desire of busy hearing board members to hear as many cases as possible on any given evening, even if it meant going late into the night, prevented comprehensive, fair hearings in many instances.[14] Unlike deportation hearings where transcripts were regularly kept, the absence of transcripts or records with justifications from hearing boards often prevented Attorney General Biddle from fairly determining whether to uphold or overrule the board's recommendation. Thus, although both types of proceedings lacked the due process of a criminal hearing, there were some procedural mechanisms in place in deportation hearings, at least theoretically, to afford aliens of nonenemy countries greater protections than enemy aliens.[15] In the alien enemy hearings, board members could base their recommendations for internment on information in FBI reports, which subjects were not given the opportunity to refute. For example, admissible hearsay evidence might be that of an anonymous informant who attended a meeting of the Sons of Italy and reported to an FBI agent that a subject alien spoke with fervor about Fascism. Such occurrence could not be verified but was acceptable evidence for the proceedings.

The case of Biagio Farese, a radio announcer born in Italy in 1897 who was among the first aliens to be apprehended in Boston, illustrates the differences between deportation and alien enemy proceedings, and how they operated separately within the Justice Department. As we saw in the social profile of the civilian internees, at least ten of them had undergone deportation proceedings by the time they were interned or labeled a "criminal deportable alien enemy." Farese simultaneously underwent deportation proceedings through the INS and alien enemy hearings through the Alien

Enemy Control Unit. His case shows how the legal distinction between an alien and an *enemy* alien affected the procedural rights afforded him.

Farese's story is also important because it illustrates the long reach of the Alien Enemy Act and highlights the complicated issues that holding multiple citizenships caused Italians who migrated to the United States through other locations on the American continent. Since the Alien Enemy Act applies to "all natives, citizens, denizens, or subjects of the hostile nation or government," it did not matter that Farese had more recently become a citizen of either Canada or Great Britain, both friendly nations. All that mattered was that he was born in Italy, a country at war with the United States at the time.

Farese came to the attention of the FBI because of his uncertain citizenship status as well as his associations with organizations and individuals believed to be promoting Fascism in Canada and in the Boston area. In 1929, seven years after illegally entering Canada by deserting an Italian ship, Farese became a naturalized citizen of that country. There he was an editor of an Italian newspaper printed in Montreal called *Il Cittadino*, a pro-Italy paper alleged to have spread Fascist ideology. He entered the United States in 1936 by train into upper New York under the temporary status of a visitor, without a visa, certificate or other documentation, but ended up residing first in New York and then in the Boston area where he registered as an alien under the Alien Registration Act of 1940. In Boston he engaged in the radio advertising business with a fellow Italian, which allegedly allowed him to broadcast pro-Fascist propaganda, and produced a comedy portraying an Italian family.[16]

How Farese proceeded to navigate the immigration system, claiming three different citizenships at separate hearings, shows how the war context created difficulties for individuals who followed a transmigratory path to the United States. When war between Great Britain and Italy made his return to Canada unfavorable, Farese sought the assistance of U.S. Congressman Thomas A. Flaherty to obtain a visa from Cuba to permit his migration to the United States from that country.[17] That effort never came to fruition because in October 1940 Farese was arrested for illegal entry and for overstaying his leave from Canada, initiating multiple deportation hearings. At the first hearing in December 1940, with the representation of counsel, he claimed to be a Canadian citizen. The outcome was a recommendation of deportation to Italy.[18] At the second hearing held in May 1941 to consider his application for suspension of deportation or for voluntary departure, topics of questioning included his presidency of the Federation of Italian World War Veterans in Boston and his association with the Italian consul. He denied all allegations of Fascist or "un-American" activities, stating that his solicitation of funds on behalf of the federation was to benefit innocent women and children who were the victims of war in Italy.[19] Believing that he had lost his Canadian citizenship due to his absence from Canada for over a year, and anxious not to return to Canada where he was certain that he would be interned along with his Italian comrades, Farese stated that he was an Italian citizen.[20] A third hearing was held in October 1941 to allow Farese to answer certain allegations made by the Royal Canadian Mounted Police and the FBI regarding potentially Fascist activities. Again with the assistance of counsel, he denied joining the Italian army to engage in the Italian-Ethiopian War and denied ever being a member of the Fascist Party.[21] The outcome of the three hearings was a recommendation for deportation to Italy since he appeared to be "inimical to the welfare of this country."[22]

While Farese's immigration status was pending final determination by the immigration headquarters in Washington, he came within the custody of the Alien Enemy Control Unit when he was arrested under presidential warrant on December 8, 1941. He subsequently underwent a hearing on January 17, 1942, and received his internment order on January 31.[23] At his alien enemy hearing, he claimed British citizenship. Even though he had lost his Canadian citizenship due to his absence from Canada for six years, he remained a British subject under Canadian immigration law.[24] As in the deportation hearings, at issue were his prior military service for Italy, his employment history, and his involvement in the Federation of Italian World War Veterans.[25] Although both alien enemy and deportation proceedings were under the jurisdiction of the Justice Department, since the hearing boards were separate judicial bodies, they followed their own rules and regulations. During the course of Farese's internment in August 1943, the Board of Immigration Appeals determined that "because he [was] being interned as an alien enemy," he should be deported to Canada based on his violation of the Immigration Act of 1924 by remaining in the United States for longer than permitted.[26] This logic was reversed some months later when the Board of Immigration Appeals suggested to the attorney general that if he continued Farese's internment, the deportation of Farese would be deferred until the end of the war.[27] In Farese's case, a favorable camp record at Ellis Island, his final place of internment, showing that "he remained aloof from the known ardent Fascists" and cooperated with questioning from camp officials, did not appear to have a positive bearing upon the status of his deportation case.[28]

Through good camp demeanor, favorable performance on work projects off the camps, and association with known anti-Fascists in the camps, Farese eventually earned parole in August 1944. At a hearing on Ellis Island before a Special Alien Enemy Hearing Board in the summer of 1944, he asserted his disgust with Mussolini and loyalty to the United States, making his continued internment unnecessary for the protection of the internal security of this country. The conditions of his parole were that the INS supervise him closely and that he refuse employment in radio broadcasting. Farese told his district parole officer that while interned he delved into the principles of the Fascist government and came to the realization that the progress claimed by Mussolini's government toward improving Italy was a sham, leading him to appreciate democracy and to hope for Italy to have a similar form of government some day. He claimed that his support of Italy had been out of pride for his homeland. Farese's only complaint was that the terms of his parole kept him from finding employment in his line of work, and due to his being interned during the war, he had difficulty convincing people that he was anti-Fascist.[29] Farese was finally released from the custody of the Alien Enemy Control Unit in November 1945, six months after the end of the war in Europe.[30]

With internment behind him, Farese's deportation case was reopened in May 1947 for further consideration of his application for discretionary relief based on the economic detriment that his deportation would cause his wife, a naturalized citizen, who was in poor health. As an alien in the deportation proceedings, Farese could assert family circumstances as a reason to avoid deportation, an opportunity that was not available to him as an enemy alien in the internment process. By this time, Farese and his wife were living in New York City where he was employed as a radio script writer and part-time actor on a radio station. In July 1947, the presiding inspector of the INS issued an opinion proposing that Farese's outstanding warrant of deportation be withdrawn and that he be given an opportunity to depart voluntarily from the United States on the basis of discretionary relief due to his wife's circumstances.[31] Thus, after multiple hearings at which Farese could address the allegations against him and through various procedural mechanisms, Farese was able to obtain suspension of the deportation order and ultimately relief. Farese eventually became an American citizen in 1951 in Boston, and was residing in New York at the time of his death in 1969.[32]

Farese's case and the case studies that follow reveal how the operation of the administrative system appeared to the internees to be built on faulty logic of presumed guilt, which placed suspicion on par with probable cause, causing them frustration when they were powerless to affect the outcomes of their cases. These sentiments, juxtaposed with evidence of the government's efforts to achieve fairness in the adjudicatory process, provide a story of tension among the parties involved in internment. Before examining the cases of other internees, it is useful to outline the perspectives of Justice Department officials and legislators about the process of justice they were creating even months after hearing boards across the country had begun examining aliens. These opinions created the policy, although they did so in dialogue with the relevant legal precedents regarding constitutional protections for aliens.

The Long Reach of the Alien Enemy Act of 1798 and "Courtesy" Alien Enemy Hearings

Director Edward Ennis of the Alien Enemy Control Unit established the procedures for hearing and reviewing cases of resident Italian aliens who had been arrested. The hearing board in every federal judicial district was to consist of "three citizen civilians at least one of whom should be an attorney, appointed by the Attorney General."[33] The hearings were adversarial in nature. A U.S. Attorney was to act as "the administrative officer of the Board [to] present to it the facts bearing on the alien enemy's case," and representatives of the INS and FBI were to be present with the board.[34] The boards included university presidents, deans and professors of law schools, newspaper publishers, and prominent businessmen among their members.[35] Hearing board members received a token $1 a year plus travel expenses.[36] It was considered an honor for "respected and outstanding men in each federal judicial district" to serve the country in this capacity.[37]

A typical case file assigned to a U.S. Attorney consisted of a summary report on the subject alien from the FBI, the alien's INS file, and an "Alien Enemy Questionnaire."[38] Aside from hearing the facts of each case presented by the U.S. Attorney, the board was authorized to interrogate the alien and to decide whether to recommend internment, parole, or release on the basis of affidavits from the alien, witness statements, documents, and statements of the INS officer and FBI agent.[39] The instructions stated that the alien could not have attorney representation and was not permitted to object to the hearing, any questions asked of the alien, or other evidence adduced.[40] In his memoir, Francis Biddle explained that the exclusion of attorneys from the proceedings "greatly expedited action" and put the hearing on a "common-sense basis."[41] The board was to transmit its recommendations to Attorney General Biddle, who made the final decision on each case. Its recommendations were to follow general guidelines: internment was for those of "dangerous character"; those "considered not so dangerous" were granted parole with or without bond and had to report periodically to a parole officer where they lived; and those "found to be harmless to the public safety" were released from government custody.[42] While such nebulous categorizations left much discretion in the hands of hearing board members, the standard to be followed by the hearing boards dictated that any doubts about an alien's loyalty were to be resolved in the government's favor.[43] As of May 1942, the disposition in approximately 42 percent of Italian alien enemy cases was internment.[44]

The following discussion among Chairman Tolan, Dr. W. G. Everson (who was the chairman of the Alien Enemy Hearing Board in Portland, Oregon), and a member of the Tolan Committee explains how the alien enemy hearing boards were to be conducted in each federal judicial district. It raises the issue of the type of procedure owed an enemy alien and how proceedings would differ from court trials.

THE CHAIRMAN: Doctor, is there anything obligatory on the Justice Department to turn these cases over to you?

DR. EVERSON: No.

THE CHAIRMAN: In other words, can they intern them without coming to you at all?

DR. EVERSON: Yes. The alien is not entitled to hearing; it is not a trial. It is a courtesy that is granted to the enemy alien by the Government. The Government is under no obligation to conduct a hearing in any of these cases.

THE CHAIRMAN: What you are trying to fix is the loyalty or disloyalty of the particular aliens who come before you?

DR. EVERSON: We are trying to determine their present loyalty to the United States, or possible subsequent acts of disloyalty.

MR. SPARKMAN: And these people who are interned so far, are what might be classed as dangerous enemy aliens, aren't they?

DR. EVERSON: We feel that they have done things that indicate they are disloyal to the United States Government, or, perhaps they have done things that would lead us to believe that they would be dangerous if left in their communities.[45]

The Tolan Committee was cognizant that rights under the Constitution endure in wartime, stating that "suspension of this writ [of habeas corpus in cases of rebellion or invasion] does not abrogate the fifth and fourteenth amendments, which provide for due process and equal protection of the laws" because "even aliens are guaranteed certain protection afforded by the Constitution."[46] Yet Attorney General Biddle recognized a distinction in the treatment of *enemy* aliens, that is, citizens of countries at war with the United States, as opposed to any alien, instructing that "all alien enemies are subject to detention and internment for the duration of the war without hearing."[47] The Alien Enemy Act of 1798 allows the government to detain and deport aliens of enemy countries without any hearing or lawyers for the suspect. No individualized finding of culpability, dangerousness, or suspicion is required; the government need only prove citizenship of a nation at war with the United States.[48] Nonetheless, hearings were provided "not as a matter of right, but in order to permit [the alien enemies] to present facts in their behalf."[49] This was consistent with the policy established by the Justice Department and the War Department in November 1941 that there be a hearing before internment "under alien enemy proceedings."[50]

Before considering what constituted a fair hearing in the context of alien enemies, a look at developments in the law's treatment of aliens is informative. Congress has not narrowed the provisions of the Alien Enemy Act despite Supreme Court rulings that the Constitution affords certain protections to persons who are in the United States but are not citizens.[51] Under the plenary power doctrine, the federal government has exercised substantive power to exclude and deport aliens, which was not subject to judicial review.[52] However, in cases in the late nineteenth century and early twentieth century, the U.S. Supreme Court interpreted the Constitution as protecting all "persons," that is, citizens and noncitizens, who were in the territorial United States.[53] It considered aliens "persons" within the meaning of the Fourteenth Amendment.[54]

With respect to the procedural rights of aliens, the law made a distinction between proceedings for deportation, which is not punishment for a crime, and criminal proceedings in which aliens could benefit from the protections afforded by the due process clause of the Fifth Amendment.[55] But in 1903, the Supreme Court questioned the plenary power doctrine in the context of deportation as well, holding that the due process clause applied to deportation proceedings to determine an alien's right to remain in the United States.[56] As legal historian Kunal Parker suggests, with this decision the "Court recognized that over time, territorially present immigrants might acquire a stake in American society and slowly become insiders themselves."[57] However, the Department of Labor's Committee on Administrative Procedure reported in 1940 that "the law with respect to what constitutes a fair hearing in immigration, as in other administrative, hearings is still in a state of flux."[58] The law left administrative agencies with little guidance on how to conduct hearings. The Committee on Administrative Procedure was concerned in particular that the Labor Department assumed "that any hearing which may be accorded an alien is a privilege and not a right."[59]

Even though the alien enemy hearings were a "courtesy," Attorney General Biddle felt that the first wave of examinations of arrested Italians by alien enemy hearing boards for a determination of internment, parole, or release fell short of his minimal expectations. He did not believe that the hearing boards assisted him in the way that he had intended. On several occasions, Biddle had to ask the hearing boards to provide him with more data on which they based their internment opinions because their reports were too sketchy for him to make a fair assessment of the board's recommendation. He called for a "sufficiently full summary of the testimony or other matters brought out at the hearing . . . [to] be set forth to permit [him] to make that independent judgment on the facts which the regulations require."[60] Deficiencies in the records transmitted to him not only jeopardized the fairness of the internment process but slowed down the processing of people in detention facilities who were awaiting an order from the Justice Department.

A factor contributing to the inconsistency of the proceedings across the districts appears to be the variance in the backgrounds and attitudes of board members.[61] For instance, board members who lived and worked among Italians, such as those in regions of the United States with larger populations of Italians, seemed able to contextualize information from FBI reports better than board members who encountered Italians only in the adversarial setting of the hearings. This observation helps explain how the hearing boards in Boston and New York City functioned, as shown below. This is not to say, of course, that any board escaped the pressures of their important role in helping to ensure the security of the nation, pressures that necessarily infused distrust into the process of determining the loyalties of the aliens before them. Unfortunately, the lack of data in the records from a sampling of hearing boards about what impressions they formed of the aliens they examined and why they formed these impressions makes a regional comparison of board approaches nearly impossible.[62]

Another issue to consider in the analysis of how hearing boards conducted proceedings is the lack of information provided to them about the mission, structure, and homeland ties of the Italian American organizations with which membership or affiliation often formed the basis of recommendations for internment. According to one historian relying upon an army report, the hearing boards, the army, its intelligence division, and the commanding generals of the defense commands did not have sufficient information on Italian American organizations until "many months after war started."[63] With respect to such organizations, Attorney General Biddle guarded against unfair presumptions based on membership alone in instructing that "the activity of the individual rather than the nature of the organization" should be scrutinized. The citizenship and standing in the community of witnesses who spoke on behalf of the alien were also to be noted for purposes of credibility and the precise nature of their relationship with the alien.[64] But barring evidence of specific acts of disloyalty or threats to the public's safety, the board's determination of loyalty through interrogation of the alien enemies was necessarily flawed.

Beginning in December 1941, Erwin Griswold, a professor at Harvard Law School at the time and later the law school's dean, served on the Alien Enemy Hearing Board for the District of Massachusetts in Boston.[65] In numerous cases of Japanese, German, and Italian aliens, Griswold expressed his views on whether evidence of the alien's past activities or contacts were indicative of future espionage or subversive activities. For example, in the case of a forty-eight-year-old Italian alien who had lived in the United States for thirty years and was believed to have associated with Fascist sympathizers, Griswold recommended parole as opposed to internment because there was no evidence that the alien was or had been "an agent or operative of the Italian or any other government" or had frequented the Italian consulate.[66] Griswold stated that the alien was not unlike other Italians in the United States who not long before the outbreak of World War II were "pro-Italy" as opposed to "anti-America."[67] Griswold appreciated the difference between having associations with the enemy and actively participating in initiatives against the United States, and took a cautious approach in recommending internment only for those alien enemies who fell in the latter category. This same level of scrutiny can be seen in the cases of German aliens before his board. For example, in a case where Griswold parted company with the rest of the board in recommending parole instead of internment, he noted that the German alien ceased "active sympathy with the Nazi government" around 1935 and became an anti-Nazi. He explained that this was a case where "the risk, on all of the evidence, appear[ed] to be so small that it [was] difficult to reach the conclusion that internment [was] required in the public interest."[68] In this manner, Griswold appears to have upheld the spirit of due process standards in the hearings.

The matter of Ubaldo Guidi-Buttrini, a sixty-four-year-old accountant turned Boston radio show host and correspondent for the Italian newspaper *Il Progresso*, provides an instance where the board went to great lengths to achieve justice in the hearing process. The board carefully weighed evidence, going so far as to give Guidi-Buttrini the benefit of the doubt concerning his loyalty to the United States. This approach ran counter to the standard established by the Alien Enemy Control Unit of deciding doubtful cases in favor of the government, effectively providing Guidi-Buttrini greater rights than the law owed him. At the time of Guidi-Buttrini's arrest on December 9, 1941, he expressed his love for Italy and indicated that he had no intention of becoming an American citizen. The findings of the Boston board after hearings on January 7 and 10, 1942, were that Guidi-Buttrini had been "an ardent advocate of Fascism" who, as a member of the media, posed a threat in "the effect his utterances may have upon his fellow countrymen residing here." Astonishingly, board members had reservations about internment and recommended parole with supervision. Attorney General Biddle overruled this decision and ordered internment on February 19, 1942.[69]

By Guidi-Buttrini's second hearing on December 14, 1942, which occurred upon motion of the board in Boston, additional FBI reports were put into evidence. In this rare instance where the file contains a transcript of the rehearing, we are provided some insight into how the board evaluated evidence. The board felt that reports of Guidi-Buttrini's efforts at gathering Italians in New England to protest the League of Nations' sanctions against Italy during the Ethiopian campaign and his organization of a program to collect gold for the Italian government pointed to his leadership in subversive activities. However, the board believed that favorable witnesses outweighed this evidence. Members were impressed with the stature of the witnesses who spoke to his fine character in the community, which included two Massachusetts Superior Court judges and counsel for the city of Boston. One of the judges was Massachusetts Superior Court Judge Felix Forte, who was "supreme venerable" of the Order of the Sons of Italy, a position that very likely put him in the same social circles as Guidi-Buttrini.[70] The board viewed Guidi-Buttrini's speeches in Italian over the radio and at public events as indications of pride in his Italian descent and love of his homeland, rather than opposition to democracy or ill will toward the U.S. government. Their view was supported by the fact that two of his sons and both of his sons-in-law served in the U.S. armed forces. It was only out of "abundant caution" that the board recommended parole because it believed that "the alien's absolute release would involve no danger to our war effort."[71] Griswold challenged the government on the charge that Guidi-Buttrini received payments from the Italian consul by pointing out that the allegation lacked evidentiary support, particularly since Guidi-Buttrini and his daughter had already explained the sums of money deposited in their Boston bank account as funds for advertising.[72] In effect, the Boston hearing board expected the government to prove beyond a reasonable doubt that Guidi-Buttrini was engaged in seditious activity against the United States.

Although the political clout of the Massachusetts judges and Boston city attorney may have influenced the Boston hearing board to decide in Guidi-Buttrini's favor, it did not persuade the Office of the Attorney General that he was not dangerous. In this, as in many internee cases, Attorney General Biddle exercised his power to overrule the decision of the local hearing board. Despite two findings by the Boston hearing board that Guidi-Buttrini should not be interned, Biddle decided that he should remain interned through the duration of the war. It appears that the most damaging allegations against him were that he was involved with Mussolini's secret police force, OVRA (*Opera Voluntaria Repressione Anti-Fascista*), an allegation first heard before the Dies Committee in the late 1930s, and charges that he was a Fascist propagandist paid by the Italian consul. Unfavorable reports from army camp officials and immigration inspectors indicating that he subjected other internees to his ardent Fascist views must have also convinced the Justice Department that he continued to be a security risk.[73] In the last two years of his internment, Guidi-Buttrini's situation was unchanged despite inquiries from the director of the National Catholic Welfare Conference (NCWC) and his state representative to the Attorney General's Office, and appeals of his son, who was serving overseas, to President Roosevelt.[74] Ultimately, even the support of many prominent politicians did not guarantee a favorable outcome for Guidi-Buttrini because the government believed he was in a unique position to persuade other aliens to be pro-Italy and anti-America. The Alien Enemy Control Unit did not believe it was safe to parole him until May 1945, by which time relations between the United States and Italy had changed dramatically. In addition, the factors of his advanced age and his family of loyal citizens convinced government officials that he no longer presented a security risk.

There were miscommunications between the hearing boards and Attorney Biddle's office with respect to how their duties were to be performed, as verified by Griswold's correspondence with the Alien Enemy Control Unit pertaining to the alien enemy cases in general. In response to complaints directed at the Boston hearing board about the form of the recommendations, namely that evidence was not discussed in full, Griswold explained that he and other board members understood that the cases were to be heard within ten days, and mistakenly thought that the hearing board in each district made final decisions, which were relayed to the Justice Department only for a stamp of approval.[75]

Although the final authority on the outcome of each case rested with the Justice Department, the alien enemy hearing boards appeared to have discretion in the form and substance of the questions posed to the aliens, resulting in different experiences before the boards across the federal districts. A transcript from a hearing before Alien Enemy Hearing Board No. 1 for the Southern District of New York, chaired by Edward Corsi, who had a long career in government in the areas of immigration and social welfare, indicates that board's efforts to understand the alien's views on Italy's government versus that of the United States.[76] First, it is worth mentioning that Corsi was an Italian immigrant who had been naturalized. It is surprising that the government was unconcerned that a naturalized citizen of Italian origin might sympathize with the persons he was examining and jeopardize the fairness of the hearings process. That fact aside, Corsi's aim in the hearings was sensible. He stated that the purpose of the hearing was "to determine the measure of [the alien's] views toward America" and one's "attitude toward our own democratic system in the United States and . . . the very important fact that these two systems are at war at this time."[77] Questions investigated the heart and mind of the alien by asking what membership in the Fascist Party meant to him, his hopes for the future of Italy, and whether he intended to become an American citizen.[78] This board's approach of searching the mind-set of the alien was to treat lying as evidence bearing on both the alien's character and the ultimate question of how great a danger he was to public safety.[79] Memoranda to the Alien Enemy Control Unit from Corsi's board members reveal the same level of thoughtfulness with respect to the German aliens before them. They carefully evaluated witness statements, compared the circumstances of various cases to assure consistency in results, and reconsidered their recommendations of internment once new evidence surfaced at rehearings.[80]

benefit of stenographers, pens, pencils, paper, and clergy.
We did think, however, that it was clear to all the United
States Attorneys that the Boards were not to render final
decisions so that even in the absence of adequate directions
we could expect them to send us sufficiently full discussions
of evidence. The reason we were confident about that was
that we in this office had felt strongly that the Boards should
render final decisions subject to check-up; and when we were overruled
we all had the feeling that everybody must know about it, there
having been quite a fuss.

I should like very much to have a chance to discuss
some of these cases with you, since we have some difficulty in
catching the flavor of what goes on at the hearings. I get
the impression that the Boards vary widely with respect to the
keenness with which they probe the evidence and bring out the
character of the accused. Indeed, there are some Boards upon
whose judgment of persons we rely almost implicitly. There are
others from which we can get no impressions at all and I am
anxious to talk with somebody who has seen the lay members of a
Board in action to find out whether there is anything we can
do from this end to suggest fruitful methods of questioning. I
am inclined to doubt it but I think in some districts we are
going to have to try something. I would appreciate any contributions you had time to make to the further instructions to hearing
boards we are presently attempting to draft.

Sincerely yours,

Thomas M. Cooley II
Chief of Review Section
Alien Enemy Control Unit

These two paragraphs are taken from a letter written by Thomas M. Cooley II of
the Department of Justice to Harvard Law School Professor Erwin Griswold, who
served on the Alien Enemy Hearing Board in Boston. Cooley addressed the
misunderstanding of some hearing boards that they were rendering final decisions
as opposed to recommendations on each individual, as well as the variability among
boards in how thoroughly they examined the alien's character. (Detail of letter,
Thomas M. Cooley II to Professor Iwrin and Irwin [sic] N. Griswold, February 3,
1942, Erwin Griswold Papers, 1925–1994, Box 73, Folder 8. Courtesy of the Historical
& Special Collections, Harvard Law School Library.)

The Alien Enemy Hearing Board No. 4 in New York City, chaired by
Nicholas Kelley, a former secretary in the U.S. Department of Treasury and
a lawyer specializing in arbitration and labor law, was primarily interested
in political activities and affiliations both in Italy and the United States.[81]
This board's questions also probed the alien's ties to family members in Italy, why they did not come to the United States, and the nature of com-
munications with the alien's homeland.[82] In some cases, the board asked the

alien if he would do anything to harm the United States if requested to do so through Italian channels.[83] Without the benefit of transcripts, however, there is no way to surmise how the alien's answers to specific questions may have affected the outcome of the hearing.

In mid-February 1942, after more than 100 Italians had been interned, the Alien Enemy Control Unit addressed the lack of transcripts through supplemental instructions to the alien enemy hearing boards to take a transcript "of all the testimony," particularly "in doubtful cases." It also requested that instead of merely summarizing reports, the board "should attempt to transmit its impressions on matters arising at the hearing, such as the demeanor of the alien, its judgment on the testimony of the witnesses and specific grounds which form the bases for its recommendation."[84] Thus, Director Edward Ennis emphasized the importance of a record for Attorney General Biddle's proper assessment of cases. The Justice Department went so far as to remove hearing board members whom it believed were too lenient in their evaluations of the security risk presented by each individual.[85]

By late August 1942, when over 200 Italians had already been interned, the Justice Department adopted a policy by which alien enemy hearing boards would rehear cases if authorized by the director of the Alien Enemy Control Unit or the U.S. Attorney responsible for the alien. The granting of a new hearing could be based upon several factors. The first factor was abuse or misconduct at the first hearing, namely disallowing witnesses to testify. Other factors to be considered in granting a rehearing were insufficient notice of the hearing; pertinent evidence not produced at the first hearing; a lack of uniformity in how early cases were conducted as compared to later cases; the illness of the alien making internment difficult and the danger of parole or release less likely; and the age of the alien. For those aliens already in internment camps, a rehearing could occur in their absence since the procedure was "a matter of grace and not of right."[86] Undoubtedly, the practice of not giving some internees the chance to be present at their rehearings in order to provide personal testimony contributed to their feelings of injustice.

As late as March 1943, the Justice Department reported to all alien enemy hearing boards that after a review of 10,000 cases, it determined "that the source of complaint most frequently encountered is the fact that alien enemies are not sufficiently informed of the charges against them." In some cases, this procedural deficiency resulted in internment that could have been prevented if the subject understood the circumstances that the board deemed suspicious and had an opportunity to refute the allegations. In response to this problem, Director Ennis notified all alien enemy hearing boards that in future hearings "full and detailed disclosure of all charges against the alien enemy" were to be made, and if requested by the alien, "an opportunity to rebut the charges by direct evidence" was to be afforded. The board was to withhold the names of informants and any other information that might jeopardize the FBI's investigation, but it retained discretion in deciding when to disclose the charges since it might obtain more truthful responses if disclosure did not occur until after the alien's testimony.[87]

Beginning in August 1943, pursuant to instructions of Attorney General Biddle, a Special Alien Enemy Hearing Board, composed from the pool of approximately 400 members of the Alien Enemy Hearing Boards across the judicial districts, convened at the internment camps to rehear cases of internees when a sufficient number of cases at any one camp warranted the time and expense.[88] At the conclusion of the rehearing, the special board was required to submit its report and recommendation with a transcript to Biddle and the U.S. Attorney for the district where the case originated. The original hearing board then had the opportunity to review findings made in the rehearing and consider them along with any new evidence before submitting its report to the attorney general.[89] Thus the final recommendation rested with the original hearing board. This new protocol would of course delay a final decision. Edward Ennis altered the protocol by advising that orders could be entered based solely on the special hearing board's recommendation as the original hearing boards could offer value to the reconsideration only if they had relevant information concerning that alien's local community. But he met with resistance from those who felt the original hearing boards should retain some control over internees who had initially appeared before them.[90] For example, the U.S. Attorney in the Southern District of New York pointed out that good conduct at an internment camp was not "a sufficient guaranty against a clever alien's working later to undermine the firmness of our people in carrying on the war."[91] Ultimately, it was left within the discretion of the U.S. Attorney whether to consult the original board.[92]

The case of Angelo Gloria, a radio personality and one of the most vocal Fascists among the internees, exemplifies the extended role that an original hearing board could play. The Justice Department paid heed to Edward Corsi's opinion that Gloria was "just one of those fellows who may have done things that might now indicate an attitude of disloyalty to the Country but who fundamentally are harmless and innocuous." Corsi wrote: "I do not believe there is any danger in releasing him if that is possible."[93] Gloria was paroled a few days after Corsi wrote to the Justice Department, completing almost two years of internment, and died shortly thereafter.[94] Given Gloria's reputation, his parole before the end of the war speaks to the influence that Corsi had. Regardless of whether Corsi's Italian heritage allowed him to better evaluate Gloria's mind-set and the likelihood that he would commit sedition or if it unfairly influenced the decision about Gloria's internment, the outcome in Gloria's case illustrates the ad hoc nature of the process.

The Justice Department's continual reevaluation of the structure of the hearings and the method for reaching decisions shows an effort to create a uniform system of justice for evaluating the loyalty of the Italian aliens. However, the majority of Italian internees who underwent initial hearings in the first six months of the U.S. entry into the war were not afforded the benefit of the perfected hearing process. Instead, this study reveals that they were forced to await rehearings by special hearing boards that did not occur until after they had spent at least a year in internment, and, as the case of Francesco Fragale illustrates below, there was the risk that biases of the initial alien enemy hearing board would continue to taint the process.

Hearing Boards Provide Rough Justice for Italian Enemy Aliens

Turning from issues of process, we examine specific case files of Italians who came before the alien enemy hearing boards, which provide valuable insight into how the boards at both the local district level and the special boards in the internment camps reached individual determinations of disloyalty and national security risk. In most cases, as evidenced by the series of remedial instructions the Justice Department sent to the hearing boards, the decision-making process was flawed because there was not an opportunity for a full development of facts and circumstances surrounding government allegations. As Pericle Chieri's case exhibits below, subjects could not rebut charges that were not revealed to them. Boards relied upon FBI reports of anonymous informants who had gathered information about the aliens' affiliations and employment, leading to presumptions about an individual's connections to Mussolini's government and beliefs in Fascism. The hearings failed to base decisions upon evidence of specific acts of disloyalty, and in some instances did not take into consideration letters and affidavits attesting to the internee's good character and loyalty. In the cases of aliens employed in the media, hearing boards often had the benefit of translations of editorials and radio shows that they could scrutinize for pro-Fascist and anti-American rhetoric that might stir up the national pride of Italian immigrants and turn them against the United States, but information was not necessarily contemporary. For example, sources from the mid-1930s, when the U.S. views of Mussolini's government were favorable, might not have presented an accurate picture of the alien's sentiment at the time of his hearing.

The following case studies also illustrate the extent that appeals of politicians, religious leaders, family, and friends influenced decisions of hearing boards, which contributed to discrepancies in the rendering of justice across the districts. For members of the media, such as Guidi-Buttrini, who were under the greatest suspicion, such patronage proved to be of minimal help in accelerating an alien's release date. Many former Italian newspaper editors and radio announcers who were interned or paroled throughout the war were released by the Justice Department only after Italy's position in the war had weakened so much that the government believed they no longer had any sway over the sentiment of Italian communities. For Italian aliens in lower-profile professions, such as a baker in San Francisco's North Beach or a butcher in Boston's North End, the good word of a city official or district attorney about their reputation in the community and commitment to family could go a long way in saving them from internment.

As detailed earlier, the professions of the Italian internees ran the gamut from unskilled laborer to sophisticated and highly successful businessman. The case of Pericle Adriano Carlo Chieri, a thirty-seven year-old mechanical engineering professor who was interned for nine months in 1943, shows the sort of employment activity and expertise that could bring someone to the attention of federal authorities and draw suspicion from the hearing board.[95] It also provides an example of how the government's failure to state charges against a subject could have prejudiced the case. Like Farese, Chieri was simultaneously undergoing internment proceedings and deportation proceedings due to his alien status. He came to the attention of authorities as a result of an arrest upon an immigration warrant. Chieri's initial internment hearings occurred in December 1942 and January 1943, before the Justice Department's pronouncement several months later that subjects were to be informed of charges against them. Chieri maintained that he was unaware of the grounds for internment and therefore could not have known what information to provide in his defense.[96] If he had been notified of charges in the initial alien enemy hearing, his internment of approximately nine months might have been avoided.

A native of China and a citizen of Italy, Chieri was admitted to the United States on July 20, 1939, as a nonimmigrant alien under section 3(1) of the Immigration Act of 1924. In deciding upon his request for a change in his immigration status and his application to be employed, the State Department considered him a "dangerous enemy alien." The alien enemy hearing board had the following information about Chieri's history: he worked as a technical secretary-clerk at the Italian Embassy in Washington, D.C., from 1939 to 1941 under the direction of the Italian Air Attaché, compiling information concerning aviation matters in the United States; he served in the Engineer Corps of the Italian Air Force as a lieutenant in 1937 and from 1938 to 1939; in 1933, he became a member of the Fascist Party in Italy, and he last paid dues to the party in 1938, which he explained was a requirement for his job with a shipping company in Italy. The government's concern appears to have been that Chieri had access to blueprints of air bases in the United States and could copy them for the Italian government.[97]

The Alien Enemy Hearing Board in Detroit decided in early February 1943 that internment was in order. Board members believed that the circumstances of Chieri's departure from the Italian Embassy were not clear and wondered why he kept a job at the embassy when he claimed he did not want to do anything contrary to the interests of the United States. In particular, hearing board members felt that "his experience as an officer of an Italian-Chinese aircraft company makes it clear that his professional careers have been in competition with American interests." Instead of allowing Chieri the opportunity to explain aspects of his employment history that concerned board members, they appeared to rely upon adverse reports of other departments of the government, leading them to conclude that he was an agent of a foreign country and "potentially dangerous to the security of the United States."[98] Chieri had been under FBI surveillance for several years since he was suspected of espionage. As revealed in later proceedings, Chieri's employment at the Italian Embassy merely required him to translate technical articles into Italian for the press and technical magazines, and none of the articles were of a confidential nature concerning national defense. He claimed never to have obtained information on foreign planes for the Italian government.[99]

In his request for a rehearing, Chieri expressed his plan to remain in the United States so that he could be with his wife, an American citizen, in South Carolina. Upon rehearing Chieri's case in June 1943, despite favorable testimony from his wife, the Detroit board again recommended internment.[100] It believed that Chieri sought American citizenship only when it became evident that it would be to his best advantage after release from service in the Italian Embassy.[101] Chieri was held in detention facilities in Detroit, transferred to Chicago, then to Camp McCoy in Wisconsin, and he ended up in Fort Missoula, Montana, where in September 1943 he went before a special hearing board. Chieri testified that his sympathies were with the policies of the United States in the months before hostilities with Italy, which led the board to conclude that he was a man of integrity. In light of his favorable record from Camp McCoy and Fort Missoula, his demeanor, general attitude, and disposition toward the United States, his marriage to an American-born citizen, and the responsible character of his sponsors, the board recommended his release the following month.[102] The surrender of Italy on September 8 likely played a role as well in Chieri's release. After a long battle, Chieri finally obtained his American citizenship in 1952.[103]

Like Chieri, Aldo Ghirardi, who was taken from his San Francisco home on the day after the attack on Pearl Harbor, had been under FBI surveillance, which led to his arrest.[104] Ghirardi's case exemplifies the problem of a hearing board's reliance upon evidence of Fascist sympathies from many years earlier, which may not have accurately reflected the alien's state of mind by the time of the hearing. On February 12, 1942, he was brought before the Alien Enemy Hearing Board for the Northern District in San Francisco on charges of dangerousness. Ghirardi, an elevator operator and building manager, was apprehended on the basis of reports from FBI informants that he was a member of the Fascist Party and was promoting Fascism through his affiliation with the Sons of Italy. Among evidence of his Fascist views was a letter from the Italian consulate acknowledging his donation of three silver medals for the Ethiopian War, an application for a medal from Mussolini for participating in the March on Rome in 1922, and a photo of Ghirardi with the Blackshirts on the march. Despite the passage of time since these events, the San Francisco hearing board noted that "the subject appears to be an enthusiastic Fascist and speaks of Fascism with pride and loyalty." On September 24, 1943, after almost two years of internment, a special hearing board at Fort Missoula recommended unconditional release based on reports of favorable behavior and cooperation in the camp as well as Ghirardi's expressed desire to remain in the United States, become a citizen, and serve in the armed forces. After living in the United States as an alien for over twenty years, Ghirardi became an American citizen in 1947.[105]

In some instances, the alien enemy hearing board did not consider available letters of recommendation and affidavits of the alien enemy's character in the initial hearing. Like numerous other Italian internees, Mario Giovanni Favoino was employed in the media as an Italian newspaper and magazine editor, author, and radio commentator.[106] Apprehended in Mount Vernon, New York, on December 9, 1941, Favoino was the subject of FBI reports from a "highly confidential informant in June 1940," which stated that he "scorned democracy and exalted Fascism" as a radio announcer for a New York City station. Transcripts of his radio programs in his file indicate that he "insinuat[ed] that the system of government in the United States has broken down, and when a machine has broken down, the thing to do is to 'get a good mechanic' to repair the damage and operate the machine."[107] Such expressions of political ideology did not receive First Amendment protection, as it was seen as dangerous propaganda, unfavorable to the Allies' cause. Also considered suspicious were his memberships in the Squadristi, a Fascist militia in Italy, and in the New York branch of the Italian Fascists Abroad, in which he served as secretary. A note in Favoino's case file indicates that the Alien Enemy Hearing Board of the Southern District of New York did not make letters of recommendation and affidavits concerning his character part of his record when it examined him on January 7, 1942. After Favoino received an order for internment on January 26, 1942, he made the usual circuit of camps, first interned on Ellis Island and Camp Upton in New York, then Fort Meade in Maryland, and finally Fort Missoula in Montana. Edward Ennis promised Favoino's wife that the review section of the Alien Enemy Control Unit would examine the additional evidence concerning her husband, but it is unclear from the file whether it was actually considered. On September 14, 1942, the review section recommended continuing Favoino's internment, reporting that the hearing board had formed a bad opinion of Favoino when he asked for an interpreter since he claimed he did not speak English well. The review section found that Favoino was a "dangerous alien enemy who has been actively engaged in the distribution of propaganda unfavorable to the cause of the Allies and the prosecution of the present war."

The absence of the letters and affidavits, at least in the initial hearing, certainly gave the subject and his family the impression that the process was unjust, but there is no telling whether this missing evidence was positive enough to outweigh the damaging information already before the hearing board. Favoino was paroled in November 1943, two months after Italy's surrender, and was not fully released until two years later, on November 15,

1945, after the war had ended.[108] Favoino was never naturalized. He repatriated to Italy where he died in 1967.[109]

The case of Francesco (Frank) Larencesco Fragale illustrates how a poor first impression on the hearing board could taint an internee through the duration of the war despite favorable affidavits from military officers and personal friends evidencing a change of heart and patriotism toward America. Fragale was a twenty-year-old waiter when FBI agents apprehended him in Milwaukee, Wisconsin, on December 9, 1941, making him one of the youngest Italian civilian internees.[110] The hearing board that examined Fragale on January 13, 1942, had an FBI report stating that he was a member of the Fascist Youth Movement in Italy, upon his arrival in the United States he worked for his uncle who was the former Italian consul in Milwaukee, and corresponded with the Fascist government in Rome concerning his organization of Fascists in Milwaukee. In his "enemy alien questionnaire," he claimed to have owned and operated an Italian newspaper, *Il Corriere Italiano*. When FBI agents had questioned him about the newspaper articles' extreme Fascist views, he claimed they were copied from other sources. Despite a reference from his manager at the Hotel Astor in Milwaukee that he never showed pro-Axis tendencies nor spoke against the United States, Fragale gave the hearing board the impression that he was the "'cocky' type," and a witness of "shiftiness and evasiveness."[111] The board reached a unanimous decision, reporting Fragale "was an opportunist who was willing at one time to follow the 'party line' and try to keep the Italians of Milwaukee lined up with the fatherland. He seems a willing tool, and potentially dangerous."[112] A report of his conduct at McAlester Internment Camp confirmed the board's impression as military officers gave him "unfavorable" ratings in the following categories: "Character of associates or groups of associates among internees"; "Expressed views with respect to the position of the United States in the present war"; "Reaction to war news favorable to the United States."[113] Such reports indicate that camp officials observed internees carefully for any signs of disloyalty or behavior unbefitting a potential American citizen.

When the alien enemy hearing board considered his request for a rehearing in September 1943, apparently the only document before it was a report of camp conduct with a notation about an army report stating Fragale was a "good worker," but "liable to passing information he obtains to other internees."[114] The board unanimously denied Fragale's request for a rehearing because his anti-American statements and association with an extreme Fascist group in camp were consistent with activities that warranted his internment in the first place.[115] Fragale pursued the matter with the Department of Justice. He wrote that he hoped to obtain parole and go live with a relative, claiming that he had done nothing "that may have been considered harmfull [sic] to the safety of this Nation" nor made statements that could be considered "against the principle and the Constitution" of the U.S. government. He had in fact received his first citizenship papers in January 1943 while interned.[116] He had also produced numerous affidavits from military officers from the camps where he was interned attesting to his trustworthy and cooperative character as well as confirmations of his loyalty to the United States from a school administrator, a shop superintendent, a priest, and relatives, but they did not effectuate parole.[117] Although a Fort Missoula parole officer recommended in May 1944 that Fragale be paroled because he was an honest and dependable worker off station who had expressed loyalty to the United States and a willingness to fight in the armed forces, Fragale did not receive a parole order until November 30, 1944. Given Fragale's alleged former Fascist activities, he was paroled under the strictest supervision on the condition that he agreed not to work for a newspaper or radio station.[118] Once paroled, Fragale showed himself to be true to his expressed intentions by joining the U.S. armed services. He finally received his release order on July 3, 1945.[119] He served in the army from 1945 to 1947, receiving his American citizenship in Seoul, Korea, in 1946. He died in Milwaukee in 1988.[120]

What is remarkable about Fragale's case is the delay in his parole, despite overwhelming testimony from military officers and members of the community that he held allegiance to the United States. He could not overcome the impression that he left on the initial hearing board that he was of the " 'cocky' type" and that he espoused Fascism when the United States was on the brink of entering war against the Axis powers. His allegedly close associations with Mussolini's government are likely what kept him interned for so long, as he was one of a few internees who received two consecutive internment orders. Successive hearing boards seemed to view his case through the lens of the initial board, specifically that there was a sizable Italian population in Milwaukee at the time, approximately 25,000, whom Fragale could potentially influence. They continued to believe that Fragale was in a strategic position, as a writer and as the nephew to the former Italian consul, to turn many Italian immigrants away from the American cause, despite evidence that his views had changed.[121]

Pauline Tedesco was one of two women interned on her own account. The only other female internees were Latin Americans who volunteered to be with a male family member. A middle-aged Italian alien from Scranton, Pennsylvania, who identified herself as a housekeeper separated from her husband, Tedesco was ordered interned in March 1942.[122] Her case is interesting not only for the fact of her being a woman interned for over a year, but also for the insight that it provides into how one board made a connection between morally objectionable behavior and the likelihood of committing sedition against the United States.

Tedesco, who went by numerous aliases, came to the attention of the government for several reasons, the most important of which was her practice of prostitution and operation of houses of prostitution in at least six locations in the late 1930s, for which she paid fines and served short-term jail sentences. Her business reportedly made her a wealthy woman, but she admitted to never paying income taxes. She also admitted to violating the 1940 Alien Registration Act by failing to register as an alien and traveling without a permit, and to possessing a shortwave radio in violation of wartime restrictions on Italian aliens. In addition to citing all of these legal violations and FBI reports of Tedesco's alleged un-American statements and pro-Italian sympathies as grounds for her internment, the Alien Enemy Hearing Board in Nanticoke, Pennsylvania, also found her personal circumstances questionable. Her undocumented marriage to a man from whom she had been estranged for over twenty years and more recent cohabitation with another man appear to have been factors contributing to the board's opinion that Tedesco's "underworld associations" made her "potentially dangerous."[123]

Tedesco was detained at the Gloucester City Detention Center in New Jersey until September 1942 when the INS Border Patrol transferred her to the internment camp at Seagoville, Texas. She remained there in better facilities until her parole in May 1943.[124] At the rehearing of her case in October 1943, despite favorable testimony from neighbors that Tedesco appeared to be loyal to the United States and did not associate with any subversive organizations, the Alien Enemy Hearing Board in Scranton determined, on the basis of her past criminal record, that she should not be unconditionally released.[125] She continued on parole status. When interviewed by an INS inspector almost a year later, Tedesco, who had obtained a job at a carpet company as a parolee in an attempt to rehabilitate her former reputation, stated her belief that the U.S. government "unjustly persecuted" her because of her past reputation which she felt "in no way reflect[ed] against her loyalty to this country."[126] Local resentments may have played a role in identifying her as suspect as they had in many cases. Her profession in and of itself would not have indicated a propensity to commit sedition against the United States.

In December 1944, Tedesco was released from alien enemy parole but remained subject to regulations of the immigration authorities as a deportable alien.[127] She did eventually obtain her American citizenship in 1962 in Brooklyn and was living in Manhattan at the time of her death in 1990.[128] In evaluating her case, the facts that her siblings had obtained their U.S. citizenship and that she had family members serving in the war were not enough to convince the Justice Department that she too could be a loyal American citizen. Despite her efforts at rehabilitation, Tedesco could not erase the immoral nature of her prior crimes. In addition, the hearing board placed undue significance upon her marital status and liaison with another man, betraying a presumption that a woman who was not lawfully married to a man was suspect.[129] With so few women internees, however, it is difficult to test any theory of a pattern in evaluating women in the alien enemy process or to make an overall conjecture that the government underestimated women's agency in the national security state.[130]

In cases of individuals who did not have a prior criminal history, the involvement of an Assistant U.S. Attorney or Assistant District Attorney in submitting affidavits attesting to their good character may have accelerated their parole or release. Calogero Carolo, a fruit peddler in New York City for close to twenty years who had intentions of returning to Sicily, was apprehended on a presidential warrant on June 19, 1942.[131] His file with the Justice Department indicates that he was affiliated with the Fascist Lictors, a member and vice president of *Circulo Francesco Crispi*, a branch of the Italian Blackshirts, and that he had no strong bonds to the United States. FBI agents thought it was significant to a determination of his loyalty to America that he had a copy of the Italian newspaper, *Il Grido della Stirpe* (The Cry of the Ancestry), as well as the sheet music of a Fascist hymn. Carolo had a small farm in Sicily where his family lived and made two trips back and forth to Italy even though he had permanent residence status in the United States. A "salient fact" in the evaluation of the alien enemy board in New York was that Carolo's sole purpose in the United States was making money to send back to Italy and that he had planned on eventually returning.[132] Thus, Carolo's lack of interest in obtaining American citizenship made an unfavorable impression on the board. After being interned for over a year, he had a rehearing at Fort Missoula in September 1943 at which time the board considered affidavits that had been sent to the U.S. Attorneys Office regarding Carolo's honorable character and hard-working attitude.

The favorable reports appear to have sped up his parole order, issued on November 4, 1943, but he was not ordered released by Attorney General Biddle until June 28, 1945. Carolo never became an American citizen. He repatriated to Italy where he died in 1978.[133]

Further evidence in the interviews of two government attorneys of Italian descent in San Francisco, taken by Stephen Fox, confirms the extent of influence that persons with political clout had on the fate of the internees. They were able to convince the boards that certain Italian aliens with whom they were familiar were upstanding citizens who retained no allegiance to Italy, thereby saving them from internment. In recalling his involvement in these proceedings, Alfonso Zirpoli, who had been an Assistant U.S. Attorney during World War II, said that he presented the cases of aliens detained at an INS facility at Sharp Park in Pacifica, California. "Some of those who testified would say, 'I'm a good friend of Assistant U.S. Attorney Zirpoli. We're members of the same club—*Il Cenacolo.*' "[134] The familiarity that government employees of Italian heritage had with the Italian community may have helped educate boards about the particular mind-set of the Italian immigrant or inform them on matters such as the mission of Italian American organizations or the extent of influence that the Italian media had.

John Molinari, who served as a deputy district attorney in San Francisco during World War II, presents another example of the political influence of Italian Americans in the hearing process.[135] Molinari recalled receiving phone calls from mothers and wives whose sons and husbands had been taken into custody and then going to the Salvation Home in San Francisco to see if he could vouch for people he knew. He described the hearings he attended as follows: "They had military tribunals to screen them. It was sort of an informal hearing. Some of the hearing officers were reserve lawyers that I knew, who were reserves in the judge advocate department of the military." When Molinari was able to describe the individual being examined as "loyal" or "not a problem," he was released within a few days.[136] In comparing the current litigious society to the 1940s, he said: "Nobody ever attacked [J. Edgar] Hoover on whether the FBI had probable cause [to arrest these people] or not. . . . In those days, you were a little hesitant about taking on the government in wartime. You might be accused of being disloyal if you took the cudgels from one of these persons."[137] Molinari's references to military tribunals and probable cause most likely describe exclusion hearings discussed earlier, which were conducted by a board of three military officers for naturalized citizens under suspicion or for those who lived in a military zone. Regardless of the type of hearing, however, Molinari confirms the power of having a respected government official vouch for a suspect's loyalty and good character, and attests to the flexibility in institutional standards that the ad hoc form of justice of the wartime hearings allowed.

Although all interned Italians were categorized as "alien enemies" in the Provost Marshal General files, there were a number of civilian internees who had become naturalized U.S. citizens prior to their arrest. As a naturalized citizen in the Territory of Hawaii, Mario Valdastri presents a case unique from the other internees profiled in this chapter because the process given to a U.S. citizen should have been greater than that afforded an enemy alien.[138] His story gives us an opportunity to understand civil-military relations during wartime. The U.S. government's treatment of U.S. citizens in the Territory of Hawaii relied upon the pronouncement of martial law there after the attack on Pearl Harbor as the Hawaiian Islands were considered a war zone. One feature of martial law was the imposition of military tribunals; military commissions and provost courts tried all criminal cases without the rules of evidence or constitutional guarantees afforded defendants, including trial by jury and attorney representation. Because habeas corpus had been suspended, civilians could be held without being informed of charges.[139]

Valdastri was born in Italy in 1896, and as a teenager in 1909 came to the United States where he resided continuously. In 1918, he became an American citizen when he enlisted in the U.S. Army to serve in France during World War I, receiving an honorable discharge the following year. Upon his return to civilian life, he married an American citizen of Italian origin, had two children, and built a successful contracting business in Honolulu. Federal agents arrested Valdastri on December 8, 1941, at his home in Honolulu.[140]

At his hearing at Fort Shafter on Oahu before a board of army officers and civilians, Valdastri appeared without counsel. While Valdastri was out of the room, an FBI special agent gave testimony that upon his return from a trip to Europe in 1933, "he expressed himself as quite pro-Fascist, which attitude has become more pronounced since the start of the recent war," as well as pro-Nazi, and even held meetings of local Italians at his home "to forward the cause of Fascism in the Islands."[141] Most suspicious was his allegedly close friendship with the former secretary to the Italian consul in Honolulu, who was suspected of espionage activity. After the president's closure of Italian consulates, it was believed that the Italian consul asked Valdastri to carry on some of the activities of the consulate. In response to questioning by the board, Valdastri admitted to expressing pro-Fascist leanings until 1935 but stated that since then he "detested the movement of Fascism" and had "nothing to do with the Germans" or Nazism. He admitted to his acquaintance with the consul's secretary, but characterized the nature of his meetings at the consulate as relating to the development of commerce and the financial business of the Italian Club, which he later disbanded for political differences, rather than representing the actions of the governments of Germany and Italy.[142] Despite Valdastri's explanations, the hearing board felt that his alleged ties to Fascist government officials and his former leadership of the Italian Club with its Fascist leanings were too recent for the U.S. government to trust his loyalty to the United States. Since Valdastri fit the profile of someone capable of inciting others because of his prominence in business and political circles, U.S. authorities chose not to take a risk with him.

After three months of detention at the Honolulu Immigration Station and a facility on Sand Island (within Honolulu proper), during which time Valdastri was not allowed to have visitors, he was transferred to two army camps for internment, first Fort McDowell on Angel Island in San Francisco and then Camp McCoy, Wisconsin.[143] In an appeal to the American Civil Liberties Union (ACLU) in New York, Valdastri spoke of the injustice he experienced, stating that he had never been formally charged and that, as an American citizen, he felt that he was entitled to "an opportunity of having my case brought before a regular court and of assuring my defense."[144] There is no evidence in Valdastri's file that the ACLU came to his defense.

In a letter to President Roosevelt from his camp barracks, Valdastri expressed his disillusion that he, a U.S. citizen and veteran of World War I, was given a sham hearing during which he was never formally charged with an offense. He explained: "In Honolulu, I was given a so-called hearing which lasted five minutes. No formal accusation against which I could have defended myself was ever brought against me, nor were the reasons for my arrest ever disclosed to me." He found it "profoundly shocking to be treated in my own country like an enemy alien and to have been subjected to proceedings unworthy of American administration."[145]

Upon his return to Sand Island in June 1942, Valdastri's daughter Frances wrote to Allen Gullion, the provost marshal general during most of World War II. She requested her father's release after Valdastri's own letter to Gullion went unanswered.[146] Major General Gullion assured Frances Valdastri that her father had undergone a hearing before a board of three civilians before his internment, under the jurisdiction of the commanding general of the Hawaiian Department. Speaking of Valdastri as if he were an alien enemy instead of a naturalized U.S. citizen, Gullion explained that the hearing was "not held as a matter of right but was allowed in order to avoid injustice." Gullion cited "considerations of national security, dependent upon the military factors involved" as governing the decision to intern Valdastri. His release was dependent upon a determination by the Hawaiian Department that "such release would in no way endanger the public safety of the United States or be detrimental to the war effort."[147] Finally, in late February 1943, after a second hearing board concluded that Valdastri was not a danger to the United States, he was released. One of the factors contributing to his release at that time was that the military needed Valdastri's skills in construction. Valdastri chose in 1967 to retire with his wife in Italy; he lived to be eighty-two.[148]

There could be a lot of variety in the nature of the hearings across the districts and over time. In some cases, aliens complained that the hearing board was not sensitive to their poor command of the English language which necessitated at least a translator, if not representation by an attorney to inquire into exact charges and to communicate a defense.[149] There were also complaints from members of the alien enemy hearing boards who were concerned with the overwhelming numbers of cases that they were expected to hear. A proposal called for as many as 500 boards (as opposed to the approximately 100 boards that existed) nationwide and suggested that the boards would not have to include lawyers or specialists.[150] A decentralization of the hearing board system would have charged district attorneys with reviewing cases, instead of the Attorney General's Office, or an appeals board in each district could have been set up.[151] While such changes in the system might have achieved a more expedient resolution for each enemy alien, there would have been even less uniformity in the process across the districts without the input of the attorney general.

Italy surrendered on September 8, 1943, and, most Italian internees in the United States were at least paroled by the end of 1943. Data from this study shows that the exception was the group of Italians identified as the most ardent Fascists and perceived as influential leaders in their community. These individuals, particularly those in the media, were among the first to be apprehended and the last to be released from internment. By March 1944, Director Ennis wrote to the attorney general, recommending the parole of Italian seamen and civilian internees. With respect to civilian internees, his justification was that "even the few internees who are not politically demoralized by Italy's fall know that their Fascist views are completely discredited in their communities and they would not be a danger to their community if returned on parole."[152] In the subject group, sixty-four Italian internees were not released until 1945. Given that most of the members of the subject group were apprehended in the first six months of the war, those remaining had spent at least three years in internment camps. There were only a handful of men who remained in INS custody by the fall of 1945.

In assessing the justice of the process of selective internment of Italians during World War II, it is also instructive to consider what internment was like in other Anglo countries overseas and in Canada. In Great Britain, at least 74,000 German and Austrian refugees, many of whom were Jews persecuted by the Nazi regime, were interned without process. This example was foremost in Attorney General Biddle's mind when he established the American style of individual determination, which seems relatively fair in comparison.[153] At the time, approximately 19,000 Italian nationals lived in Great Britain, some of whom had been there for decades.[154] Most of the 4,000 Italians interned there were sent to camps on the Isle of Man.[155] At the height of internment, over 20 percent of Italian nationals in Great Britain were interned, which is overwhelmingly larger than the percentages interned in the United States and Canada. By Britain's armistice with Italy in September 1943, there were still around 1,500 Italian internees, although releases sped up after this point.[156]

In 1939 to 1940, the Australian internment policy mirrored that in Britain, but by 1942 to 1943 the policy was relaxed, reflecting the "milder U.S. practice and the fact that wartime events had pushed Australia from being a child of the British Empire to a new role as client of the United States."[157] Overall, the Italian community's situation in Australia was much more grave than it was in the United States. Similar to Great Britain, approximately 20 percent of Australia's Italian population was interned on suspicion of Fascist sympathies or because of the subject's occupation. Although tribunals were established to hear petitions in late 1940, releases from Australian internment camps came slowly.[158] There were few proponents of liberty and due process for the Italian internees among the Australians, whose "existing prejudices" about Italians as both cowards and violent were strengthened by how and when Italy entered the war.[159]

The picture in Canada looks similar to the one in the United States. By the end of 1940, approximately 500 individuals of the 112,625 Italian Canadian population were interned on suspicion of Fascist leanings. This figure represents about four-tenths of one percent of the population, as reported in the 1941 census, which is much closer to the ratio interned in the United

States than to the percentages of the Italian population held in Great Britain and Australia.[160] A comparative study of the legal processes in these common-law countries for evaluating the loyalty and status of suspects and of conditions in internment camps, specifically the extent that the host country chose to abide by the 1929 Geneva Convention's provisions for prisoners of war in its treatment of internees, would allow us to better evaluate the U.S. commitment to democratic and humanitarian ideals. Consideration of the influence of each country's legal traditions outside of constitutional protections might provide a cross-temporal dimension to the analysis as well as a cross-national one.

The story that follows of what life was like on a day-to-day basis for internees held in U.S. camps shows how their understanding of democratic principles gave them hope. Many internees believed that a rehearing at the camps would once and for all clear their names and restore their normal lives. While some sought to prove their loyal and obedient character through cooperation in camp duties or in work projects off site, others composed letters to Justice Department officials explaining what aspects of their prior lives could have been mistakenly construed by the government as suspicious. Above all, they sought to prove that they were in fact loyal to the United States and would be upstanding citizens if released.

CHAPTER FOUR

Bocce behind Barbed Wire

Checks on Government Power in the Camps

All accounts of life in the internment camps, whether in INS reports, memoranda of camp officers, or in the letters of internees, paint a picture of the resiliency of the Italian aliens in bleak surroundings. The sense of normalcy that the internees created through volunteering for work projects, participating in musical and sports activities, celebrating their cultural heritage in meals and in holiday traditions, and forging friendships with fellow internees allowed them to regain their dignity and gave them a sense of agency while confined.

Although their agency was limited by the strictures of the camp environment, that environment was itself ameliorated by U.S. commitments to international law. As noted in a previous chapter, member states to the 1929 Geneva Convention were not obligated to extend the treaty's prisoner of war protections to civilian internees, but the United States did so, following a proposal of the International Committee of the Red Cross and thereby affording the internees checks on government power in the camps. The 1929 Convention guaranteed prisoners safe and humane treatment, a good standard of living, and a means of redressing complaints about their conditions.[1] Moving beyond the protections of the treaty, however, the Italians took initiatives to influence their fate so that they might gain freedom. In the face of the government's preponderance of power—internment without notice of charges, frequent movement from camp to camp, interference in family relationships through censorship of mail and monitoring of visits—the Italian aliens individually sought to prove that they could be loyal American citizens through their work ethic, their cooperative demeanor, and by expressing their patriotism in camp and in letters to the Justice Department. In some cases, such efforts may have secured an earlier parole or release, while in other cases the government's adherence to damaging FBI reports prevented aliens' explanations for suspicious information about their past from having any positive effect on their fate. Thus, while the Italian aliens frequently challenged the power asserted by Justice Department officials and military personnel, the government ultimately had the upper hand. This chapter tells stories of how Italians challenged governmental power and ways in which the government retained power, and by doing so, narrates the personal consequences of the legal and political manipulations described in the preceding chapters.

This account of camp life draws upon multiple sources of varying degrees of reliability. Whereas INS reports provide information on the structure of camp life as well as the administrative history of operational decisions, they better reflect the aspirations and goals of the system than the actual experiences of the internees. The accounts of Jerre Mangione are more reliable because he had the advantage of visiting every INS camp and speaking with and observing camp officials and internees, and he wrote about camp conditions when he was no longer employed as the public relations director for the INS. The letters between internees and their loved ones do a much better job of giving us a picture of how the internees felt and how they spent their time; however, both the system of censorship and the internees' desire to paint a rosier picture of camp life to save their families from worry compromised the truth of what they wrote. In contrast, government officials did not censor internees' appeals to the Justice Department, the State Department, or to the Swiss Legation as the Protecting Power, lending more veracity to these statements about confinement. Finally, accounts provided in interviews of former internees and their family members many years after internment may be truthful because there was no risk of reprisals for criticizing the government, but the passage of time undoubtedly altered their memory of events.

Camp Barracks and the Structure of Internment Life

The INS, under the jurisdiction of the Department of Justice, had detention facilities in almost every large port in the United States and converted space in county jails and other publicly owned buildings for the purpose of holding enemy aliens. It had custody of all enemy aliens until the Alien Enemy Control Unit reached a decision to intern, parole, or release each individual. Those sentenced to internment were turned over to the U.S. Army for detention at their camps, with the exception of women internees who remained in INS custody.[2] As explained below, the Latin American internees also remained at INS facilities.

At the outbreak of the war, the INS was already operating internment camps at Fort Stanton in New Mexico, Fort Missoula in Montana, and Fort Lincoln in Bismarck, North Dakota, all of which had been established to detain Italian and German seamen taken in 1939 and 1941 from vessels in

American ports and the Panama Canal to prevent sabotage.[3] Just after the United States entered World War II in December 1941, Italians and Japanese from the West Coast were sent to Fort Missoula.[4] INS reports indicate that Fort Missoula housed 1,317 Italian seamen in all.[5]

The other permanent INS internment camps or facilities considered suitable for long-term detention were as follows: Santa Fe in New Mexico; Kenedy, Seagoville, and Crystal City in Texas (the last camp established for family groups such as those from Latin America pursuant to the State Department's agreement); Sharp Park outside San Francisco; Kooskia in Idaho; Algiers in Louisiana; Gloucester City in New Jersey; and Ellis Island in New York. In the latter part of 1942, the State Department and the provost marshal general requested that the INS assume custody of civilian internees being held in army camps since the army was preparing to house hundreds of prisoners of war. On February 27, 1943, the attorney general and secretary of war agreed to return the civilian internees, numbering approximately 4,200, to INS custody.[6] By June 1943, 4,029 had been transferred back to the INS.[7] In March 1944, the remaining Italian civilian internees at Fort Missoula were moved to Ellis Island, and the army regained custody of this camp on July 1, 1944.[8] As late as May 31, 1945, there were twelve persons of Italian nationality held in Crystal City.[9]

The files of the provost marshal general for Italian civilian internees indicate that they were held at the following army camps: Fort George Meade, Maryland; Fort McAlester, Oklahoma; Fort Sam Houston, Texas; Camp Forrest, Tennessee; Camp McCoy, Wisconsin; and Fort McDowell on Angel Island in San Francisco Bay. In most instances internees stayed at multiple army camps over the course of their internment, being forced to move every few months, apparently the result of bureaucracy and logistics. As explained above, custody of the enemy aliens was initially split between the INS and the army, but the army's need for space for prisoners of war required the shift in custody back to the INS. The shuffling of internees also occurred as a result of reuniting families from Latin America at the INS camps designed for family units, as well as the staggered parole dates for internees, which freed up housing at various times.[10] As a general rule, the U.S. government disapproved of American wives joining their alien husbands in internment camps.[11]

The treatment of internees at INS camps differed from that at army camps. Any differences in protocol may be attributed to the fact that the army camps functioned under military regulations, while the U.S. Border Patrol operated the INS camps under less stringent standards. However, in his letter to the editor of the *Honolulu Star Bulletin* detailing the experience of Italians and Japanese taken from Hawaii, Mario Valdastri recognized "the considerate attitude and human understanding of the officers" at the army camp at Fort McCoy, which undoubtedly influenced the mutual respect that internees showed one another.[12] Valdastri's entire letter expresses positive sentiment about his camp experience, but its reliability is compromised by the filter of censoring he knew his letter would have to pass. In this respect, the policies for censorship of correspondence entering and leaving the INS and army camps resembled each other.[13]

The United States abided by the terms of the 1929 Geneva Convention with respect to the setup and organization of internment camps, and to all aspects of the day-to-day existence of the internees such as the provision of food, canteens, recreation, and education. The permanent internment camps followed a fairly standard pattern of organization: headquarters, internal security, surveillance, services and supplies, maintenance, and medical.[14] Crystal City, known as the family camp, did not fit this organizational structure because families required additional services, such as a maternity ward, adequate schools for children, a more complex system of issuing clothing, and more diversified production projects.[15]

On his tour of internment camps, Jerre Mangione visited Seagoville Internment Camp, formerly a federal minimum-security reformatory on the outskirts of Dallas, and reported that the $1.8 million facility on an 830-acre tract resembled a "prosperous college campus."[16] The one- and two-story red brick buildings with cream-colored limestone trim were in the architectural style of contemporary southern colonial and faced on two quadrangles.[17] Intended as the internment camp for aliens who would be repatriated at the end of the war, it first housed families from Latin America, then predominantly single women who lived in comfortable dormitories, and couples who lived in eighteen-foot-square "victory huts." Seagoville had an auditorium where women performed ballet and theater, a library with an extensive collection of foreign-language books, a weaving room, and a garment factory. Letters screened by staff censors reveal that internees at least claimed to be pleased with the food and housing at Seagoville, especially those Latin Americans who had been living in poverty in their native countries, and many found the American staff "considerate" and "gentle."[18]

In sharp contrast to the attractive setting of Seagoville stood Kenedy Internment Camp in south Texas, which housed mostly Japanese and Germans as well as a diverse group of Latin Americans. The first group of internees that arrived in April 1942 included 456 Germans, 156 Japanese, and 14 Italians.[19] Kenedy was an abandoned federal facility built by and for the Civilian Conservation Corps with nine barracks measuring 20 by 120 feet and some smaller structures on twenty-two acres. Remodeling involved the construction of more than two hundred prefabricated huts to house five or six persons, and the building of a dining hall, kitchen, hospital, headquarters, accommodation for officers and nurses, warehouses, and latrines.[20] Mangione described how the "tall barbed-wire chain fence and guard towers surrounding [the camp] dominated the desolate landscape like a harbinger of doom."[21] As at the other INS camps, clothes, shoes, linens, toiletries, and smoking tobacco were issued to internees pursuant to the terms of the Geneva Convention.[22] Internees could purchase food products and other items at the camp canteen at local market price.[23] The whereabouts of internees at Kenedy were monitored day and night. Elected captains assisted internees in lining up at 9:00 A.M. and 4:30 P.M. for head counts when the sirens sounded, and the staff conducted three or four bed checks nightly.[24] Of the twenty attempts at escape in the history of the INS internment program, none of which were successful, three occurred at Kenedy.[25] Interestingly, no Italian or Japanese enemy aliens attempted to escape; German nationals were responsible for all twenty attempts.[26] Despite its bleakness, the camp's improvised wooden chapel contained a vivid mural depicting the life of Christ and his resurrection, which Mangione found to be "the only visual symbol of hope" in all the camps.[27]

The third internment camp in Texas, Crystal City, was the largest INS detention facility, housing the families with children from Latin America, including a few Italian families. Wives of interned husbands volunteered for internment here with their children to keep their families intact. Located on a former migrant farm labor camp consisting of 41 three-room cottages, 118 one-room structures, and service buildings, Crystal City grew with the construction of 219 temporary duplex, triplex, and quadruplex housing units, 15 additional three-room cottages, and 103 plywood huts. The total capacity of the camp was 962 families, most of whom were Japanese. Each housing unit was equipped for cooking, and materials were supplied to the internees to construct furniture and furnishings. Communities were established based on nationality and race.[28] Mangione described Crystal City's atmosphere as "almost cheerful" in its resemblance to a bustling southwestern town with a school, hospital, community center, bakery, and stores. Since it contained a polyglot population of diverse ethnicities and ages, it presented challenges in medical services and dietary offerings. Families were provided a weekly allowance to buy their own food.[29]

This photo of Fort Missoula, taken from outside the camp on a wintry day, illustrates the bleakness of confinement and the loss of freedom. Because internees had been taken under exigent circumstances from the comfort of their families and homes, internment for months and even years in primitive barracks without being told what they had done wrong caused them to feel disillusioned with the U.S. government. (*Fence around Barrack Buildings at Fort Missoula*, 1941–1943. Peter Fortune Collection [2001.048.187]. Courtesy of the Historical Museum at Fort Missoula.)

Mangione was impressed with the community's self-governance through democratic procedures whereby each language group in the camp elected its own council with a spokesperson who served as an intermediary between the internees and the administration and as a liaison to designated foreign emissaries for issues that infringed on internee rights under the Geneva Convention.[30]

Set in the picturesque mountains of Montana, Fort Missoula had the largest population of Italians among the internment camps. Ironically labeled *Camp Bella Vista* by the Italians, Fort Missoula was barricaded by 2,400 feet

of chain-link fence topped by barbed wire, and had sixty-foot guard towers at the north and south gates staffed all day and night. A fifty-foot iron
searchlight tower overlooked the barracks consisting of housing units, each
accommodating fifty men in double bunks, a hospital, a school, a library, a
theater, a mess hall, and a recreation hall.[31] The men woke at 6:00 A.M., ate
breakfast in shifts, and answered roll call at 8:00 A.M. and 8:00 P.M. They
were expected to participate in jobs necessary for the operation of the camp,
such as serving food, on a rotating basis. Internees could earn eighty cents
a day for specialized work such as carpentry, mattress making, sewing, furniture making, and construction work.[32] The Italian internees had a general council, a governing board of twenty-eight members elected by the men
themselves, including a mayor, police chief, parks commissioner, and sani-
tation commissioner.[33]

Early reports on Fort Missoula in 1941 when it housed seamen and the
foreign employees of the 1939–1940 World's Fair were positive, conveying
the picture of a camp that allowed the internees much autonomy and time
for leisure.[34] Alfredo Cipolato, one of the men who worked at the World's
Fair and one of the first to be interned at Fort Missoula, described life as
calm with few disruptions among beautiful facilities such as the library and
tennis courts.[35] After Pearl Harbor, however, when Japanese, Germans, and
Italians were interned together at Fort Missoula, conditions seemed to
change. Mangione had an opportunity to observe the "lack of love" among
these groups of men. While the Japanese ignored the Germans and Italians,
the latter two groups showed contempt for the Japanese and dislike for each
other, sometimes descending into fist fights.[36] A contemporary report of
conditions at Fort Missoula confirms Mangione's impression of animosity
among the national groups. A *Wide World* news reporter who visited the camp
revealed that the Italians and Japanese shared no camaraderie as fellow members of Axis powers; instead they were known to "glower at each other."
Camp guards observed that the Italians never said so much as "good morning" to the Japanese.[37] While the Japanese had their own mess hall where the
staples were rice, soybeans, and fish, the Germans and Italians shared a mess
hall but also maintained separate menus.[38] The Italians "turn[ed] up their
noses at sauerkraut," while the Germans showed their distaste for spaghetti.[39]

The impressions that each ethnic group made on camp officials, specifically how "Americanized" they appeared in terms of their work ethic, found
their way into reports on each internee for use by hearing boards recon-
sidering each internee's status. Upon interviewing the camp commander at

The Italian internees shared a mess hall with the Germans but maintained their own cuisine and could partake in their unique cultural traditions. (*The Italian Mess Hall at Fort Missoula*, 1941–1943. Peter Fortune Collection [2001.048.111]. Courtesy of the Historical Museum at Fort Missoula.)

Fort Missoula, Mangione learned that Italian internees fit the stereotype of their ethnic group as temperamental but also "the most human," while the Japanese proved to be the most cooperative in participating in menial chores like scrubbing toilets, regardless of social rank.[40] The fact that the first item on the Alien Enemy Control Unit's form report for internee behavior at the camp was "general attitude and cooperativeness with Camp authorities" proves the importance of a cooperative attitude in evaluating whether an internee presented a security risk. Camp officials also typically commented on whom the internee associated with and whether the internee was a good influence on other internees.[41] For example, army reports on the behavior of Ubaldo Guidi-Buttrini, the Boston radio commentator profiled in the previous chapter, indicated that he was a bad influence on other internees with his Fascist speeches. He was blamed for the army's failure to enlist the seamen with whom he was interned at Fort Missoula to man Allied merchant vessels or Italian ships bound for Italy.[42]

From the reports of internees who spent time at numerous army camps, operated by the Provost Marshal General's Office and the War Department, and from accounts of family members who visited them, we learn that security was comparable to that at the INS camps. The daughter of a former internee recalled Fort Sam Houston's intimidating aura upon visiting her father; the camp was surrounded by "a double-fenced enclosure made of heavy cyclone fencing with barbed wire across the top," and two armed guards stood in towers at each corner of the camp.[43] However, the accommodations at the army camps were generally more primitive than those at the INS camps. Living quarters at Fort Meade and Fort Houston consisted of tents instead of housing structures.[44] In Carmelo Ilacqua's letters home, he wrote positively of the tent he shared with three other Italians at Fort Houston and commented that he was treated better there than at Fort Missoula "where authorities attitude was as though we had broken laws."[45] Thus the type of treatment internees received most likely colored their feelings about their physical surroundings. Likewise, Valdastri was pleased with the barracks at Fort McCoy. He described how quarters housed forty men each, equipped with beds and linens, Cannon heaters, and writing tables, and were kept "immaculately clean" by room service on a rotating schedule.[46]

There appear to have been more restrictions on internees' movement at the army camps as opposed to the INS camps where internees wore civilian clothes and could work outside the camps for pay. Internees at Fort Meade reportedly had to wear shirts with "POW" printed on the back.[47] At Fort McCoy, internees had to answer to frequent roll calls, as opposed to just morning and evening. But the daily routines and organizational structure at the two types of camps were similar. Just as the INS established rules for the daily work routine of its internees, the army camps created work rosters. At Fort McCoy, rosters assigned internees shifts to work in the mess hall or to clean up the camp grounds. Similar to the system of self-governance observed at Fort Missoula and Crystal City, nationality groups at Fort McCoy elected leaders to represent their respective interests.[48]

Reports of the extent of care for the physical and mental well-being of internees varied among the camps. While some camps had medical specialists on hand, others did not. Certain types of illnesses, namely mental insanity, cancer, and tuberculosis, required the removal of afflicted internees to proper medical facilities, often Public Health Service Hospitals.[49] Valdastri described a regimen of frequent physical exams by a staff of three Japanese doctors who prescribed a healthy diet and exercise routine for the men at Fort McCoy, as well as dental examinations.[50] However, at Fort Missoula, getting competent medical care proved to be a continual problem. After a stint by an Italian doctor from one of the ships proved unsuccessful, in late 1941 a professionally incompetent and temperamentally unsuitable doctor was assigned to the camp.[51] Camp directors also had difficulty getting eye doctors or dentists for the internees due to the lack of availability as well as a lack of interest in working with patients with language barriers, apparent neuroses, and unreasonable demands.[52]

The files of the provost marshal general indicate that at least seven men in the subject group of 343 Italians selectively interned died in the camps. Mental illness was common and often marked by frequent complaints of indefinable physical ailments. There were eight men among those studied who were diagnosed with psychosis and committed to mental institutions during the time of their internment. More common, of course, were cases of depression and anxiety, likely caused by the internees' frustration at being held against their will and exacerbated by increasingly longer periods of separation from loved ones.

As for the moral and spiritual well-being of the internees, reference could be made to the Geneva Convention, which granted "complete freedom in the performance of their religious duties, including attendance at the services of their faith."[53] Army chaplains performed services, and the internees' own Christian, Buddhist, or Shinto priests were permitted to conduct services in their native languages.[54] Papers of the National Catholic Welfare Conference (NCWC) indicate that U.S.-based Catholic missionaries, the Maryknoll Fathers, Sisters, and Brothers, proposed having an actual presence in the internment camps and living on the compounds to carry on religious care of the interned. The Catholic organization particularly expressed a spiritual responsibility to the Japanese while they were confined. But the federal government did not comply with this request.[55] More successful were efforts by the NCWC to provide organized Catholic faith services and to make Catholic books in the specific foreign languages available in the prisoner-of-war camps so that Germans, Italians, and Japanese alike could satisfy their spiritual needs.[56] The War Department's response was favorable; the provost marshal general arranged for the office of the chief of chaplains to coordinate visits by Catholic clergy and agreed to have camp commanders distribute Catholic prayer books and other religious literature.[57]

By all accounts, living conditions were generally good, although the internees judged their treatment relative to their lives prior to internment or what their confinement protected them from, such as service in the Italian army or life in a war-torn country. The United States took its obligations under the Geneva Convention seriously, which led to some resentment in the American population, as we shall see below. Through the function of reciprocity, the U.S. government had to abide by the convention's assurances of safety and humane treatment of internees to protect Americans who were prisoners in enemy countries. The monitoring system of neutral protectorate countries made enemy nations that were signatories to the treaty accountable to each other. For example, the United States decided to follow the convention's standard for prisoners of war that the food be "equivalent in quantity and quality" to that served to U.S. troops at base camps.[58] This meant that internees were served food, such as meat, that was strictly rationed for Americans.[59]

Beating Barbed-Wire Sickness

The INS recognized that internee labor was a good administrative policy for a number of reasons. First, a work program could utilize internee labor without creating competition within the civilian workforce because at the time there was a severe shortage of unskilled labor in some sections of the country. Second, it would reduce internment costs without impacting supervision at the camps. And finally, employment would combat the "psychoneurotic tendencies among internees," by engaging them in productive activity that got them away from the camp and took their minds off of their confinement.[60]

Under the terms of the 1929 Geneva Convention, prisoners of war could be employed in work for which they were physically fit.[61] The Detaining Power was responsible for "the maintenance, care, treatment and the payment of the wages of prisoners of war working for private individuals."[62] According to the Regulations Governing Civilian Internees pursuant to the convention, internees working outside the camp could earn wages at the rate of eighty cents per day. Money earned was to be credited to the internees' accounts and not paid directly to them until their release or repatriation, or in the case of death, to their heirs. Subject to the approval of the commanding officer of the internment camp, the internee could draw on his account up to ten dollars per month, which was issued in the form of canteen coupons.[63] Thus pleas by family members who wished for their interned loved one to work in order to help support his family at home were futile because the system did not allow money earned through work projects to leave the camps.[64]

The Geneva Convention allowed arrangements to be made for internees to work for the Western Montana Beet Growers Association, which was badly in need of help during the war. Approximately 300 Italian seamen interned at Fort Missoula in 1942 were the first group of internees to be employed in the sugar beet fields, returning nightly to the internment camp.[65] Initially, the workers were transported under heavy security to the beet fields, but eventually policies became more relaxed.[66] The success of that program, both in increasing the productivity of the farms and in improving public relations in Missoula County, led to a more expansive program the following year. In March 1943, when funds became available, the INS established a pay-work program whereby internees could voluntarily work both on projects at the internment camps and off site for private employers and other government agencies at the rate of ten cents an hour, not to exceed an eight-hour workday. Any internee who wished to work in the pay-work program had to get approval from the Alien Enemy Control Unit, which reviewed issues of internal security.[67]

Not only did the program put money into the camps, it had a great effect on the morale of the internees. The establishment of this program coincided with the transfer of all remaining civilian internees from army camps to INS custody. Thus the swollen population of internees at INS camps filled a void in unskilled and semiskilled labor across the country, particularly for farms around Fort Lincoln and Fort Missoula. In addition to work on farms, the projects ranged from forest service jobs to railroad maintenance to work in hospitals.[68] Alfredo Cipolato recalled being trained as an orderly at St. Patrick's Hospital in Missoula since most of the orderlies and doctors were in the military. Although it was a unique opportunity, he and his fellow internees were restricted from going beyond one block in each direction from the hospital.[69]

At Crystal City, located in a climate suitable for agriculture, internees had more opportunities than those elsewhere to participate in a pay-work program. Some planted and tended large vegetable crops, while others worked in the production of eggs and poultry, or did other jobs, such as curing meats, preparing baked goods, repairing shoes, or manufacturing furniture. Internees could also do office work and even served as instructors as part of the work program.[70]

The Justice Department litigation files for each internee indicate that an internee's performance and attitude on the job were factors examined by the alien enemy hearing boards on reconsideration of an internee's status. Hearing boards interpreted a good work ethic as synonymous with good citizen potential. For example, reports of Francesco Fragale's cooperative behavior while working for the forest service at Missoula, later as a bell-boy and waiter at a Missoula hotel, and finally at the factory for the American Crystal Sugar Company where he was described as "hard-working" and "dependable, trustworthy, ambitious," figured into the decision to finally parole him in late 1944. As was the case with other internees on a particular work project, Fragale was allowed to live off the internment camp at the hotel where he worked, and therefore had the benefit of reports from his landlord that he was "a good tenant and well behaved."[71] Thus, in some instances, work projects offered internees the opportunity to assert some control over their fate by exhibiting qualities that could positively influence the reviewing board's opinion of their loyalty to the United States and potential to be good American citizens.

Aside from work opportunities, entertainment and group activities were the best method to combat the "barbed-wire sickness" of boredom.[72] In both the INS and army camps, internees were allowed to organize musical groups, sports activities, and to engage in educational and cultural activities. Valdastri described evenings of entertainment where there was a cultural exchange of music as part of the social life at Fort McCoy, saying sounds from the Orient created "a strange mood of baffled amazement to ears which never heard them before."[73] Thus, music served to aid in each nationality's appreciation and understanding of the other. Perhaps the camp with the best music was Fort Missoula as a number of famous Italian musicians were interned there, including musicians from the World's Fair and seven violinists who had been entertainers on the Italian luxury liner *Conte Biancamano* seized in the Panama Canal. Every night after the 5:00 P.M. supper, a band played while other internees sang.[74] Each concert held at the recreation hall open to the public raised close to $300 for the Italian welfare fund. Theater was also common among both the Italians, who favored heavy drama, and the Germans, who preferred lighter entertainment.[75]

The activities that were most successful in lifting the spirits of the Italian internees were sports like soccer and bocce ball, particularly in the summer months, and boxing or skating in the winter.[76] But young and old also formed teams with internees of the other nationalities to compete in the

To beat "barbed-wire sickness," Italian internees engaged in soccer as well as other sporting matches. (*Aerial View of Football Match at Fort Missoula*, 1941–1943. Peter Fortune Collection [2001.048.128]. Courtesy of the Historical Museum at Fort Missoula.)

all-American sport of baseball. Valdastri captured the spirit of men regaining their dignity through athletics in describing how "young men showed remarkable feats in beautiful teamwork, old men seemed to be rejuvenated until there was no resemblance to the little heaps of misery beaten down by an unmerciful fate who had left Hawaii mentally and physically broken only a short time ago."[77] Despite this display of control by the internees, the government had the upper hand even in the arena of sports and other recreational activities. Although the activities were organized and directed by the internees themselves, camp officials could withhold the opportunity to participate in recreation if internees failed to cooperate in the camp and perform all expected duties.[78]

The internees also creatively devised ways to pass the time in a variety of hobbies, from handicrafts like sandal making, to building bird nests in empty cans salvaged from the camp, to collecting rocks for polishing and painting.[79] Other internees occupied themselves in educational courses in practical skills, such as those for Italian seamen seeking advancement in their careers, as well as language courses in English, Spanish, German, and Italian.[80] Valdastri reported that "lectures about professional topics and classes of various languages" were offered at Fort McCoy.[81] Newsletters advertising activities and events, which were circulated among internees, contributed to a sense of community.[82] At some camps, the internees even got passes on occasion for visits to town, initially accompanied by guards, to shop at places like the Missoula Mercantile, where Italians and Japanese were reportedly well received.[83] All of the above served as morale boosts for the internees.

But what internees craved most was to see and hear from their families. Visits home were granted only in extreme circumstances, such as a death in the family. More frequent were visits by family members to the camps, but the visits were restricted in number and held under strict surveillance. The military advised internees that they could have only two visitors per month and that each visit could last no longer than twenty-five minutes.[84] The following description that Lucetta Berizzi Drypolcher gives of her visit to her father, Louis Berizzi, at Fort Meade shows how uncomfortable these meetings could be: "We could only speak English. The meeting room was cold and crowded, and he didn't look well. He was underweight—just not the same, in a fatigue uniform with "PW" on the back. There was sort of a general room where we met with him. The internees would come from their quarters. They were behind barbed wire, we could see that as we entered. We were very close, so it was very difficult being there."[85]

Undoubtedly visits were unsatisfying for both internees and family members. The meetings gave no opportunity for internees to express their feelings about internment or to tell their loved ones how things really were in the camp. Certainly the prohibition against speaking Italian added to the strangeness of visits given that many family members were accustomed to communicating in their native tongue.[86] Ubaldo Guidi-Buttrini's daughter Temi merely asked her father *come stai* (how are you?) before receiving a rebuke from the officer monitoring her visit.[87]

Mario Valdastri was not allowed to see his family from the time of his detention at the Honolulu Immigration Station in early December 1941 and his first stay on Sand Island in the Territory of Hawaii through his transport to the mainland.[88] Valdastri's son recalled visiting his father at Sand Island after he had returned from the mainland in late 1942. After crossing Honolulu harbor by boat, visitors had to walk about a half mile to the camp which was surrounded by double, twelve-foot barbed-wire fences. He met his father at a picnic table in a tent that housed Italians. In December 1942, Valdastri's daughter Frances was killed in an automobile accident. Valdastri was allowed to view his daughter's body for only an hour in the funeral home with the escort of two armed guards. Sadly, Valdastri had not been allowed to attend his daughter's wedding, which had occurred shortly before.[89] Such stories reveal how internment completely disrupted family relationships.

Depending upon the size and location of the facility, the INS camps utilized a variety of methods for monitoring conversations between internees and their visitors. In camps such as Ellis Island, which were located near the homes of the internees' families and friends and received the most visitors, officials were able to reduce the number of guards needed for monitoring by requiring that "conversations were held across a table which was partitioned to prevent the unseen passage of messages."[90] At other camps, the internee and his visitor sat on benches facing each other with a small space in between for observation, or they were allowed to sit together in the presence of a guard.[91]

Internees were entitled to receive a quota of authorized publications. Once that quota was reached, camp officials had the authority to cancel additional subscriptions. For example, Mario Ricciardelli, who occasionally wrote articles for the weekly Italian newspaper *Il Grido della Stirpe*, believed to be the voice for Fascist propaganda, lost his subscription to the *Washington Sun* when the adjutant at his camp determined that his publications quota had already been filled.[92] It must have been demoralizing to an internee used to staying abreast of news to have limits placed on his sources to the outside world. Valdastri described the eagerness of internees to get updates on what was happening outside the camps. Since not every internee could obtain newspapers in their native language or knew English well enough to understand news over the radio, a few of the most literate internees prepared daily news reports.[93]

As internees were not allowed to make or receive telephone calls at the camps, their only form of communication with their friends and family members was the mail system. Internees were permitted to write two letters and one postcard a week. Photos from the camps were prohibited.[94] Officials at the INS internment camps recorded and examined all mail to and from internees for any trace of plans for subversive activity, a method of screening allowed under the Geneva Convention.[95] Mail destined for locations outside the continental United States was sent under seal to the Office of Censorship for additional review by personnel competent in the Japanese, German, and Italian languages. The system of censorship allowed the INS to determine the "general attitude, possible improper plans, conditions of health and morale, and identity and addresses of close relatives and friends of the internees." If any suspicious excerpts were found in an internee's correspondence, they were forwarded to the INS Central Office and the director of the Alien Enemy Control Unit, and in special cases, to the FBI, military and naval intelligence, and to the Special War Problems Division of the State Department.[96] Regulations published on April 15, 1942, which were designed to standardize the censorship practices between the INS and other agencies, directed that "malicious and false complaints regarding conditions of detention" should be deleted from letters, but there would be no censorship of letters addressed to the Justice Department, the State Department, or to the Protecting Power.[97] Thus, internees did enjoy the freedom of speech with respect to communicating their feelings about their confinement to government authorities.

The file of Mario Ricciardelli presents an example of an uncensored letter. In a letter to H. E. N. D. Borgus, the Swiss minister, Ricciardelli wrote of the "abuse and humiliation" of being handcuffed at a train station when being transferred from Fort McAlester for a rehearing at an INS facility to determine whether he might be released from internment. He requested to know whether such treatment of a civilian internee was in violation of the Geneva Convention.[98] As Lawrence DiStasi points out, the presence of this letter in Ricciardelli's file indicates that it was either forwarded to or intercepted by the U.S. government and ended up in the War Department.[99] The fact that Ricciardelli received a second order of internment on December 30, 1942, and was not paroled until September 15, 1943, confirms that his rehearing was not successful.[100] The effect of his letter to the Swiss minister on the result of the rehearing is unclear.

Family members tried to keep their interned loved ones abreast of all events at home, important happenings like births, marriages, and deaths, updates on the development of the internees' children, and other more mundane issues like how productive the gardens were at home. They sent items that they thought the internees might enjoy such as candy, cigarettes, and books. In turn, internees reported on the state of their health and diet at the camps as well as on musical or sports events. However, the internees were prevented from relating any negative accounts of internment as indicated in numerous examples of deleted messages in correspondence. Notes of camp officials reviewing internees' correspondence indicated the sender and intended recipient and the deleted passages in Italian, with rough translations. For example, a note in the file of Alfredo Tribuiani, a news reporter apprehended on December 8, 1941, indicates that camp officials deleted Tribuiani's sentiments about the conditions of his internment from a letter to Adele Tribuiani. He wrote that conditions at his internment camp were "better than Gloucester [Gloucester City detention facility in New Jersey], however the lack of LIBERTY oppresses one's heart and soul."[101] Similarly, the following thoughts of Filippo Romano, a journalist for *Popolo Italiano*, written in a letter to his loved one, Mrs. Maria Romano, were deleted: expressions of *il nostro dolore* (our grief) and *l'umanità* (inhumanity) of censorship of letters which has *agravando la nostra tragica situazione* (aggravated our tragic situation). In an earlier letter, deletions included his resentment that the government interned "the barons, dukes, counts, artists, and professional people who represent the Flower of Italy, who have come here I know not why, while the true criminals continue to amass millions of dollars."[102] Camp officials gave particular attention to the correspondence of internees in the media profession since they feared the influence of these internees who were adept at expressing their opinions, and as public figures, probably still had a following outside the camps.

Letters coming into the camp were scanned for sentiments, whether of emotional attachment or complaints about their loved ones' fate, out of fear that they might negatively affect the morale of internees. In some cases, the deletions were understandable in view of this concern. For example, Velleda Guidi's complaint to her father—"it was very mean that we were allowed only 25 minutes with you . . . Imagine, we traveled 30 hours straight to be allowed only 25 minutes with you"—was deleted probably because it might have served to anger Guidi-Buttrini and make him less obedient toward military officials.[103] On the other hand, some deletions by military officials censoring letters seemed to work against this purpose. Censors deleted from a letter written to Alfredo Tribuiani a verse titled "Let's Keep Smiling," which spoke of brightening the day with a smile and keeping courage up, presumably positive sentiment for an internee, for the reason that it had "possible hidden meaning."[104] Similarly ambiguous was the deletion of Mariana Fabbri's cartoons of herself and her dog in letters to Alessandro Fabbri, a business manager from New York City and a veteran of the Italian army who spent about a year and a half in internment.[105] What is certain is that censoring violated the personal relationships of internees and their loved ones and made both sides wonder what information was kept from them.

The internee letters did not always express despair about their confinement. For example, in his conversations with Dr. Amy N. Stannard, the officer in charge of Seagoville who received information from the staff censors, Jerre Mangione learned that many of the Latin Americans who had been living in poverty expressed gratitude in their letters for the good food and housing at Seagoville. However, what these letters had in common with the letters Italian aliens sent to their friends and family in the United States was anguish over being parted from loved ones.[106] Many internees assured their loved ones that they were fine and that there was no need to worry. Carmelo Ilacqua said they were "meeting this storm with courage and fortitude, we will be able to withstand it and we, too, will see the sunshine again."[107]

Many families of internees not only worried about the welfare of their loved ones in camp, but also wondered how they were going to survive at home. Without their husbands' income, many wives faced severe financial problems. We know from the file of Giovanni Maiorana, a fisherman from San Francisco, that in some cases the Federal Reserve Bank, pursuant to the direction of the Secretary of the Treasury, could arrange for the accounts, safe deposit boxes, and securities of internees to be blocked.[108] Such restrictions would necessarily affect family members. There was a federal assistance program, officially called "Services and Assistance to Enemy Aliens and Others Affected by Restrictive Governmental Action," established through presidential allotment in February 1942, which continued through June 1944. The intention of the program was to assist enemy aliens and their families affected by the government's relocation of persons from military areas and detention or internment. The Bureau of Public Assistance administered the program through state public assistance agencies operating on behalf of the Social Security Board.[109]

As other scholars have discovered, however, the number of enemy alien families who actually received government aid and the amount of that aid are unclear, suggesting that the program was not regularly administered to families in need. Rose Scherini asserted that the families of internees "were given no financial assistance by the U.S. government, although there were reports that the American Red Cross and the Federal War Relief Agency would help the families."[110] Stephen Fox was unable to retrieve detailed records of assistance to Italian and German aliens in 1942, but he determined that payments across counties in California were inconsistent. The fact that some counties disbursed almost nothing explains why many aliens do not recall that the program existed.[111] Further evidence that families were unaware that aid was available exists in the file of Anthony Pidala. Apparently Mrs. Pidala, upon inquiry about receiving the wages from her husband's work while interned, learned for the first time from the colonel in the Aliens Division that assistance could be sought from the regional office of the Federal Security Agency in Chicago.[112] Family members having financial difficulties were also referred to the office of the commissioner of the INS.[113]

As we have already seen in the case studies, internees made pleas to politicians and others in positions of influence for help in getting released or at least paroled. Inquiries by the American Committee for Protection of Foreign Born to the Alien Enemy Control Unit about the status of alien groups or particular aliens who had been interned indicate that this organization was monitoring the situation throughout the war.[114] The NCWC deserves highlighting because it had a continual role in the handling of the nationals of all three Axis powers, from the government's announcement of mandatory registration of aliens in 1940 through the relocation and internment of enemy aliens. The papers of the NCWC indicate the organization considered the particular circumstances of each individual when determining which Italian internees to aid. In the case of Prince Boncompagno Boncompagni-Ludovisi, an export broker interned at Camp Meade, the NCWC refused his request to solicit a letter from high ecclesiastical authority vouching for his character and good standing. The NCWC would not support Boncompagni-Ludovisi because he was implicated in an allegedly illegal exchange of Italian currency that could only be handled by the Italian government.[115] In the case of Ubaldo Guidi-Buttrini, Bruce Mohler, the NCWC's director of the bureau of immigration, carefully qualified the organization's position as not being able "to judge the innocence or guilt" of Guidi-Buttrini when he presented a favorable letter from the internee's son, an American serviceman, to Edward Ennis.[116] However, the NCWC was willing to assist a former seaman, Guglielmo d'Amico, interned at Fort Missoula, by supplying favorable information about him so that the apostolic delegation could contact Edward Ennis to discuss his parole.[117] It appears that the NCWC could justify coming to the aid of the seamen who were interned solely on the basis of being on the crew of an Italian ship taken by the U.S. government, whereas the Italians selected for internment after December 7, 1941, on the basis of their professions and associations presented a much greater ethical dilemma. The NCWC also took an interest in the plight of the Latin American internees by assisting their efforts with the Department of State to return to their families and homes in Latin America.[118]

Instead of relying on outside organizations to assist them in getting paroled or released, many internees wrote directly to the Justice Department to describe their backgrounds and explain any suspicious associations or activities that may have gotten them interned. These internees felt that they could reverse their fate by forcing the government to understand their circumstances and realize that they were in fact patriotic to the United States. For example, Diego Riggio, a tailor originally from Sicily who had lived in the United States for close to twenty years, suspected that his internment was based on his affiliation with a "social club," *Circolo 9 Maggio*, a small organization of Italians in his Brooklyn neighborhood. He explained that this group "had never a political character" nor did he hear any "comment unfavorable to the United States," but in fact it encouraged American citizenship, which he had sought through the help of his daughter. To further prove his loyalty to the United States, Riggio claimed to be a member of the Labor Party, to have participated in the campaign to reelect Roosevelt in 1940, and to have financially contributed to Mayor La Guardia's election.[119] Whether this appeal sped up his release in April 1944 is a matter of speculation.[120]

Dr. Domenico Rosati, who was interned for a month, released, and then interned again after a rehearing, tried to convince the attorney general and the Alien Division of the War Department that his profession was "to serve humanity, more so in time of war than in peace, and it can never be dangerous." He expressed a willingness to serve at hospitals "under close surveillance."[121] Presuming that his internment was based on his service in the Medical Commission at the Italian consulate, where he examined disabled war veterans, and on his offer of services during the Ethiopian crisis, he explained that he withdrew from colonial activities after 1937 and retained only a "business and social" relationship with the consulate thereafter. When the State Department offered him repatriation, he stated his desire to remain in the United States. As further proof of his loyalty, he registered with the American Medical Association to serve in the army in September 1940, and later registered with the Procurement Service, listing the army as his first choice and the health service as his second choice.[122] Unfortunately, Dr. Rosati's arguments on his behalf were not successful, as he was one of the last internees to be released, in June 1945, almost two years after Italy had abandoned the conflict.[123]

Michael Angelo Scicchitani also touted his refusal to repatriate to Italy as evidence that he had adopted the United States as his home and desired "to observe and respect the laws and principles of this Nation and to become an [sic] useful member of its vast and productive family." He explained his military service in the Italian army during the Ethiopian War to the federal attorney assigned to his case as "the result of a political upheaval of which I was an obedient participant . . . just obeying orders," which was the circumstance of many other internees who had no choice but to serve a mandatory term in the service. He further explained his membership in the Italian War Veterans, another organization targeted by the U.S. government, as "merely spiritual" since he became a member with "the sole intention of bringing closer ties between the Italian War Veterans and those of the former comrade-in-arms from America."[124] What probably kept Scicchitani interned until June 1945, however, were, among other things, his alleged involvement as a squad leader for the Fascist Party, his solicitation of members for the Spanish Civil War, and commendation by Fascist leaders for his devotion to the cause for which he offered no explanation, all of which occurred over five years before his internment.[125]

The Alien Enemy Control Program was a system that placed great weight on the appearance of Fascist sympathies, often tied to an alien's associations, no matter how much earlier they had occurred and regardless of whether they were social rather than political. Internees may have felt empowered when they made appeals to the Justice Department and asserted that they had not been given the opportunity to explain the exact nature of their suspicious affiliations, but in reality the government had the upper hand. As the following section reveals, the Geneva Convention provided the aliens an instrument for their grievances regarding their living conditions in camp, but it did not provide grounds for protesting the fact of their internment without notice of charges and without a hearing that conformed to due process guarantees.

Complaints on Both Sides of the Fence

At the start of the war, public knowledge of the conditions of internment of enemy aliens was limited.[126] Generally the media abided by the Justice Department's warning that publicity would interfere with the government's adherence to the terms of the 1929 Geneva Convention, as well as threaten national security.[127] Thus the INS felt that it was best to follow an overly cautious policy of no publicity about the camps out of concern that the average person would think the internees were being pampered while American prisoners abroad were being treated very poorly. Camp officials enlisted the cooperation of the local press and influential people in the surrounding communities to squash criticisms and rumors. Their compliance was assured by the fact that the camps boosted their towns' economies.[128] In the special case of Fort Missoula, public relations with the town were strengthened by the opening up of musical and theatrical performances at the camp to the public.[129]

Ellis Island's location in New York Harbor, visible by binoculars on a clear day from Battery Park or the Staten Island ferries, presented an exception to the low profile of internment camps. In an article accompanied by a photo of Axis nationals boarding a boat for Ellis Island, a reporter for the *New York Times* wrote of hundreds of Italians, Germans, and Japanese "inside the wire of their bleak and treeless exercise ground" marching in endless circles on the island, "the trade-mark of a concentration camp." Presumably based on firsthand encounters with them, the reporter described the internees as having "faces of small professional and business people," among whom there were a few Germans and Italians who would be at home "behind the counters of corner delicatessen shops or plying shaving brushes in barber shops." The privileges granted to internees, namely visits and correspondence with family and friends and access to books in any language caused the author to remark that the island's "concentration camp" was "as humane as such places can be made, far more humane than German and Italian camps."[130] Despite the reporter's caveat, even making this comparison must have angered the families of American servicemen held as prisoners of war overseas.

There were, in fact, complaints from the public that the U.S. government was pampering enemy aliens. Negative sentiment for the internees can be traced in the *Boston Daily Globe* toward the end of World War II. A July 26, 1944, article expressed the outrage of the state commander of the American Legion who, responding to news of "outbreaks" of Italians from internment camps, called for the treatment of Italian prisoners "like prisoners of war rather than guests enjoying the hospitality of a nation." Particular resentment was felt among American veterans of World War I who had been held in Italy under much less desirable circumstances and treated with much less leniency. The Legion presented a resolution to the Veterans of Foreign Affairs "deploring the coddling of foreign prisoners," while Natick, Massachusetts, mothers of servicemen being held as prisoners of war abroad demanded a ban on the entertainment of Italian internees in that town.[131] Such complainants were most likely unaware of the Geneva Convention guarantees that the United States extended to the internees. The International Committee of the Red Cross and Protecting Powers supervised the treatment of internees. Their records indicate that delegates made regular visits to the Ellis Island and Crystal City camps to inspect the internees' living conditions and to confirm that they met required standards.[132] A typical inspection report indicated whether improvements had been made since the last visit and commented on the state of medical care, food, work opportunities, amusements, and education. Inspectors held interviews with the camp chiefs to determine the relationship between camp authorities and the internees.[133] There were also charges by the public that camp officials were excessively lenient in their discipline of the internees.[134] Under the Geneva Convention, the laws, regulations, and orders of the Detaining Power's armed forces provided the measures to be taken in case of acts of insubordination.[135]

From his discussions with internees at Fort Missoula, Jerre Mangione determined that the least likely Italian internees to complain were the seamen, who arrived before the Italian aliens apprehended by FBI agents in the United States. While the long-term resident Italians questioned their misfortune at being chosen from among the approximately 700,000 Italian aliens living in the United States to be interned, the seamen did not question the U.S. government's right to intern them during the war, "an attitude which enabled them to accept their detention with far more grace than the civilian Italians." Some were openly supportive of the United States and hoped to become permanent American residents after the war.[136] The seamen were generally young men used to being away at sea for long periods and living in cramped quarters, which made them appreciate the more favorable conditions at Fort Missoula as well as its distance from the war.[137] Their positive experience at Fort Missoula has been chronicled by Umberto Benedetti, a former crewman on the *Conte Biancanamo*, who claimed that accommodations at Missoula "far exceeded the guidelines set down by the Geneva Convention"; there was no food rationing at the camp, and "the internees were accepted by the community," many choosing to make it their home once released.[138]

In contrast, the Italian aliens who had been pulled away from their established homes and professions in the United States complained vociferously about the conditions of their confinement. Under the terms of the

Geneva Convention, a prisoner of war—and by extension, an internee—could not be punished for submitting a complaint either to military authorities or to representatives of the Protecting Power about the conditions of his captivity.[139] When the Swiss Legation became aware of complaints, such as those about medical and dental service, they would investigate the situation during periodic visits to the camps.[140] Other than medical issues, the most common complaints were those regarding the mail system—the limitation on the number of pieces of mail that internees could send and the delays experienced by internees and their family members in receiving mail due to censorship. Francesco Panciatichi, a newspaper editor from Long Island, served as a spokesperson for the Italians at his military camp, appealing to Attorney General Biddle to eliminate mail delays, which could be as long as thirty-eight days. He not only described the uneasiness and worry of the men in his group on account of not hearing from their loved ones, but also the "torturing anxiety" of "our families whose members are mostly American by birth."[141] In response to Panciatichi's appeal and a letter from Panciatichi's wife regarding delays on her end, Edward Ennis suggested to Brigadier General B. M. Bryan Jr. that the War Department adopt the same procedure as INS camps, which used their own personnel to censor domestic mail instead of employing the longer process through the Office of Censorship, which already screened international mail.[142]

Common complaints of older Latin American internees were that their work was too strenuous. They were only allowed relief from their duties if they had a medical reason. Some Italians who had been under the impression in Latin America that they would receive the same treatment as diplomats insisted that they should be lodged in hotels where they would not be expected to operate kitchens and provide their own janitorial and maid service. Such complaints proved to be futile, and accommodations were not altered to suit the desired status of any internee. Other complaints, specifically those about the high prices for items at the canteens and a lack of variety of merchandise, eventually subsided as camp administrators made improvements to increase the popularity of the canteens.[143]

Those internees protesting the fact of their internment and the process that brought them to the camps faced much greater hurdles. Many complained to the Justice Department of their inability to have a rehearing at the camps. In one appeal to Attorney General Biddle, Frank Caracciolo, a sewing machine mechanic who had lived in the United States for over twenty years, asked for reconsideration of his case and a chance to prove his sincerity and devotion to the United States. Caracciolo explained that he was never "mixed up in any political movements," but was a member of an Italian society only to gain Italian clientele when he sold olive oil after losing his job. He argued that the greatest testament to his loyalty to the United States was his refusal to repatriate when the Swiss Legation, unbeknownst to him, placed him on a repatriation list. Caracciolo begged for a rehearing so that he might have "an occasion to further demonstrate [his] fidelity to this Nation, the Country of [his] adoption, the Country of [his] children."[144] Likewise, Ilidio Di Bugnara, a tailor from Brooklyn, wrote to Edward Ennis and the U.S. District Attorney in Savannah, Georgia, from Fort McAlester for an opportunity to have another hearing to demonstrate that he was not an enemy of the United States, but willing to participate in the American war effort if he were to be released on parole.[145]

In some instances, internees filed joint complaints. When a group of men at Fort Missoula witnessed the release of approximately 130 of their fellow Italians by the end of 1943, they presented a petition to the Honorable Ugo Carusi of the Justice Department for clemency in view of the upcoming holidays. Expressing their discouragement "at the sudden slowing down of further releases," and perplexity over why rehearings expected in the prior month had not occurred, they claimed inconsistency in the Justice Department's handling of cases. They believed that the only factor setting them apart from the released men was that most of them were single.[146]

The most legitimate and organized complaint that Mangione became aware of during his visits of the camps was a petition to President Roosevelt and Attorney General Biddle by twenty-five Germans at Fort Lincoln who had been interned without a hearing. The objections that the complaint raised with respect to the rights of the interned to be informed of specific charges against them, to face their accusers, to examine the evidence against them, and to prepare a defense with legal counsel were equally applicable to the many Italian aliens who were apprehended by FBI agents and detained in the days following the Japanese attack on Pearl Harbor. The German petitioners eventually were granted hearings before civilian hearing boards, but none of the procedural rights that they claimed were granted for the reasons of executive privilege under the Alien Enemy Act of 1798 and the absence of constitutional guarantees for alien enemies, as discussed earlier.[147]

Although internment frustrated and bewildered them, the internees maintained their spirit by making the most of their time in the camps and retaining their sense of identity. Some even planned for their lives once released, although that time came later than they had hoped. Their greatest concerns were reconnecting with their families and rehabilitating their reputations in their communities. How they would be received upon their return home, however, remained uncertain.

Conclusion

In May 1942, the Tolan Committee concluded that with respect to Italian and German aliens, it was wrong to make assumptions about loyalty and national security risk based on ethnicity and citizenship status. Referring to testimony specifically about Italian aliens' commitment to the United States, the committee reported: "This testimony has impressed upon us in convincing fashion the fundamental fact that place of birth and technical non-citizenship alone provide no decisive criteria for assessing the alinement [sic] of loyalties in this world-wide conflict."[1] Many Italians who had lived in the United States for a number of years had not become American citizens by the start of World War II, not due to any continued allegiance to Italy, but because their illiteracy prevented them from passing the citizenship exam. Yet because they were classified as enemy aliens, the United States questioned their loyalty and placed various restrictions upon them to ensure safety within its borders. Against the backdrop of wartime emergency, the federal government felt compelled to remove from the general population all aliens who could potentially present a security risk. The Italian community as a whole fared better than other alien enemy groups in the selective internment process since only a fractional percent of the 700,000 aliens nationwide were interned. However, those who underwent the internment process faced hearings that often failed to provide a fair opportunity for evaluating each subject's loyalty to the United States. By the time the Office of the Attorney General corrected problems in the hearings process, it was too late to change the fate of the hundreds of Italians already interned.

The government applied policies of selective internment and individual exclusion from military zones to Italian and German aliens and naturalized citizens, but it did not impose mass evacuation and internment as it did with persons of Japanese descent. What saved Italians and Germans from this fate were the overwhelming logistics of relocating their large populations and the drain on government resources that such a plan would have entailed. The relative absence of racist feeling against the European alien enemy groups when compared with feelings against the Japanese also cannot be underestimated in an assessment of government policies. In comparison with the Japanese population, Italians generally had an easier assimilation into American society and by the 1940s had begun to enjoy the public's favorable perception of their work ethic and allegiance to this country, best reflected in testimony before the Tolan Committee. In contrast, discrimination against persons of Japanese descent, already present before World War II, heightened considerably after Japan's attack on Pearl Harbor. Racist statements regarding the Japanese, expressed in meetings and correspondence among military and civil leaders in California, and California Governor Olson's assertion that the identification of the loyalty or disloyalty of Italians and Germans was easier than that of persons of Japanese descent, reflected a common attitude that the Japanese did not deserve the same protection of their civil liberties as was granted to other groups.

While the government did not treat Italians on the whole as poorly as it treated persons of Japanese descent, there was a noticeable difference in the treatment of Italian aliens on the West Coast as compared to those on the East, mostly resulting from the perceived threat in those regions of the country. The location of crucial airplane factories and naval shipyards and relative proximity to Pearl Harbor were all important factors in the placing of greater restrictions on Italians on the West Coast. Only on the West Coast were more than 10,000 Italians relocated for a period of time without first being given the chance to undergo a loyalty hearing. They were forced to uproot their families for a time and move to an unfamiliar area because of their nationality and residence in what the military designated as prohibited zones, rather than any finding of disloyalty. As suggested in chapter 2, the different philosophies of the defense commanders, the more stringent philosophy of General DeWitt versus the individualized approach of General Drum, also accounted for the greater disruption of Italian communities on the West Coast. Data from the social profile of internees shows that proportionately more Italian aliens from the West Coast were interned than were those from the East Coast. This varying implementation of government policy reflected the crisis in which decisions had to be made quickly by one sector of government and put into action in an ad hoc manner by another, resulting in disparate treatment nationwide.

Equally important to the government's policies with respect to the Italian community was the political clout enjoyed by prominent Italians in the United States. We saw how Italian anti-Fascists Count Carlo Sforza and Carlo Tresca were trusted by the Roosevelt administration to provide valuable intelligence information for identifying individual Fascist individuals and organizations in the United States. Arturo Toscanini conducted many concerts to raise money for U.S. war efforts, effectively becoming a spokesperson for America's democratic ideals. Italian Americans who held political office, such as San Francisco Mayor Angelo Rossi, vouched for Italians' value to the war effort, both in terms of contributing soldiers and working in war industries, which helped convince the Tolan Committee that a policy of wholesale evacuation was not appropriate. Germans' relative political power on the East Coast also contributed to saving them from relocation en masse, but the government's perception that Italians as a group were loyal to the United States gave them an advantage. Perhaps the greatest demonstration of how politics influenced government policy was that Attorney General Biddle chose to announce the removal of Italians from the category of alien enemies on Columbus Day, October 12, 1942. The lifting of restrictions allowed Italian aliens whose citizenship applications were on hold to finally become naturalized citizens and opened up new job opportunities at factories previously closed to persons of Italian ancestry.[2] By all accounts, it was "a masterly stroke of international statesmanship *and* good politics."[3]

The removal of alien enemy status in October 1942 applied only to the Italian alien population, suggesting their preferential treatment among the alien enemy groups in the United States. Further supporting this conclusion is the data we have seen showing that Italians were selectively interned in far fewer numbers than were Germans and Japanese. Most compelling is the statistic that only approximately five-hundredths of one percent of the Italian alien population in the United States was interned.

Although the statistical data indicates Italians fared better than the other ethnic groups during World War II, this book documents numerous injustices, namely the relocation of more than 10,000 Italians on the West Coast without investigations and problems in the selective internment process. The evaluation of alien enemy hearing boards conducted herein suggests that the greatest source of injustice in the adjudicatory process was the unreliability of the FBI's methods in the Custodial Detention Program for identifying suspicious persons and of the evidence collected by the FBI on each subject. The FBI's lists cast a wide net among Italian aliens—often based on mere membership in an Italian organization—pointing to men who had lived for many years in the United States, were loyal to their adopted country, and cherished democracy. Well into the alien enemy program, Attorney General Biddle came to believe that the FBI's classification system was flawed in how it designated individuals who might threaten the country's security, and that the FBI's lists should not be used for any purpose. He found the evidence upon which the classifications were based "inadequate," the standards for the evidence "defective," and claimed that a determination of "how dangerous a person is in the abstract and without reference to time, environment, and other relevant circumstances is impractical, unwise, and dangerous."[4] The hearing boards' reliance upon FBI reports of anonymous informants alleging Fascist affiliations or activities when making their recommendations of internment led to deprivations of civil liberties, specifically the political freedoms of speech and association. Boards often did not have information on the particular context of subjects' seemingly anti-American or pro-Fascist statements, their associations with certain organizations, or their participation in political activities that gave rise to suspicion. In cases where there was no conclusive evidence of subversion, the policy set by the Alien Enemy Control Unit was to decide in favor of the government, leading to the internment of persons based on assumptions rather than on information that had been vetted.

Examination of individual cases in chapter 3 reveals inequities in the alien enemy hearings. An imperfect process was created as a result of the urgency of the perceived wartime security threats and the Justice Department's delegation of authority to approximately one hundred districts nationwide through a series of contradictory instructions. Internees were frustrated at not having the chance to prove their loyalty, and hearing board members lacked clear direction from the attorney general on how to conduct the hearings. As indicated in debates among members of the Tolan Committee about what alien rights under the Fifth and Fourteenth Amendments might survive in wartime, evidentiary standards of criminal trials in courts of law did not have to be applied to enemy aliens. The Alien Enemy Act of 1798 allowed the government to detain and deport aliens of enemy countries without any hearing or lawyers for the suspect. Thus the hearings, which followed ad hoc form procedures similar to administrative hearings for deportation, were merely a courtesy for enemy aliens, rather than a right. They met statutory requirements and even contained some semblance of due process in their inclusion of an attorney on the board to assess evidence. Yet the case files reveal that the procedure set by the Justice Department did not allow the aliens, many of whom were illiterate, to answer to suspicions of disloyalty since attorney representation was prohibited in the hearings and translators were not routinely provided. The result was that the hearings before alien enemy boards did not consistently function in a manner that would discover the truth behind allegations or anonymous tips that appeared in FBI reports.

To its credit, the Justice Department continually reevaluated the structure of the hearings and the method for reaching decisions in an effort to create a uniform system of justice for evaluating the loyalty of the Italian aliens. Attorney General Biddle tried to correct the mishandling of justice by communicating to the alien enemy hearing boards the necessity of evaluating each alien's particular activity and by maintaining for himself the right to render the final decision in each case. However, Biddle could not remedy the misjudgments that hearing boards made because they lacked information on the mission of many Italian American organizations and the particular role that each suspect Italian alien played in that organization. Some boards based their recommendation of internment on evidence of a subject's Fascist leanings from the prior decade. Biddle's efforts to make the adjudicatory process fairer—by advising boards to arrange for transcripts of the hearings and to state specific grounds in their recommendations, by granting rehearings where the original hearings were defective, for instance, in not admitting witness testimony, and by directing boards to state charges against subjects and allow rebuttal evidence—came much too late to effectively insert greater due process into the internment proceedings. By the time internees had rehearings before special boards, they had already spent at least a year in internment, and in some cases, the biases of the initial alien enemy hearing board continued to taint the process. Not having a fixed term of internment increased the internees' anxiety and sense of injustice.

Not surprisingly, hearing boards took varying approaches to procedural due process. This contrast is seen in the case of Pericle Chieri in Detroit, where the hearing board did not give him an opportunity to explain his employment history, as opposed to the hearing of Ubaldo Guidi-Buttrini in Boston, where the board allowed the testimony of influential witnesses to outweigh the FBI evidence. In still other cases on both the East and West Coasts, the presence of Italian American hearing board members, like Edward Corsi who chaired an alien enemy hearing board in New York City, and government attorneys, such as John Molinari in San Francisco who presented cases to the boards, raises questions as to whether the hearing boards were able to engage in unbiased adjudication.

I could not find any evidence that the Justice Department prosecuted any Italian alien for engaging in subversive activities in the United States or for providing aid or threatening to give aid to Italy in support of Fascism. But of course we will never know if the removal of suspect Italians from the general population prevented the commission of seditious acts. As for naturalized citizens, I uncovered no evidence that any Italian American who was under exclusion orders lost his citizenship. Apparently neither fraud in the naturalization process nor disloyalty during the war could be shown.[5] There were undoubtedly Fascist sympathizers in the United States who could have given the federal government legitimate reason for concern, if they had been able to amass sufficient support. As seen in the case studies, several internees in the subject group who had worked in the Italian media made anti-American and antidemocratic statements that alerted the government to a potential risk. These twenty-nine aliens, given their means to influence other members of the Italian community, were considered the most dangerous among the subject internees. The fact that radio transcripts and newspaper and journal articles provided evidence of their anti-American sentiment distinguishes members of the media from most of the other subject internees for whom evidence of a subversive mentality was speculative.

It was not until April 1942, after many Italian aliens had been interned and many more had been relocated from their homes on the West Coast, that government officials considered that they might have missed targeting the most potentially dangerous elements of the Italian communities, namely members of the younger generation, alien and citizen.[6] The average age of the subject internees was forty-three, indicating that the government focused on older, more established members of the Italian communities who could more easily be identified through employment and membership in Italian organizations than could those of the younger generation. The business, educational, and social leaders of the Italian communities seemed like the most obvious suspects, but they might not have been, in fact. This cannot fairly be judged in hindsight.

In addition to the potential miscalculation of the age of persons who might present a security risk, there is also the question of whether the government overlooked persons because they were American citizens. As explained earlier, through the process of individual exclusion, suspicious naturalized citizens were identified and ordered to move from designated areas of the country, but the Justice Department chose to prosecute few of these cases. Indeed, FBI reports concerning a number of the subject internees associated them with out-and-out pro-Fascist naturalized citizens.[7] If it were true that there was more danger among American citizens, both foreign- and native-born, then investigations beyond the alien population could have been warranted. The irony of a policy that distinguished citizens from noncitizens is that aliens intent on committing sabotage could have pursued naturalization so that they might gain access to areas, such as the California coast, that were off limits to aliens.[8]

An overriding reality throughout these events was the integration of Italian Americans into the fabric of American society by the start of World War II. That Italian Americans constituted a substantial voting bloc and were represented in the legislative and judicial branches on the state and national levels influenced the government's policies. Supportive testimony from prominent Italian American politicians at hearings before the Tolan Committee attested to this influence. Further, the government had come to perceive Italians as loyal sons of America. One of the most celebrated World War II veterans, U.S. Marine Gunnery Sergeant John Basilone was the son of Italian immigrants. A recipient of the Medal of Honor for his leadership on Guadalcanal, Basilone became a celebrity stateside and served as the poster boy for the American war effort on a War Bond Tour.[9] A number of Italians were even trusted to have access to classified materials in the United States because the government needed people who understood European culture.[10]

World War II solidified Italians' increasing identification as Americans, most noticeably through their representation in the armed forces. When interviewed about growing up in Italian households, Italian American veterans expressed common themes of their parents' disapproval of Mussolini, and how their parents nurtured a sense of patriotism toward the United States, even refraining from teaching them Italian so they would learn English and become integrated in the local communities.[11] They did not think of themselves as having a different nationality. As one veteran explained: "Your loyalty was here. But, of course, after a while, even though you're feeling that you're somewhat different, ethnically, once a person of my generation became involved with the war and served, we felt that, I no longer had a feeling that I was a minority . . . . I was just as much an American as anyone else and part of the system."[12] Mussolini and Fascism did not have any great influence on their families or their communities. Nor did Italian Americans think of the people of Italy as enemies of the United States. Another veteran recalled the sentiment as follows: "It was very interesting because never did we ever associate with Italians as being the enemy. They were just there. They were kind of non-existent. They were not part of the German regime, and there was no bias whatsoever."[13] This ordering of enemies that placed Italians behind Germans in terms of threat is consistent with how the government perceived the military strength of these countries, as well as the danger posed by their nationals on American soil.

President Franklin D. Roosevelt receives the Four Freedoms Award from the Italian American Labor Council, signifying the positive relationship FDR had with the Italian community. Luigi Antonini (on right in flowing tie), president of the council, presents the plaque. Others in attendance include William Green, president of the American Federation of Labor (second from left), and Attorney General Francis Biddle (center rear). (Herbert K. White, October 18, 1944, AP Images.)

Italians on the home front did their part for the American cause in wartime industries, and Italian American labor unions played a role in the anti-Fascist movement. In particular, Luigi Antonini, the president of the Italian American Labor Council, remained committed to the Roosevelt administration.[14] The forming of the Italian American Victory Council in Chicago, consisting of societies, clubs, fraternal orders, and trade unions that held rallies and other supportive programs, signified the mobilization of Italian Americans behind the war effort.[15] As a result, there was "a more widespread acceptance of Italians as full-fledged Americans."[16] The war brought Italians full employment and high wages. Work in war industries and military service drew the younger generations of Italian Americans out of the "Little Italies" and allowed them to interact with all types of Americans.[17] Their outward embrace of democratic ideals and appreciation for the civil liberties that they enjoyed as U.S. citizens, or hoped to enjoy once naturalized, were important factors in saving the Italian population from mass internment. Thus, their growing adoption of an American national identity convinced the government that, as a whole, Italians were a loyal immigrant group.[18]

Yet those Italians who drew the suspicion of the federal government and suffered the disgrace of internment experienced barriers in their path of assimilation as they felt that the outside world resented them. In the eyes of internees, the general population believed that they were disloyal and would have to prove their allegiance to the United States once released and they resumed normal lives. This sentiment was reflected in a letter written by Vincent Lapenta, a surgeon and chemist from Indianapolis, to the captain at his internment camp. Lapenta spoke of his grief at being placed "in such a detestable position before [his] fellow citizens." He hoped to regain his reputation in his community where he had lived for close to thirty years by participating in the war effort and thereby "vindicate [his] name as a loyal living cell in the glorious body of this nation."[19]

Fears of a cold reception upon returning home were not merely imagined. Indications of a lasting hatred for nationals of the Axis powers can be seen in an initiative by the Massachusetts American Legion to prevent former Axis soldiers from establishing permanent residences or obtaining American citizenship. Coined the "Alien Hatred Issue," the resolution stated that it "forever prohibits any individual who at any time bore arms against the United States, from establishing a permanent domicile in this country or obtaining citizenship papers here."[20] Although the applicability of such provisions is unclear, the discriminatory intent against Japanese, Germans, and Italians was unmistakable. Recognizing the resolution as an unacceptable form of alien hatred, however, prompted other members of the group to fight against its adoption.[21]

Ironically, a number of former internees either served in the U.S. armed forces upon their release or were employed in other capacities domestically. For example, Carmelo Ilacqua, who had been employed by the Italian consulate before internment, went to work for the U.S. Army as a teacher of the Italian language to officers in training at Stanford University who were assigned to occupy Italy.[22] In another example of the government utilizing former internees' skills, the military employed Mario Valdastri in construction, giving him access to military bases and construction areas in Hawaii merely days after his release from internment.[23]

But the majority of internees, some of whom had been away for several years, had difficulties finding employment and regaining their former lives when they returned home. Once paroled, Biagio Farese, the radio broadcaster from Boston, did his best to convince people that he was anti-Fascist. He complained that the terms of his parole kept him from finding employment in his line of work, causing him "to take a few dollars from his wife every day in order to have pocket money."[24] Prospero Cecconi, a pastry man from San Francisco who spent close to two years in internment, came home emotionally bitter and physically sick from his experience. He suffered from peritonitis, associated with the stomach ulcers for which he was hospitalized at Fort Missoula. With no family, he relied upon the care of his parole sponsor, a social worker at the Italian Welfare Agency. His first attempt at obtaining citizenship in 1945 failed, but he eventually became a citizen the following year. In 1951, Mr. Cecconi left the United States for good, choosing to spend his retirement in his hometown in Italy, even after he obtained the long-coveted American citizenship.[25] Several other former internees, including Mario Valdastri, chose to retire in Italy.[26]

Accounts of those Italians and their families who suffered from individual exclusion also indicate that the financial and emotional damage from the wartime experiences was permanent. Even though the period of exclusion from his home was temporary, Nino Guttadauro and his family continued to suffer from the economic hardship of being forced to leave his job as an accountant in San Francisco and search in nonprohibited states for an employer who would trust him with financial matters. His first job following exclusion was as a grocery clerk in Salt Lake City. As his son described it, his father's psychological scars resulting from how the experience diminished his value to himself, his family, his community, and his society, remained with him for the rest of his life.[27] Like Guttadauro, Renzo Turco, an attorney in San Francisco who was forced to close his law office and move to Chicago when he received his exclusion order, had difficulty finding employment because prospective employers were leery of his trustworthiness since he had to report weekly to the FBI as a "potentially dangerous" person. He eventually found a job through friends as an auditor for the Internal Revenue Service.[28] Another San Francisco attorney, Sylvester Andriano, whose public profile included service on the local draft board, the police commission, and the Italian Chamber of Commerce, and leadership in the Catholic Church and in the Italian language school in North Beach, was excluded from Military Area No. 1. He moved at least five times in a little more than a year, followed at every step by an FBI agent, until the army canceled his exclusion order in December 1943 and allowed him to return to San Francisco.[29] In California alone, twelve Italian Americans holding prominent positions were ordered by General DeWitt to leave the state, causing great disruption to their professional and personal lives.[30]

Italian communities also changed because of the events of World War II. After the war, Italians were less likely to join fraternal organizations like the Sons of Italy and other social organizations that had drawn suspicion during wartime. Italian communities such as North Beach in San Francisco spread out as families moved to the suburbs. John Molinari recalled that prior to the war, North Beach was "a homogenous community where . . . you knew what was going on." He attributed the change after the war to the relative inactivity of the Italian media. Prior to the war, there were "two daily Italian newspapers, two or three Italian radio programs daily, and morning and afternoon papers, in Italian." But after the war, the San Francisco newspapers merged into one, which eventually went out of business.[31] Thus Italians' means of staying connected with their communities in the United States and events in their homeland were drastically reduced. While this may have been the natural result of Italians' further assimilation into American culture, the passing of older generations, and a deflated pride in Italy, the lesson of Italians' wartime experience was that showing loyalty to American ideals and the democratic form of government was not only safer, but also more advantageous for the prosperity of their families.[32]

For most Italians, whether they were subject to internment, exclusion, relocation, or other restrictions on their freedoms, the entire wartime experience was "blanketed in silence."[33] A common theme in the oral histories taken by Stephen Fox in the 1980s and the stories gathered by Lawrence DiStasi is that the events from World War II were not spoken of in Italian families because family members were ashamed to have been treated as if they had done something wrong. Many years after World War II, when they were willing to talk about it, those affected felt lingering pain but not anger. Although recognizing that the past could not be changed, Italians involved in the initiative to obtain acknowledgment from the U.S. government of violations of civil liberties believed that formal recognition in the Wartime Violation of Italian American Civil Liberties Act could help put the matter to rest.

Italians as a group did not suffer the extent of injustices experienced by other groups more widely affected by government policies during World War II. But certainly anyone forced to leave family, friends, and a job for several years while interned felt the disillusion that accompanies the loss of freedom and separation from society, and any children separated from their father or any wife from her husband for an indefinite period of time shared in the anguish. The experience of Italians during World War II is one of resilience in the face of adversity and determination for a greater identity as Americans.

Afterword

The story of the internment of Italians during World War II raises the same question we ask today about how modern liberal democracies may wage war and remain true to democratic values. As we grapple with the question of what rights are due individuals residing in this country whose ties to terrorist organizations at war with the United States cast suspicion upon their activities, the process of selective internment during World War II provides valuable lessons.

Immediately after September 11, 2001, legal scholars feared that the reasoning of the United States Supreme Court's 1944 *Korematsu* decision could permit limits on the civil liberties of Arab immigrants and potentially some Americans of Arab descent. Referencing that case, in which the Supreme Court gave deference to government decision-makers to determine national security policies, critics of the proposals from President George W. Bush's administration to increase law enforcement to fight terrorism drew parallels between the government's treatment of Japanese and Japanese Americans in the 1940s and persons of Arab descent post September 11.[1] The U.S. Commission on Civil Rights was keenly aware of the dark cloud of internment that loomed over the country, prompting one of its members to address the debate by stating that the best way to avoid a return to *Korematsu* was "to make sure that there is a balance between protecting civil rights, but also protecting safety at the same time."[2]

Ensuring that government leaders not repeat the mistake of making broad inferences about disloyalty toward the United States based on national origin was an appropriate response to the crisis. But worrying about the vitality of *Korematsu* and a repeat of World War II programs likely obscured the true lesson of the "fundamental error" of that episode in American history about the great extent of deprivations imposed on persons of Japanese descent on the basis of an inference of suspicion.[3] Certainly we felt the resonances of this period in history in the aftermath of the events of September 11, when the fear of sleeper terrorist cells resulted in discriminatory application of immigration laws, including long-term detentions, final deportation orders, and special registration requirements, in an effort to screen out dangerous terrorists from law-abiding communities.[4] The vast majority of the more than 1,200 noncitizens detained were Middle Eastern, Muslim, and South Asian. Identified as suspicious based on perceptions of their racial, religious, or ethnic identity, none could be connected to terrorist activity.[5] Legal scholars criticized federal law enforcement tactics of rounding up Arab and Muslim noncitizens, which "reinforce[d] deeply-held negative stereotypes—foreign-ness and possibly disloyalty" about these groups.[6] Perhaps the worst long-lasting effect is that overzealous investigations placed both U.S. citizens and noncitizens from Arab and South Asian communities in fear of the government.[7] However, in efforts to preempt this problem, President Bush and his staff sought to learn about the American Muslim culture, reaching out to Muslim leaders and their organizations. Although the effort was controversial because of the radical nature of some of the Muslim groups befriended by the Bush administration, the goal of the "Muslim outreach" was to prevent the victimization of Arab Americans and to win the hearts and minds of pro-American Muslims.[8] Interviews of young male Arab aliens for the purpose of gaining information about terrorists could also be touted as a government program meant to open up the channels of communication between the Bush administration and members of Arab communities.[9]

In the first year of his administration, President Barack Obama used different language in outreach to Muslims and in his rhetoric for proclaiming faithfulness to the rule of law, but he did not actually remake the antiterrorism policy of the previous administration.[10] However, in August 2011, the White House released the first national strategy to "counter violent extremism" (CVE) domestically, with an aim to build partnerships among local government, law enforcement, religious leaders, the private sector, and universities for preventing the nurturing of violent extremists at the community level.[11] President Obama appeared to be sensitive to the problem that such engagement with Muslim American communities may serve to stigmatize them if they are the only minority group singled out for CVE programs, and that the communities may interpret the program as a cover for surveillance.[12]

I can find no trace of recent policy-makers consulting the historical example of the selective internment process during World War II. Yet this book raises questions that continue to have relevance today. Arguably the most significant legacy of the 2001 terrorist attacks is the cost to civil liberties imposed by legislation intended to make Americans safer, namely the USA PATRIOT Act of 2001, which allows, among other things, electronic surveillance, warrantless searches, and indefinite detentions in certain circumstances.[13] In particular, the case studies in chapter 3 explore how the U.S. government assesses the loyalty of individuals—what role various categories of citizenship play, what types of evidence are productive and predictive, and what form of process is to be afforded in the determination of loyalty.

On the first question of the significance of national citizenship to government policies, evidence in the case of Italians shows that alienage could have been a result of illiteracy or backlogs in the INS rather than a conscious decision to hold onto one's foreign citizenship out of loyalty to Italy. The great number of Italian American men in the armed forces whose parents were aliens provides the best proof that using alienage as the primary indicator of disloyalty to the United States was seriously flawed. Certainly persons who were potentially greater security risks could have been shielded by their legal status of citizenship. Yet if the U.S. government had not made distinctions based on citizenship with respect to the Italian population, then it would have made the process of becoming an American citizen, which requires the act of renouncing allegiance to one's foreign nation, less meaningful. It also would have undervalued rights that come with citizenship. In the case of Japanese American internment, it was irrational for the government to ignore the significance of citizenship.[14]

Today the analysis of whether citizenship should be taken into account in formulating law and public policy designed to investigate and prevent terrorism is complicated by the fact that the United States' adversaries are not nations but criminal organizations that may be adversaries of many of the Arab and Muslim nations, namely Saudi Arabia, Pakistan, and Egypt, whose citizens the U.S. government has investigated, detained, and deported.[15] Thus persons of interest today cannot be distinguished as easily as were aliens of enemy nations during World War II.[16] The other reality regarding the status of noncitizen threats is that U.S. intelligence officials believe American citizens who have become radicalized on their own or through association with a foreign terrorist organization present the greatest terrorist threat domestically.[17] National security analyst Peter Bergen predicts that we are likely to be facing the problem of "homegrown jihadists" who present a "low-level terrorist threat" for many years.[18]

The case of the Italian civilian internees offers guidance in the identification of persons posing national security threats. Understanding the problems that government officials encountered in evaluating reasonable suspicion of a national security risk posed by individual Italian internees can provide insight for today's military detention of individuals, citizens and noncitizens, outside normal criminal processes. Thus, we are at my second question: what types of evidence are productive and predictive in assessing the loyalty and potential terrorist threat of individuals and organizations? The case studies show that the questionable reliability of FBI reports tainted the process of investigating the loyalties of Italian aliens during World War II. FBI field agents gathered information on their Italian subjects' expressions of sympathy or admiration for Mussolini and regarding any ties they had with the Italian government through work or membership in Italian organizations, but often referred to unsubstantiated accusations by a single individual. Alien enemy hearing boards relied upon uncorroborated reports of Fascist support and did not have specific information on the mission or activities of the Italian organizations in which membership was treated as a proxy for subversive inclinations.

The modern-day counterpart is the government labeling groups as "terrorist" and imposing penalties, such as freezing assets and criminalizing transactions, without giving the designated organization an opportunity to offer evidence in its defense in court.[19] Lists of designated terrorists have been created in secret using criteria undisclosed to the public, and persons associated with terrorists are presumed guilty by association.[20] The government argues just as strongly today that leads about terrorist threats must remain confidential so it can pursue ongoing counterterrorism operations as it argued with respect to alien enemy hearings during World War II. Yet tribunals that do not employ a fair method of discovering why particular organizations exist and what missions they pursue fail to recognize the constitutional principle that individuals deserve the chance to rebut evidence against them before losing their liberty, regardless of citizenship status.[21]

The form of process is the third issue for consideration. Although the Alien Enemy Act provides for the summary detention and deportation of alien enemies without due process or any hearing at all, for that matter, the hearings were afforded in the selective internment process for individualized determinations of disloyalty or proclivity for sedition against the United States, instead of relying upon race or ethnicity to infer disloyalty. Given the serious consequences of internment and repatriation, the Italian internees' demands for greater procedural guarantees, namely a statement of charges against them and an opportunity to rebut government evidence, were in keeping with the promises of the democratic society where they had chosen to live. As this book demonstrates, the Justice Department responded to those demands in the spirit of the democratic ideals that this country strives to promote, albeit too late for most internees.

Debates more recently center on how the legal status of individuals detained by the military on suspicion of terrorist connections determines the extent of due process guaranteed.[22] The U.S. government has the power to detain citizens and noncitizens determined to be "enemy combatants." The justification for confinement of such persons indefinitely is the opportunity for interrogation to gain intelligence as well as preventing detainees from engaging in future terrorist activity.[23] The U.S. Supreme Court has determined that detainees who are U.S. citizens have rights of minimal due process, instilling hope that incarceration without process will not occur in the name of national security.[24] Yet for civil libertarians, confinement for an American citizen, and perhaps noncitizens in the United States as well, without attorney representation typical of a criminal trial and court review of "enemy combatant" status is still unacceptable.[25]

As we moved farther away from September 11, a "second generation of scholarship" found firmer middle ground for critique between outrage over civil liberty abuses and complacency over deference to the administration in the name of national security by reflecting on constitutionalism and policy-making informed by historical practice.[26] Not only has civil liberties policy varied by war, but it has also varied by issue. For example, during World War II, First Amendment rights were protected while ethnic groups were not treated equally.[27] Harvard Law Professor Mark Tushnet has identified "two interlinked problems" of wartime: "decision makers act with imperfect information, and they do so within bureaucracies that generate bureaucratic pathologies not unique to wartime."[28] In most instances, the government is retrospectively judged to have overreacted to the wartime emergency.[29] This idea applied to the administrative state during World War II is instructive. According to this wisdom, we might criticize the Roosevelt administration, the Justice Department, and the War Department for misjudging the potential threat to national security posed by members of Italian communities, but should recognize that their mistakes were based on imperfect intelligence information on individual suspects. Operating under the expediency of wartime conditions on the home front after the Japanese attack on Pearl Harbor, the Justice Department struggled to institute a fair policy for evaluating the loyalty of detained Japanese, German, and Italian aliens that would be implemented uniformly in districts across the country. The challenge of maintaining consistency and fairness in the application of government policy was not specific to wartime, but the country's administrative state was tested in unique ways by the immediate need that the Japanese attack on American soil created for a policy on handling enemy aliens. The form of hearing afforded enemy aliens suspected of disloyalty toward the United States could not be scrutinized soon enough to prevent violations of civil liberties for the majority of internees who were taken into custody in the first six months after December 7, 1941. Ultimately, however, the Justice Department strove for a selective internment program with features of liberal democracies, namely, focusing on the activities of persons being examined rather than on mere associations, and allowing rebuttal of specific charges and government evidence of a security threat.

This lesson from World War II in developing sound public policy for evaluating the security risk of individuals can provide procedural guidance for the implementation of President Donald J. Trump's executive orders concerning the suspension of U.S. entry of foreign nationals from designated countries.[30] A policy under which nationals from predominantly Muslim countries could be prevented from entering the United States without having undergone an individualized determination of security threat based on specific intelligence information raises concerns about targeting certain ethnic and racial groups and providing due process.[31] Not only might historical precedent help us evaluate the wisdom of such a policy with respect to our democratic processes, but an understanding of the past can also allow us to project ramifications on America's foreign policy.[32]

A final lesson from the case of Italians for today's policy-makers is that the government might have dispelled the sense of injustice and powerlessness experienced by internees if it had revealed its interpretation of due process, in terms of the fact-finding procedure, and standards of proof, as well as the rationale for its policy with respect to enemy aliens. Thus, in addition to hoping that the government might strike the proper balance between ensuring the nation's safety and guaranteeing civil liberties in times of crisis, we might wish for more transparency in the policies it chooses to follow. This may mean explaining the tensions and contradictions inherent in pursuing the goal of maintaining an effective intelligence operation to prevent terrorist acts while remaining true to the values and virtues of a democratic society. How the government chooses to define the country's values and virtues requires frequent reevaluation and explanation. We will be unable to judge the effectiveness of today's antiterrorism policies until many years from now. History has shown that improvements can be made, but they often happen too late to prevent civil liberties violations and the sense of disillusionment experienced by affected groups.

Italians apprehended per month

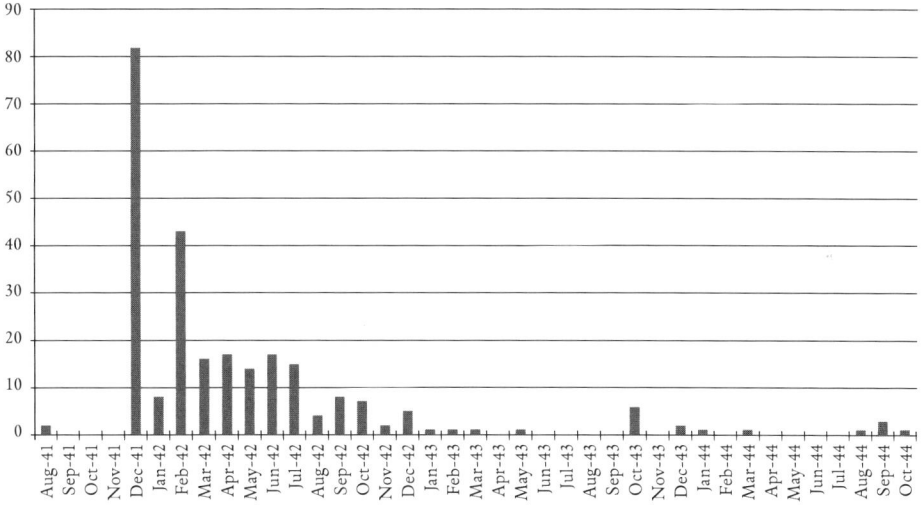

Regions/Territories of origin of Italian civilian internees

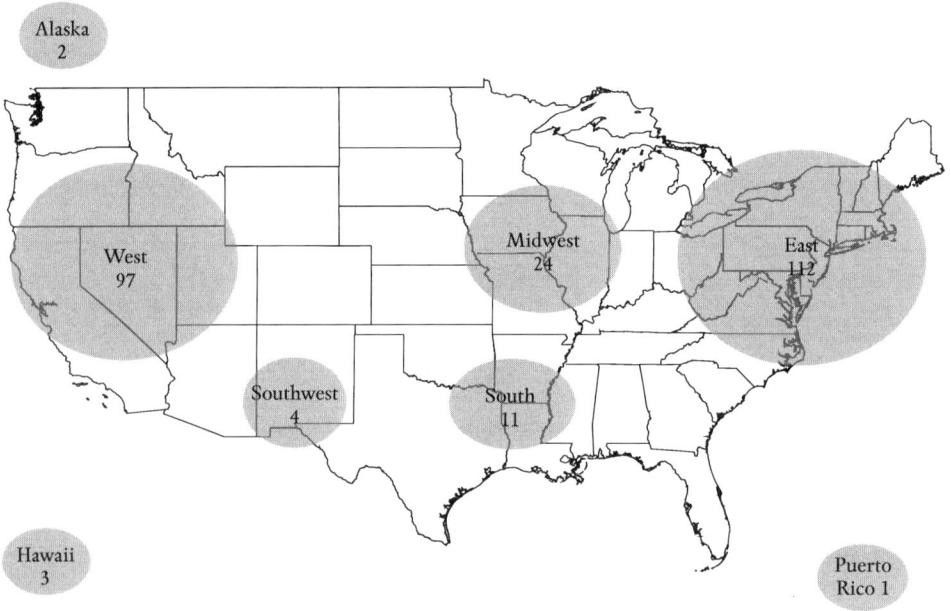

Alaska
2

West
97

Midwest
24

East
112

Southwest
4

South
11

Hawaii
3

Puerto
Rico 1

Source: Map from FreeImages.com/loompus.

Occupations of Italian civilian internees

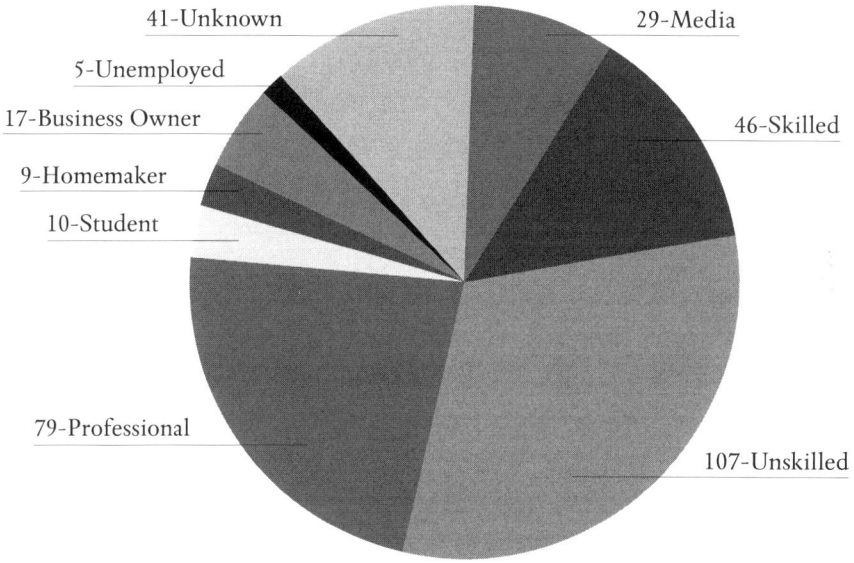

41-Unknown
5-Unemployed
17-Business Owner
9-Homemaker
10-Student
79-Professional
29-Media
46-Skilled
107-Unskilled

Timing of remedial instructions from Attorney General's Office in relation to Italians apprehended per month

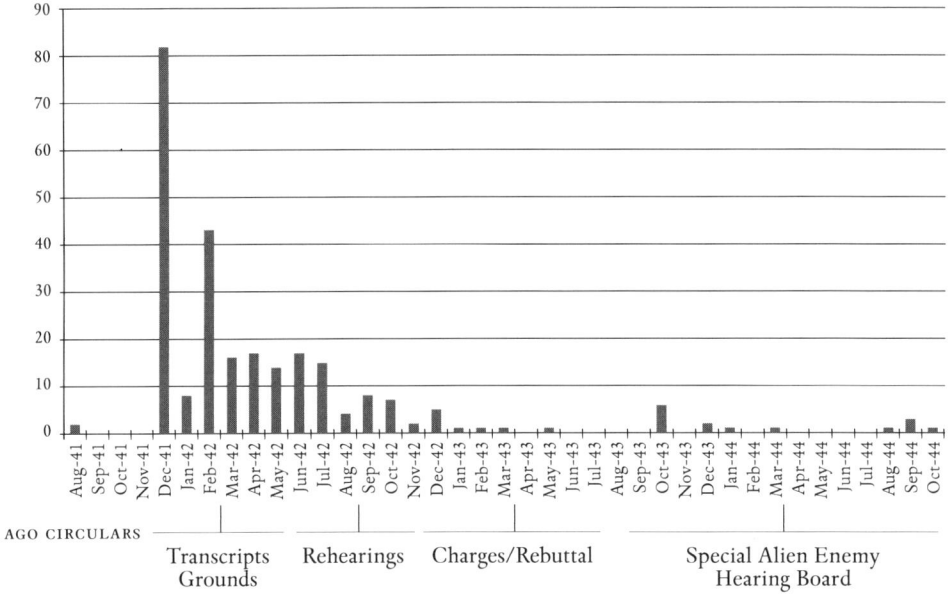

Notes

A Note on Terminology and the Subject Group

1. The Alien Enemy Act, first enacted in 1798 and amended by R.S. § 4067, 40 Stat. 531 (1918) to apply to females, became codified as 50 U.S.C. § 21 (2012). Once Congress has declared war or when invasion has occurred or is imminent, this law gives the president the power to direct the apprehension and removal of "all natives, citizens, denizens, or subjects of the hostile nation or government,"§ 21.

Under the Alien Enemy Act during World War II, nationals of Japan, Germany, and Italy were designated "alien enemies." Note that small numbers of Romanians, Hungarians, and Bulgarians suspected of disloyalty were interned, but they were designated "aliens of enemy nationality," meaning that they were not subject to the regulations concerning travel, possession of signaling devices, and other restrictions on alien enemies. See Memo attached to United States Department of Justice's "Questions and Answers on Regulations Concerning Aliens of Enemy Nationalities," Edward Corsi Papers, Special Collections Research Center, Syracuse University Libraries (hereafter cited as Corsi Papers), Box 33, Folder "ACTIVITIES Alien Enemy Hearing Board Correspondence to cases 7 May 1941 to 11 Feb. 1944."

2. Marian Smith, chief, Historical Research Branch, U.S. Citizenship & Immigration Services, e-mail message to author, October 3, 2013.

3. The census in 1940 recorded more than 1.6 million American residents as born in Italy. U.S. Congress, House Select Committee Investigating National Defense Migration, *Fourth Interim Report* (hereafter cited as House Select Committee, *Fourth Interim Report*), 241.

4. Alien Registration Act of 1940 (Smith Act), Pub. L. No. 76–670, 54 Stat. 670–71 (1940). The Act has been amended multiple times and can be found at 18 U.S.C. § 2385 (2000).

5. House Select Committee, *Fourth Interim Report*, 241.

6. "Report on Progress: Naturalization Delays Decreasing," 20. Note that Attorney General Biddle assured the alien population that there were three classes of German and Italian aliens who still could obtain naturalization: those who had taken out papers at least two years before December 8, 1941, but not more than seven years before that date; those not required to take out first papers, such as spouses of American citizens; and those whose petition for naturalization was pending in court. "Alien Curbs Aimed Only at Disloyal," 9. Biddle, quoted in the same article, told the public that restrictions on naturalization were intended "to weed out" the few enemy aliens considered subversive. In actuality, though, delays in investigations for petitions by the INS prevented even individuals in these three classes from obtaining their citizenship papers.

7. I gathered my data independently of a study by the Department of Justice which cites 418 as the number of "persons of Italian ancestry who were interned" in Appendix D, § 3(3) of U.S. Department of Justice, *Report to the Congress of the United States, A Review of the Restrictions on Persons of Italian Ancestry During World War II*, November 2001, http://judiciary.house.gov/legacy/italian.pdf (site discontinued), accessed on November 13, 2013 (hereafter cited as *DOJ Report*). The report includes appendices of lists of individuals subject to the various restrictions. The Justice Department compiled its list of internees and where they were held, if known, from government records and personal interviews. It recognizes that its list may have multiple inclusions of the same people identified by different names.

8. Note that this study includes all Latin Americans for whom I could find a file in the Provost Marshal General records at the National Archives at College Park, Maryland. Relying on correspondence from 1946 in the Special War Problems Division of the State Department, Max Friedman states that 288 Italians were deported from Latin America and interned in the United States, more than half of whom were family members accompanying the suspected Fascists. Friedman cites the other deportee figures as follows: 4,058 Germans and 2,264 Japanese. Friedman, *Nazis and Good Neighbors*, 2, 9; Compare Kashima, *Judgment without Trial*, 124, who cites the number of Italians from Latin American countries as 78 based on a 1948 memorandum of W. F. Kelly, the assistant commissioner of the Alien Enemy Control Program. One discrepancy may be in the number arrested or expelled from Latin America as opposed to the number actually interned in the United States.

9. The FBI reported that there were 1,271 apprehensions of seamen. Document 44, Federal Bureau of Investigation "Apprehensions By Field Offices, December 7, 1941 to June 30, 1945" in Tolzmann, *German-Americans in the World Wars*, 1740–49. According to INS records, Fort Missoula housed 1,317 Italian seamen. U.S. Department of Justice, Immigration and Naturalization Service, Office of Research and Educational Services, General Research Unit, *Administrative History of the Immigration and Naturalization Service during World War II*, August 19, 1946 (hereafter cited as *Administrative History of the INS*), 298.

10. See Lothrop, "A Shadow on the Land," 351. Lothrop says that 125 Italians associated with the World's Fair were detained in May 1941.

11. Records of the Office of the Provost Marshal General, Alien Enemy Information Bureau, Records Relating to Italian Civilian Internees During World War II, 1941–1946, Boxes 2–20, Record Group 389; National Archives at College Park (hereafter cited as "PMG Records of Italian Civilian Internees, NACP"). The contents of the folders for each internee vary, but each contains a "Basic Personnel Record," indicating the individual's date and place of birth, residence, number of dependents, date and place of capture or arrest, unit making the capture or arrest, occupation, education, languages, physical condition, marital status, religion, and camps where they were held. The PMG Records also contain orders of the Justice Department for internment, parole, and release, allowing me to trace the course of their custody.

12. Although army camp lists were supposed to be kept monthly, there are gaps of time in available lists in the PMG Records. What became readily evident was that the internees were shifted among camps regularly.

13. I received the Alien Registration Forms (AR-2 Forms) for specific individuals courtesy of Marian Smith, chief, Historical Research Branch, U.S. Citizenship & Immigration Services. The AR-2 Forms also provide information on aliens' arrests, military service, years of residence in the United States, memberships, and social activities.

Introduction

1. U.S. Commission on Wartime Relocation and Internment of Civilians, *Personal Justice Denied*, 2–3; compare Robinson, *A Tragedy of Democracy*, 1, estimating that "some 112,000 men, women, and children" were confined.

2. See U.S. Commission on Wartime Relocation and Internment of Civilians, *Personal Justice Denied*, 283. From January through June 1942, German submarines destroyed many American ships along the Atlantic Coast before the United States used minefield defense and antisubmarine warfare. See also Conn, Engelman, and Fairchild, eds., *Guarding the United States and its Outposts*, chap. 3, "Preparations for Continental Defense," also available at http://www.history.army.mil/books/wwii/Guard-US/, accessed on April 18, 2017.

3. Biddle, *In Brief Authority*, 207. Ironically, the FBI detained Italian opera singer Ezio Pinza, a Metropolitan Opera basso who had taken out his first American citizenship papers, and took him to Ellis Island. "Ezio Pinza Seized as Enemy Alien; FBI Takes Singer to Ellis Island," 1.

4. Hull, *The Memoirs of Cordell Hull*, 1548.

5. Corsi, "Italian Immigrants and Their Children," 105, citing 400,000 servicemen of Italian parentage; see also Scherini, "When Italian Americans Were 'Enemy Aliens,'" 21. Scherini says that some 300,000 servicemen were the sons of Italian immigrants.

6. Whitehead, *The FBI Story*, 342–43n3. There were an additional twenty-four Hungarian, Bulgarian, and Romanian aliens apprehended. Compare Diggins, *Mussolini and Fascism*, 400, who cites 228 Italian aliens interned compared to 1,891 "German-Americans" and 2,020 Japanese for the duration of the war; and Mangione, *An Ethnic at Large*, 287, 321, providing the following estimates of each alien enemy group selectively interned: 5,000 Germans, 5,000 Japanese, and 250 Italians.

7. See House Select Committee, *Fourth Interim Report*, 25. The report relies upon the 1940 census for its data, showing approximately 700,000 Italian aliens and 300,000 German aliens in the United States at the time. The total Japanese population in the continental United States in 1940 was 79,642 natives and 47,305 foreign-born. U. S. Department of Commerce, Bureau of the Census, *Sixteenth Census of the United States: 1940.* "Population," vol. 2, "Characteristics of the Population," 19, table 4. I calculated the comparative figures by using the following percentages of selective internment based on the above numbers for each alien population: 0.05 percent for Italians, 0.41 percent for Germans, and 3.2 percent for Japanese. According to the 1940 census, the population of Italian natives in Alaska in 1939 was 140, in Hawaii in 1940 it was 167, and Italian natives numbered 118 in Puerto Rico in 1940. See Alaska, 10, table 11; Hawaii, 11, table 7; and Puerto Rico, 15, table 4, *Sixteenth Census of the United States: 1940. Territories and Possessions, Population and Housing*, https://babel

.hathitrust.org/cgi/pt?id=mdp.39015079712637;view=1up;seq=9, accessed on May 5, 2017. My subject group of civilian internees includes two from Alaska, three from Hawaii, and one from Puerto Rico. I have not included data on the population of Japanese and Germans in the territories since I could not confirm the numbers of persons of those ethnic groups who were brought to the mainland for internment. Without such data, I could not draw comparisons between the percentages of each population in the territories who were selectively interned.

8. See Biddle, *In Brief Authority*, 207–8; see also Mangione, *An Ethnic at Large*, 320, footnote, who provided a larger number of 85,000 German and Austrian Jews, fiercely opposed to the Nazi regime, interned.

9. Brinkley, *Franklin Delano Roosevelt*, 90.

10. The concept of civil liberties in relation to national security can best be understood as "freedom from coercive or otherwise intrusive governmental actions designed to secure the nation against real or, sometimes, imagined internal and external enemies." R. Posner, *Not a Suicide Pact*, 4. Civil liberties are far more extensive than the rights found in the text of the Constitution since they "are shaped by statutes, regulations, and the discretionary judgments of law enforcement and national security personnel as well as by courts in the name of the Constitution" (ibid., 149).

11. See John Mancini, Co-Founder Italic Studies Institute, to Senator Alfonse D'Amato, September 28, 1995, The Dominic R. Massaro Collection, Immigration History Research Center Archives 1496, University of Minnesota, Box 96, Folder 3 (hereafter cited as Massaro Collection); see also John (Balesteri) Krollpfeiffer, Producer/Director Bauhaus Pictures, to Honorable Dominic Massaro, Supreme Court of New York State, August 8, 1995, Massaro Collection, regarding the film *A Viva Voce* recounting the experiences of Italians during World War II.

12. To Provide for the Preparation of a Government Report Detailing Injustices Suffered by Italian Americans during World War II, and a Formal Acknowledgement of Such Injustices by the President, Pub. L. No. 106–451, 114 Stat. 1947 (2000), http://thomas.loc.gov/cgi-bin/bdquery/z?d106:h.r.02442: (site discontinued), accessed on May 30, 2016 (hereafter cited as Wartime Violation of Italian American Civil Liberties Act). On July 1, 1999, U.S. Representatives Rick Lazio and Eliot Engel introduced the bill, H.R. 2442, which was subsequently referred to the House Judiciary Committee, Subcommittee on the Constitution, on September 24, 1999. After passing H.R. 2442 without amendment, the House referred it to the Senate where it passed with amendments on October 19, 2000. After the House agreed to the Senate amendments, President William J. Clinton signed the legislation into law on November 7, 2000. *DOJ Report*, iv.

13. Wartime Violation of Italian American Civil Liberties Act, § 2, par. (1), (2), and (3).

14. The process of exclusion was pursuant to Act of March 21, 1942, Pub. L. No. 77–503, 56 Stat. 173 (1942).

15. *DOJ Report*, see Appendix E.1. The DOJ admits that its list may be incomplete.

16. Wartime Violation of Italian American Civil Liberties Act, § 2, par. (6).

17. See *DOJ Report*.

18. Recent studies on the case of the Japanese include Muller, *American Inquisition*; Robinson, *A Tragedy of Democracy*.

19. See, for example, Goldstein, *Political Repression in Modern America*, 262–81. Goldstein compares all forms of political repression during World War II, merely mentioning the internment of Germans and Italians and other restrictions on these groups.

20. Compare Moloney, *National Insecurities*, 4, who argues that historically deportation policy has served as a "social filter" by defining who is eligible for citizenship in the United States.

21. Wartime Violation of Italian American Civil Liberties Act, § 2, par. (7).

22. See, for example, "Legion Head Hits U.S. Treatment of Italian Prisoners," 13, in which the terms "prisoner of war" and "internees" are used interchangeably.

23. Fox, *The Unknown Internment*; Fox, *Uncivil Liberties*.

24. Fox, *Uncivil Liberties*, 229.

25. Ibid., 227–29.

26. See Fox, *America's Invisible Gulag*, xviii, 13; Fox, *Fear Itself*, xxiv; Fox, *Homeland Insecurity*, 35–36. Fox shows that the government's "cowing" of the German community was an effective form of intimidation.

27. DiStasi, *Una Storia Segreta*, xviii; see also DiStasi, *Branded*, 271, where he argues "Japanese-, Italian- and German-Americans . . . were the ones branded as 'alien enemies': both alien to the American way, and enemies to its survival."

28. Scherini, "When Italian Americans Were 'Enemy Aliens,'" 19, suggesting that existing anti-Japanese attitudes on the West Coast "spilled over onto Italians and Germans in the early days of the war." See also Tintori, "New Discoveries, Old Prejudices," 236; David A. Taylor, "During World War II, the U.S. Saw Italian-Americans as a Threat to Homeland Security," who portrays Italians as "being targeted by EO 9066," http://www.smithsonianmag.com/history/italian-americans-were-considered-enemy-aliens-world-war-ii-180962021/, accessed on May 5, 2017.

29. See DiStasi, *Branded*, "Evacuation and Curfew," 124–94.

30. Compare Ngai, *Impossible Subjects* (discussing the differential treatment of European and non-European migrants in the legal regime of immigration restrictions beginning in the 1920s).

31. Relative political power has been cited as the reason why Germans on the East Coast and Japanese in Hawaii were not relocated while Japanese on the West Coast were. See Issacharoff and Pildes, "Between Civil Libertarianism and Executive Unilateralism," 174.

32. Compare T. Guglielmo, *White on Arrival* (arguing that Italians always were considered white in naturalization laws and the U.S. census and in the eyes of the media, employers, realtors, and politicians); Jacobson, *Whiteness of a Different Color* (model of progression toward whiteness); and Richards, *Italian American*, 185 (arguing that Italian Americans were among victims of racism that were "nonvisibly black" and that racism was directed at aspects of their moral personality, that is, ways of thinking, feeling, and believing).

33. When speaking about national security programs, President Roosevelt and his liberal congressional allies used the theme of the obligation of citizens to contribute

to defending democracy. This theme became a "hallmark of liberal internationalism." Zelizer, *Arsenal of Democracy*, 52.

34. General Records of the Department of Justice, "WWII Alien Enemy Internment Case Files, 1941–1951," Record Group 60; National Archives at College Park (hereafter cited as DOJ Litigation Files, NACP); Erwin Griswold Papers, Historical & Special Collections, Harvard Law School Library (hereafter cited as Griswold Papers), Box 73, Folder 8; Corsi Papers, Box 33, Folder "ACTIVITIES Alien Enemy Hearing Board Correspondence to Cases 7 May 1941–11 Feb. 1944"; Nicholas Kelley Papers, Manuscripts and Archives, The New York Public Library, Astor, Lennox, and Tilden Foundations (hereafter cited as Kelley Papers), Box 140.

35. See Stone, *Perilous Times*, 293.

36. Francis Biddle, Attorney General, Department of Justice, "Circular 3616, Supplement No. 1, Instructions to Alien Enemy Hearing Boards," January 7, 1942, Griswold Papers, Box 73, Folder 8.

Chapter One

1. See Smith, *Freedom's Fetters*, 11–16. The four acts were as follows: Naturalization Act, requiring proof of living in the U.S. for fourteen years, including five years in the state of naturalization; Alien Act, authorizing the president to deport any alien judged "dangerous to the peace and safety of the United States"; Alien Enemy Act, authorizing the president to apprehend and deport male alien residents to their home country at war with the U.S.; and Sedition Act, making it a crime to publish false and malicious information about the government. See Appendix to *Freedom's Fetters* for text of acts.

2. Kohn, *Eagle and Sword*, 218.

3. See Moloney, *National Insecurities*, 12–16. Moloney confirms racial bias from 1895 to 1904, stating "immigrants who were from Asia, the Middle East, Mexico, and Italy had higher rates of exclusion than those from Northern Europe" (ibid., 6). Italians had a 1.4 percent rate of exclusion compared to English and Welsh at 0.87 percent and Scandinavians at 0.14 percent.

4. See Preston, *Aliens and Dissenters*, 4; see Handlin, *The Uprooted*.

5. Fong Yue Ting v. United States, 149 U.S. 698, 709 (1893).

6. Immigration Act of 1903, Pub. L. No. 57–162, § 2, 32 Stat. 1213 (1903).

7. Preston, *Aliens and Dissenters*, 67; see Naturalization Act of 1906, Pub. L. No. 59-338, 34 Stat. 596 (1906).

8. Powers, *Secrecy and Power*, 48–49, citing *AG Report 1917*, 57–58.

9. Powers, *Secrecy and Power*, 49.

10. Ibid., 50–52.

11. Cannato, *American Passage*, 295–96, citing "Annual Report of the Commissioner General of Immigration," 1918, 14; see also, Culp, "Alien Enemy Paroles," 205, stating that 3,000 individuals were interned during World War I, of which the majority were German seamen.

12. Stone, *Perilous Times*, 151–52; see Espionage Act of 1917, Pub. L. No. 65-24, 40 Stat. 217 (1917).

13. Stone, *Perilous Times*, 173. Note that the government's standard of proof under the Espionage Act is proof of "evil intent" and falsity (ibid., 265).

14. Kanstroom, *Aftermath*, 63 and 76n85; see Immigration Act of 1918, Pub. L. No. 65-221, 40 Stat. 1012 (1918).

15. Stone, *Perilous Times*, 181.

16. Ibid., 186; see Sedition Act of 1918, Pub. L. No. 65-150, 40 Stat. 553 (1918).

17. Powers, *Secrecy and Power*, 70–71.

18. Stone, *Perilous Times*, 223.

19. Ibid., 224–26. For example, Judge George Anderson of the Massachusetts Federal District Court was a harsh critic of the Justice Department's procedures and ordered the discharge of twenty aliens held for deportation based on membership in the Communist Party.

20. See Temkin, *The Sacco-Vanzetti Affair*, 13–15; see also Gage, *The Day Wall Street Exploded*, 219–28, discussing Sacco and Vanzetti's adoption of "Galleani's brand of militant anarchism" (ibid., 219) and their possible involvement as conspirators in the September 16, 1920, Wall Street bombing.

21. Temkin, *The Sacco-Vanzetti Affair*, 110–11. In focusing on the international reactions and criticisms to the convictions and executions of Sacco and Vanzetti, Temkin brings an international dimension to the case. See also McGirr, "The Passion of Sacco and Vanzetti," which explores the international mobilization of support for Sacco and Vanzetti against the history of labor internationalism.

22. The Immigration Act of 1917, Pub. L. No. 64-301, 39 Stat. 874 (1917), imposed a literacy test for admission and barred almost all Asians. To give an idea of how many immigrants the literacy test would exclude, during the fiscal year 1909, about 56 percent of Southern Italians were illiterate. Kohler, *Immigration and Aliens in the United States*, 176.

23. Quota Act of 1921, Pub. L. No. 67-5, 42 Stat. 5 (1921); Kohler, *Immigration and Aliens in the United States*, 23–24; see also Ngai, *Impossible Subjects*, 21.

24. Wechman, *The Economic Development of the Italian-American*, 11; see Constitution of the Society for the Protection of Italian Immigrants, Article I, Corporation, Gino Speranza Papers, Manuscripts and Archives, The New York Public Library, Astor, Lennox, and Tilden Foundations (hereafter cited as Speranza Papers), Box 12, Folder "Society for the Protection of Italian Immigrants, Jan.–June." The society even maintained a legal aid department to apprise Italian immigrants of their rights and to represent their interests.

25. See Gaspare M. Cusumano, Representative, The Society for Italian Immigrants, to Mr. August V. Tozzi, Manager of the Society for Italian Immigrants, "Ellis Island Annual Report—1921," January 16, 1922, Speranza Papers, Box 13, Folder "Society for the Protection of Italian Immigrants, 1906–1923."

26. Kohler, *Immigration and Aliens in the United States*, 150. The Immigration Act of 1924 (Johnson-Reed Act), Pub. L. No. 68–139, 43 Stat. 153 (1924), did not exempt wives and minor children of resident aliens not yet naturalized from the quota, preventing them from joining their husbands and fathers in the United States.

27. Ibid.

28. U.S. Department of Commerce, Bureau of the Census, 1930 U.S. Census, http://www.census.gov/population/www/documentation/twps0081/tables/tab04.xls,

accessed on May 3, 2017. There were approximately 1.8 million persons born in Italy in a total population of about 123 million in the United States in 1930.

29. House Select Committee, *Fourth Interim Report*, 241.

30. Moloney, *National Insecurities*, 4.

31. T. Guglielmo, "'No Color Barrier,'" 32–33. I have noticed the use of race as synonymous with national origin in deportation proceedings as late as 1943. See U.S. Department of Justice Board of Immigration Appeals In re. Biagio Farese, August 28, 1943, Alien Registration File of Biagio Farese, A-3442924, U.S. Citizenship & Immigration Services (hereafter cited as Farese's A-File).

32. T. Guglielmo, "'No Color Barrier,'" 30.

33. See Nelli, *From Immigrants to Ethnics*, 127.

34. Jacobson, *Whiteness of a Different Color*, 57–59.

35. See Krase, "Ironies of Icons," 6.

36. Ferraro, *Feeling Italian*, 163. Ferraro captures the sentiment of the time in calling Southern Italians "swarthy," and "therefore not exactly white." The names "dagoes," "wops," and "guineas" were common epithets.

37. *DOJ Report*, 1.

38. Vecoli, "The Search for an Italian American Identity: Continuity and Change," 92.

39. House Select Committee, *Fourth Interim Report*, 241.

40. Gino Speranza, "The Assimilation of Immigrants," 10, Speranza Papers, Box 35, Folder "Lectures, Reports and Book Reviews."

41. Wechman, *The Economic Development of the Italian-American*, 86.

42. Cannistraro, "Generoso Pope and the Rise of Italian American Politics, 1925–1936," 270. Cannistraro cites to a national survey by *Il Progresso* in 1931, showing the following breakdown of professionals: "24,000 lawyers, 17,000 pharmacists, 14,500 doctors, 2,000 engineers, and several thousand businessmen, teachers, writers, and artists."

43. LaGumina, "American Political Process and Italian Participation in New York State," 89–92.

44. Wechman, *The Economic Development of the Italian-American*, 37–38.

45. Ignatius Seraci, Secretary, Capitol Bureau—"La Parola," June 3, 1941, Vito Marcantonio Papers, Manuscripts and Archives, The New York Public Library, Astor, Lennox, and Tilden Foundations (hereafter cited as Marcantonio Papers), Series I, General Correspondence, Box 4, Folder "Pope, Generoso." Seraci's letter indicates that accusations against Pope were raised in the examination of the Hon. Samuel Dickstein before the Dies Committee in March 1941.

46. See Cannistraro, "Generoso Pope and The Rise of Italian American Politics, 1925–1936."

47. LaGumina, "American Political Process and Italian Participation in New York State," 91.

48. Heckscher, *When LaGuardia Was Mayor*, 161–62.

49. See Joseph H. Coccaro to Honorable Mayor F. H. La Guardia, April 16, 1942, the Fiorello H. La Guardia Papers 1917–1945, Manuscripts and Archives, The New

York Public Library, Astor, Lennox, and Tilden Foundations (hereafter cited as La Guardia Papers), Series II: Mayoral Correspondence (1933–1945), reel 40 (1942).

50. See Austin G. Cocuzza to Hon. Franklin D. Roosevelt, January 3, 1942, La Guardia Papers, reel 40 (1942); and Telegram, Samuel L. Kaufman to Hon. Fiorello H. La Guardia, January 22, 1942, La Guardia Papers, reel 41 (1942).

51. Address delivered by Rabbi F. M. Isserman of Temple Israel, St. Mo., over Radio Station KXOK, March 1, 1942, La Guardia Papers, reel 40 (1942).

52. Meyer, *Vito Marcantonio*, 115, 119.

53. Telegram, Vito Marcantonio to Mr. Haywood Broun, May 3, 1937, Marcantonio Papers, Series I, General Correspondence, Box 4, Folder "Personal, The People's Voice."

54. Ennio, D'Alessandro to Gentlemen, Chairman Dinner Committee, *The People's Voice*, April 28, 1937, Marcantonio Papers, Series I, General Correspondence, Box 4, Folder "Personal, The People's Voice."

55. See Marcantonio Papers, Series I, General Correspondence, Box 2, Folder "Constituency Problems (aid requests), 1945–1946."

56. See Marcantonio Papers, Series I, General Correspondence, Box 3, Folder "General Correspondence, Italian Associations (American) (1 of 2)."

57. See Marcantonio Papers, Series II, Congressional Correspondence and Papers, 1935–1952, Box 13 (1939–1942).

58. N. C. Guccione to Hon. Vito Marcantonio, November 23, 1942, Marcantonio Papers, Series II, Congressional Correspondence and Papers, 1935–1952, Box 16 (1941–1944), Folder "Gribbon to Giuffre."

59. See Affidavit of Domenico D'Aggiola, July 24, 1942, Marcantonio Papers, Series II, Congressional Correspondence and Papers, 1935–1952, Box 16 (1941–1944), Folder "Gribbon to Giuffre."

60. Goldstein, "Charles Poletti Dies at 99."

61. Goldstein, "John Pastore, Prominent Figure in Rhode Island Politics." Pastore later served in the U.S. Senate, the first Italian American to be elected to that position as well.

62. Testimony of Angelo Rossi before Assembly Fact Finding Committee on Un-American Activities in California: Investigation into Matters Pertaining to Un-American and Subversive Activities, May 26–27, 1942 (hereafter cited as Testimony of Angelo Rossi before California Assembly Fact Finding Committee), 3455, generally 3451–71, http://www.internmentarchives.com/showdoc.php?docid=00407&search_id=77946&pagenum=2, accessed on May 3, 2017. See also LaGumina, "American Political Process and Italian Participation in New York State," 92; Issel, *For Both Cross and Flag*, 116–18.

63. Diggins, *Mussolini and Fascism*, 21.

64. Ibid., 70.

65. Ibid., 166–67.

66. Ibid., 79.

67. Nelli, *Italians in Chicago*, 239–42.

68. Handlin, *The Uprooted*, 264.

69. Nelli, *From Immigrants to Ethnics*, 156.

70. Mangione, *An Ethnic at Large*, 115. Arguments with his Sicilian family over politics are one example of the phenomenon that he describes of the children of immigrant parents feeling the tension between their parents' Old World traditions and what they learned in school, leaving them with "confused impressions of identity that were never resolved" (ibid., 369). Note that not all Italian immigrants stayed in this country. Mangione estimates that more than one million men and women returned to their native land.

71. Franklin D. Roosevelt to S.T.E. [Steve Early], January 10, 1939; President's Personal File 5763: *Richmond* [VA] *News Leader*; Papers of Franklin D. Roosevelt, Roosevelt Presidential Library.

72. Panunzio, "Italian Americans, Fascism, and the War," 776.

73. Ribuffo, "Religion in the History of U.S. Foreign Policy," 10.

74. See Diggins, *Mussolini and Fascism*, 290–91, 304–5.

75. T. Guglielmo, *White on Arrival*, 128.

76. Panunzio, "Italian Americans, Fascism, and the War," 779.

77. Diggins, *Mussolini and Fascism*, 352.

78. Roosevelt to Mussolini, July 29, 1937, Grace Tully Collection, Box 11, Folder Correspondence: Mussolini, Benito, 1933–1937, Franklin D. Roosevelt Library and Museum website; version 2013, https://fdrlibrary.org, accessed on January 10, 2017.

79. Diggins, *Mussolini and Fascism*, 360.

80. See Brinkley, *Franklin Delano Roosevelt*, 80.

81. Panunzio, "Italian Americans, Fascism, and the War," 780.

82. Diggins, *Mussolini and Fascism*, 354.

83. Henry Lewis Stimson Diaries, microfilm at University of North Carolina Davis Library (hereafter cited as Stimson Diaries), reel 6, vol. 32, p. 64, December 29, 1940, Henry Lewis Stimson Papers (MS 465), Manuscripts and Archives, Yale University Library.

84. Diggins, *Mussolini and Fascism*, 302.

85. Salvemini, *Italian Fascist Activities in the United States*, xxviii. For an interpretive history of Italian-American radicalism, see Cannistraro and Meyer, eds., *The Lost World of Italian American Radicalism*.

86. Diggins, *Mussolini and Fascism*, 106–7, citing *Commission on Un-American Activities in California: Executive Hearing* (Sacramento, 1943), III, 1447.

87. Martin Dies, "The Immigration Crisis," *Saturday Evening Post*, April 20, 1935, Marcantonio Papers, Series IV, Research Files, Box 59 (Anti-Fascism—N.L.R.B.), Folder "Research Dies Committee Folder #1."

88. Dies, *The Trojan Horse in America*, 336.

89. Ibid., 346.

90. Ibid., 337.

91. Ibid., 342, 343. He named the following: *Progresso Italiano-Americano*; *Il Corriere D'America*, New York; *Il Popolo Italiano*, Philadelphia; *l'Italia*, Chicago; *l'Italia*, San Francisco; *Le Notzia*, Boston; and *La Voce del Popolo*, San Francisco.

92. Dies, *The Trojan Horse in America*, 343.

93. Ibid., 336–37, 340. See Sexton, *The War on Labor and the Left*, 148, for a discussion of how Dies set the "rules of attack" which were carried into postwar hearings:

"denial of due process and the right to confront accusers, unsupported charges, charges relating to beliefs (often from the dim past) rather than acts, and guilt by association."

94. Note that in this section, I capitalize fascism in reference to European Fascism, while my use of the word "fascism" refers to movements in the United States, unless I am quoting other sources.

95. See Crystal Hoffer, "The Birth of Anticommunist National Rhetoric: The Fish Committee Hearings in 1930s Seattle," http://depts.washington.edu/depress/fish _committee.shtml, accessed on April 20, 2017.

96. See, for example, Roger N. Baldwin, Director, American Civil Liberties Union, "Should the Dies Committee Die?" speech delivered on WEAF, New York, January 29, 1939, and Arthur Garfield Hays, Counsel, American Civil Liberties Union, "The Dies Committee and the American Civil Liberties Union," speech delivered on WABC, New York, January 19, 1939, Marcantonio Papers, Series IV, Research Files, Box 59 (Anti-Fascism—N.L.R.B.), Folder "Research Dies Committee Folder #1."

97. See Baldwin, "Should the Dies Committee Die?" Marcantonio Papers., Series IV, Research Files, Box 59 (Anti-Fascism—N.L.R.B.), Folder "Research Dies Committee Folder #1."

98. See Vargas, *Labor Rights Are Civil Rights*, 188–92.

99. Brinkley, *Voices of Protest*, 143, 156.

100. Ibid., 274.

101. Ibid., 274–76.

102. Ibid., 278.

103. Ibid., 281, 280–82. Brinkley says that the label "fascism" has mistakenly been attached to Long and Coughlin because of the confusion surrounding the concept of fascism and due to the difficulty in finding a more suitable label for their movements. He attributes their simultaneous leanings to the left and right of the political spectrum to the contradictions of populism from which their ideals derived.

104. Diggins, *Mussolini and Fascism*, 349.

105. Gary Mormino identified this critical problem for me in comments on my final draft.

106. Diggins, *Mussolini and Fascism*, 108–9. See also Mangione, *An Ethnic at Large*, 115–16, who explained his relatives' pro-Fascism as follows: "*Fascismo* was only a word to them. Its anatomy was beyond their understanding."

107. Diggins, *Mussolini and Fascism*, 350, referring to President Franklin D. Roosevelt's 1940 University of Virginia commencement speech in which, expressing his anger over Italy's decision to enter the war with the Axis powers, he characterized Mussolini as a "backstabber."

108. Hon. Felix Forte, Superior Court of the Commonwealth of Massachusetts, to Hon. Edward Hassan, Assistant United States Attorney, December 15, 1942, with attached "Draft of Resolution" of Sons of Italy in America and Reply of President Roosevelt, Griswold Papers, 1925–1994, Box 73, Folder 7.

109. Diggins, *Mussolini and Fascism*, 350–51.

110. Donald E. Keyhoe, "Deport Criminal Aliens?" (unidentified paper or journal), La Guardia Papers, reel 38 (1941).

111. Ibid. Many of these cases fell under the 1917 Immigration Act's "hardship" provisos. For example, the Seventh Proviso allowed the secretary of labor to readmit an alien who had lived in the United States seven consecutive years.

112. Office of Government Reports, April 10, 1942 Report, "Attitudes Toward Alien Population and Other Minority Groups," in Daniels, *American Concentration Camps*, vol. 4.

113. See "The 'Enemy Alien'" and "Allow 'Enemy' Aliens To Establish Loyalty, CIO Asks Government," (undated and unattributed article), Joseph A. Labadie Collection, American Committee for Protection of Foreign Born Records, University of Michigan Library (Special Collections Library) (hereafter cited as American Committee for Protection of Foreign Born Records), Box 17, Folder 2 ("Enemy Aliens, 1942–1945").

114. See Law Aide to Mayor LaGuardia to Nick Giacomino, May 5, 1942, La Guardia Papers, reel 40.

115. "L'Attorney General Biddle Stigmatizza il falso patriottismo di certi datori di lavoro—Rifiutare lavoro agli stranieri, significa creare disunione nella nazione—afferma il Ministro della Giustizia," (Attorney General Biddle stigmatizes the false patriotism of some employers—Refusing work to aliens means creating disunity in the nation—affirms the Secretary of Justice), *La Tribuna*, January 15, 1942, 7, Corsi Papers, Box 33, Folder "ACTIVITIES Alien Enemy Hearing Board Correspondence to cases 7 May 1941 to 11 Feb. 1944."

116. "The Problem of Alien Enemies," Address by Joseph Rowe Jr., Assistant to the Attorney General, Broadcast over the Mutual Broadcasting System, Friday, February 20, 1942, American Committee for Protection of Foreign Born Records, Box 17, Folder 1 ("Enemy Aliens, 1942–1945").

117. "Tolerance Toward Aliens Urged at Annual Dinner," 29.

118. "The Attorney General Warns Against Race Prejudice and Discrimination," excerpts from speech given November 11, 1943. Attorney General Biddle emphasized the importance of public opinion supporting state and federal governments' indignation against racial discrimination and of leaders enforcing the law.

119. Gino Massagli, interview by Stephen Fox, Eureka, California, July 30, 1986, in Fox, *Uncivil Liberties*, 140.

120. Don Rafaelli, interview by Stephen Fox, Eureka, California, November 3, 1987, in Fox, *Uncivil Liberties*, 36.

121. Joseph Maniscalco, interview by Stephen Fox, San Francisco, California, May 11, 1987, in Fox, *Uncivil Liberties*, 40.

122. See Diggins, *Mussolini and Fascism*, 108.

123. *DOJ Report*, 2.

124. U.S. Senate, *Final Report of the Select Committee to Study Governmental Operations with respect to Intelligence Activities, Supplementary Detailed Staff Reports of Intelligence Activities and the Rights of Americans*, Book 3, April 23, 1976 (hereafter cited as *Senate Intelligence Report*), 394, quoting Hoover memorandum 8/24/36.

125. *Senate Intelligence Report*, 395–96.

126. Ibid., 399–400.

127. Powers, *Secrecy and Power*, 216.

128. Ibid., 215–16, 230.

129. *Senate Intelligence Report*, 412–13.

130. Ibid., 413, quoting Memorandum from Hoover to Field Offices, 9/2/39.

131. Ibid., 413–14, quoting Memorandum from Hoover to Field Offices, 12/6/39.

132. Ibid., 414.

133. See, for example, Don Whitehead, *The FBI Story*, 162.

134. Senate Intelligence Report, 403, quoting Confidential Memorandum of the President, 6/26/39.

135. Ibid.

136. Goldstein, *Political Repression in Modern America*, 248.

137. Robinson, *A Tragedy of Democracy*, 47.

138. U.S. Commission on Wartime Relocation and Internment of Civilians, *Personal Justice Denied*, 54.

139. Ibid., citing Telegrams, J. Edgar Hoover to All Special Agents in Charge, Dec. 7, 1941, FBI (CWRIC 5826, 5827, 5828), and Dec. 8, 1941, FBI (CWRIC 5784–85).

140. J. Edgar Hoover, Director, Federal Bureau of Investigation, to SACs, "Clarifying Instructions for Submitting Names of Persons Who Should Be Considered for Custodial Detention Pending Investigation in Event of National Emergency," April 30, 1941, Private FOI/PA, Department of Justice, Immigration and Naturalization Service, in Tolzmann, *German-Americans in the World Wars*, 1529, 1530.

141. Ibid.

142. *Senate Intelligence Report*, 417; PMG Records of Italian Civilian Internees, NACP. With respect to citizens, Attorney General Biddle insisted that there be probable cause that a crime had been committed before the FBI arrested them. U.S. Commission on Wartime Relocation and Internment of Civilians, *Personal Justice Denied*, 54–55.

143. Goldstein, *Political Repression in Modern America,* 248; see also Stone, *Perilous Times*, 250.

144. See Salvemini, *Italian Fascist Activities in the United States.*

145. Panunzio, "Italian Americans, Fascism, and the War," 777.

146. Retyped copy of "Membership List of German-American, Italian-American, American, and Russian Organizations," *Papers of the U.S. Commission on Wartime Relocation and Internment of Civilians*, Part 1, Numerical File Archive, University Publications of America, in Tolzmann, *German-Americans in the World Wars*, 1590–92.

147. Ibid., 1641–45, 1660.

148. Memorandum, John McCloy, Asst. Sec. of War, to Assistant Chief of Staff, G-2, April 22, 1942, in Daniels, *American Concentration Camps*, vol. 4.

149. See Bruner and Sayre, "Shortwave Listening in an Italian Community."

150. Liebmann, *Diplomacy between the Wars*, 129.

151. Ibid., 172.

152. Pernicone, *Carlo Tresca*, 253.

153. Diggins, *Mussolini and Fascism*, 7, 344–45; Pernicone, *Carlo Tresca*, 253.

154. Diggins, *Mussolini and Fascism*, 143.

155. Ibid., 414.

156. Liebmann, *Diplomacy between the Wars*, 147.

157. Diggins, *Mussolini and Fascism*, 347–48.

158. See ibid., 414.

159. Ibid., 418–20.

160. Liebmann, *Diplomacy between the Wars*, 149–51.

161. Ibid., 158, 161. See Hull, *The Memoirs of Cordell Hull*, 1551–52, for further explanation of Sforza's role.

162. Diggins, *Mussolini and Fascism*, 135–36.

163. Pernicone, *Carlo Tresca*, 254–55.

164. Ibid., 255–56.

165. Ibid., 256; Cannistraro, "Generoso Pope and the Rise of Italian American Politics, 1925–1936," 265.

166. Diggins, *Mussolini and Fascism*, 282.

167. See Cannistraro, "Generoso Pope and the Rise of Italian American Politics, 1925–1936," 285, citing telegram from an anti-Fascist committee to Roosevelt, October 31, 1935, NA, Record Group 59, Department of State, 811. OOF/227.

168. Pernicone, *Carlo Tresca*, 256–57.

169. Diggins, *Mussolini and Fascism*, 348.

170. Bayor, "Comments on the Papers by Philip V. Cannistraro, George W. Carey and Miriam Cohen," 299.

171. Pernicone, *Carlo Tresca*, 262.

172. Ibid.

173. Ibid., 263.

174. Gallagher, *All the Right Enemies*, 238–41.

175. Ibid., 237–38.

176. Taubman, *The Maestro*, 142.

177. Ibid., 158–59; 189–90.

178. Ibid., 195.

179. Roosevelt to Toscanini, April 30, 1936; President's Personal File 1370: Toscanini, Arturo; Papers of Franklin D. Roosevelt, Roosevelt Presidential Library.

180. Taubman, *The Maestro*, 230–31.

181. Ibid., 236; 238–39.

182. Ibid., 319.

183. Memorandum re. Arturo Toscanini and Thomas Mann, undated but appears to be 1942; President's Personal File 1370: Toscanini, Arturo; Papers of Franklin D. Roosevelt, Roosevelt Presidential Library. The memorandum states: "The President, Feb. 9th, sent memo. to James Rowe instructing Mr. Rowe to take the matter up with the Attorney General and the President also said 'I think there is something in the idea but we have to be careful.'"

184. Taubman, *The Maestro*, 321.

185. Stimson Diaries, reel 6, vol. 33, p. 67, March 7, 1941.

186. Ibid., 127, March 31, 1941.

187. See Valkenburg, *An Alien Place*, 2, 5–6.

188. Ibid., 6, reporting that 189 crewmen of the *Conte Biancamano* were indicted for sabotage and awaiting trial; Culp, "Alien Enemy Paroles," 208. The FBI reported that there were 1,271 apprehensions of seamen. Document 44, Federal Bureau of

Investigation "Apprehensions By Field Offices, December 7, 1941 to June 30, 1945" in Tolzmann, *German-Americans in the World War*, 1740–49. According to INS records, Fort Missoula housed 1,317 Italian seamen. *Administrative History of the INS*, 298.

189. The grounds for exclusion were (1) "an immigrant not in possession of an un-expired immigration visa as required by Section 13(a) (1) of the Immigration Act of 1924"; (2) "Executive Order 8430 of June 5, 1940, as an immigrant not in possession of a valid passport"; (3) "second paragraph of Section 30 of the Alien Registration Act of 1940 as an immigrant not in possession of any visa, reentry permit or border crossing card"; (4) "Section 3 of the Act of Feb. 5, 1917 as a person likely to become a public charge." Transcript of Board of Special Inquiry, Ellis Island, New York, April 14, 1941, 3, File of Luigi Olzai, File No. 146–13–2–44–1287, Fort Missoula, Box 37, Records of the Immigration and Naturalization Service, World War II Internment Files, Record Group 85; National Archives Building.

190. *Administrative History of the INS*, 283–84, 288, 297.

191. Sec. of State Cordell Hull to Sec. of War Henry L. Stimson, Nov. 6, 1941, Daniels, *American Concentration Camps*, vol. 1.

192. Ibid.

193. International Committee of the Red Cross, *Report on Its Activities During the Second World War*, 569–71.

194. *Administrative History of the INS*, 381. Although Japan did not ratify this treaty, the State Department reached an agreement with the Japanese government whereby Japan would apply the treaty's terms to civilian internees and prisoners of war.

195. International Committee of the Red Cross, *Report on Its Activities During the Second World War*, 570–71. There were approximately 160,000 civilians of fifty nationalities who had the benefit of a legal status and treaty guarantees. Note that the absence of a provision for *"civilian nationals of a country occupied by the enemy"* resulted in no legal protection for civilians who were eventually executed or sent to concentration camps (ibid., 570).

196. *Administrative History of the INS*, 381. Switzerland was the Protecting Power for Italy and Germany.

197. Document 49(b)i, Inspection Report of Ellis Island Camp, Visited by Mr. Alfred Cardinaux on December 3, 1943, in Tolzmann, *German-Americans in the World Wars*, 2078–79.

198. See U.S. Department of Justice Immigration and Naturalization Service, Instruction No. 58 "To The Immigration and Naturalization Service: Subject: Instructions concerning the treatment of alien enemy detainees" from Lemuel B. Schofield, Special Assistant to the Attorney General, April 28, 1942, in Tolzmann, *German-Americans in the World Wars*, 1580–89.

199. See Records of the Immigration and Naturalization Service, World War II Internment Files, Box 37. It has been explained to me by Marian Smith, chief, Historical Research Branch, U.S. Citizenship & Immigration Services, that when the internment camps closed after the war, camp files were sent to the INS headquarters in Washington, DC, on a case-by-case basis and combined with the official INS files (A-file or C-file) if that case were reopened. If the case were not reopened, the camp

file remained in the camp file set, which was eventually transferred to the National Archives. Telephone conference with Marian Smith, February 9, 2009, and Marian Smith e-mail message to author, July 18, 2016 (notes on file with author).

200. This questionnaire resembled that administered to all adult Japanese internees in 1943 by the War Relocation Authority in conjunction with the military to determine whether to grant the internees release or impose stricter confinement. See Muller, *American Inquisition*, 35. In addition to biographical and citizenship information, affiliations with Japanese and non-Japanese organizations, the questionnaires asked questions concerning willingness to serve in the American armed forces, to promise to abide by the laws of the United States, and not to interfere with the war effort of this country.

201. Memorandum, E. J. Clapp to Messrs. Arnold, Coffee and McGinnis, re: Hearings for Italian Seamen, Sept. 9, 1943, Miscellaneous Files from the Historical Museum at Fort Missoula.

202. Retyped copy of the "Joint Agreement of the Secretary of War and the Attorney General with respect to the Internment of Alien Enemies," July 18, 1941 (hereafter cited as Joint Agreement of the Secretary of War and the Attorney General), 1540, with cover letter, July 29, 1941, E. S. Adams, Major General, the Adjutant General, to the Commanding Generals, Corps Areas, Departments, and Alaska Defense Command, in *Papers of the U.S. Commission on Wartime Relocation and Internment of Civilians*, Part 1, Numerical File Archive, University Publications of America, in Tolzmann, *German-Americans in the World Wars*, 1539–47.

203. Joint Agreement of the Secretary of War and the Attorney General, par. 3.

204. Ibid., par. 4.

205. Ibid., par. 11.

206. Ibid., par. 14.

207. See Fox, "General John DeWitt and the Proposed Internment of German and Italian Aliens during World War II," 410–12; Tintori, "New Discoveries," 237.

Chapter Two

1. *DOJ Report*, 5. Later, the general procedure was that the FBI would make arrests with warrants issued by the Justice Department. With respect to Italian aliens, as of December 15, 1941, 223 warrants were issued, 41 executed, and 85 individuals were arrested without a warrant. Copy of Memorandum for the File, W. F. Kelly, Chief Supervisor of Border Patrol, December 15, 1941, in Tolzmann, *German-Americans in the World Wars*, 1572.

2. TWX (teletypewriter) message, J. Edgar Hoover, Director, FBI, to all SACs, December 8, 1941, *Papers of the U.S. Commission on Wartime Relocation and Internment of Civilians*, Part 1, Numerical File Archive, University Publications of America, in Tolzmann, *German-Americans in the World Wars*, 1554–55.

3. "Roundup of Axis Aliens," 10.

4. U.S. Commission on Wartime Relocation and Internment of Civilians, *Personal Justice Denied*, 55; Scherini, "When Italian Americans Were 'Enemy Aliens,'" 13.

5. Filippo Molinari to Carlotta [surname unknown], Arcadia, Cal., July 25, 1985, personal collection of Andrew M. Canepa, San Francisco, cited in Scherini, "When Italian Americans Were 'Enemy Aliens,'" 13. Mr. Molinari did not receive an order for release until April 20, 1945. Folder of Philip Molinari, Box 14, PMG Records of Italian Civilian Internees, NACP.

6. Presidential Proclamation No. 2527.

7. *DOJ Report*, 3, citing Thomas D. McDermott, "Aliens of Enemy Nationality," INS Training Lecture (May 13, 1943), 5.

8. Memorandum for File by W. F. Kelly, Chief Supervisor of Border Patrol, December 9, 1941, *Papers of the U.S. Commission on Wartime Relocation and Internment of Civilians*, Part 1, Numerical File Archive, University Publications of America, in Tolzmann, *German-Americans in the World Wars*, 1558; compare Map: "98 Italian Aliens Taken Into Custody By FBI," 1:30 P.M. December 9, 1941, in Tolzmann, *German-Americans in the World Wars*, 1566–67.

9. Statement of Attorney General Biddle, December 10, 1941, in House Select Committee, *Fourth Interim Report*, 28n3.

10. "Rulings on Aliens Speeded by Biddle," 23.

11. Press Release by Department of Justice, "Remember Pearl Harbor," December 13, 1941, in Tolzmann, *German-Americans in the World Wars*. Citing a report from J. Edgar Hoover, Biddle said that from December 7 through 11, FBI agents had taken into custody 1,002 German aliens, 169 Italian aliens, and 1,370 Japanese aliens. He also reported that the FBI took forty-three American citizens into custody in Hawaii.

12. Scherini, "When Italian Americans Were 'Enemy Aliens,'" 13–14; Folder of Carmelo Ilacqua, Box 11, PMG Records of Italian Civilian Internees, NACP. For Ilacqua, membership in the Fascist Party was a requirement of his consulate position in the 1930s. He was interned in camps in Montana, Oklahoma, Tennessee, and Texas before receiving parole in 1943 and final release on June 29, 1945.

13. See Translation of a Letter, Angiolina to "My dear," December 9, 1941, Farese's A-File.

14. Memorandum, J. Edgar Hoover, Director, FBI, to Messers. Tolson, Tamm, and Ladd, December 9, 1941, *Papers of the U.S. Commission on Wartime Relocation and Internment of Civilians*, Part 1, Numerical File Archive, University Publications of America, in Tolzmann, *German-Americans in the World Wars*, 1560.

15. *DOJ Report*, 5–6.

16. Instructions from J. Edgar Hoover, Director, Federal Bureau of Investigation, to all Officers except Honolulu, December 17, 1941, *Papers of the U.S. Commission on Wartime Relocation and Internment of Civilians*, Part 1, Numerical File Archive, University Publications of America, in Tolzmann, *German-Americans in the World Wars*, 1573.

17. See *DOJ Report*, 27–37; see also DiStasi, "A Fish Story," 63, 68, and DiStasi, *Branded*, 241–64.

18. *DOJ Report*, 19.

19. DiStasi, *Una Storia Segreta*, 316–17; DiStasi, *Branded*, 136.

20. *DOJ Report*, v, 25; DiStasi, *Branded*, 142–44.

21. Memorandum For The President (Draft), Subject: East Coast Military Areas, April 14, 1942, in Daniels, *American Concentration Camps*, vol. 4.

22. U.S. Commission on Wartime Relocation and Internment of Civilians, *Personal Justice Denied*, 288; see also DiStasi, *Branded*, 195–240.

23. See "Explains Benefits to Italian Aliens," 27.

24. PMG Files of Italian Civilian Internees, NACP.

25. Persico, *Roosevelt's Secret War*, 169.

26. Biddle, *In Brief Authority*, 207–8.

27. Mangione, *An Ethnic at Large*, 320. The footnote on page 320 provides 85,000 as the number of German and Austrian refugees interned.

28. G. A. Borgese, Albert Einstein, Bruno Frank, Thomas Mann, Arturo Toscanini, and Bruno Walter to President Franklin D. Roosevelt, undated, Francis Biddle Papers, 1942, Box 1, Aliens and Immigration, Franklin D. Roosevelt Library and Museum Website; version date 2013, https://fdrlibrary.org, accessed on January 10, 2017.

29. Francis Biddle to Thomas Mann, February 19, 1942, Francis Biddle Papers, 1942, Box 1, Aliens and Immigration, Franklin D. Roosevelt Library and Museum Website; version date 2013, https://fdrlibrary.org, accessed on January 10, 2017.

30. W. F. Kelly, Assistant Commissioner, Immigration & Naturalization Service, to Mr. A. Vulliet World Alliance of Young Men's Christian Associations, August 9, 1948, in Tolzmann, *German-Americans in the World Wars*, 1513. These numbers include those received from outside continental United States and those who were voluntarily interned to join the internee–head of the family. The other nationalities represented were as follows: Hungary, 53; Romania, 25; Bulgaria, 5; and other, 161.

31. See Fox, *America's Invisible Gulag*, 13.

32. House Select Committee, *Fourth Interim Report*, 229–30, Table 2, 241, citing data from the Alien Registration Division of the Justice Department. The Middle Atlantic is composed of New York, New Jersey, and Pennsylvania. New England comprises Maine, New Hampshire, Vermont, Massachusetts, Rhode Island, and Connecticut. The states of Ohio, Indiana, Illinois, Michigan, and Wisconsin make up the East North Central region. The Pacific region is made up of Washington, Oregon, and California.

33. Document 44, Federal Bureau of Investigation "Apprehensions By Field Offices, December 7, 1941 to June 30, 1945" in Tolzmann, *German-Americans in the World Wars*, 1740–49. In my comparative analysis, Italians were taken from these cities in East Coast states: Albany, Atlanta, Baltimore, Boston, Buffalo, Charlotte, Huntington, Miami, Newark, New Haven, New York, Norfolk, Philadelphia, Pittsburgh, Providence, Richmond, Savannah, and Springfield. The cities in West Coast states were Los Angeles, Portland, San Diego, San Francisco, and Seattle.

34. In the study I conducted, there were 112 internees from cities in states on the East Coast and 97 internees from cities in states on the West Coast.

35. Note that for those subjects who had multiple occupations that included the media, I only counted them in the media category in my analysis of occupations.

36. See Testimony of Gilbert Tuoni before Assembly Fact Finding Committee on Un-American Activities in California, May 26–27, 1942, 3662–65. Tuoni, an indepen-

dent film producer, testified that the government should close branches of Bank of America which he believed were supporting the Italian government, http://www .internmentarchives.com/showdoc.php?docid=00408&search_id=77937&pagenum=2, accessed on May 5, 2017.

37. Folder of Boncompagno Boncompagni-Ludovisi, Box 4, PMG Records of Italian Civilian Internees, NACP.

38. Folder of Vincent Anthony Lapenta, Box 11, PMG Records of Italian Civilian Internees, NACP.

39. Fox, *Fear Itself*, 380–81.

40. See House Select Committee, *Fourth Interim Report*, 244.

41. See Ianni, "Familialism in the South of Italy and in the United States," 105–7. "Throughout the 1920s and increasingly in the period prior to the second world war, the existence of organized crime in America which included gambling, the sale of illegal alcohol and narcotics, usury, prostitution, and the violence and corruption which surrounded these vices was attributed to an Italian American Mafia or, as it was later called, La Cosa Nostra" (ibid., 105).

42. Fox, *Uncivil Liberties*, 109–27.

43. For a description of the possible dispositions, see *Administrative History of the INS*, 414.

44. Note that for many internees, the release date came after a period of parole.

45. Friedman, *Nazis and Good Neighbors*, 9.

46. See Sidak, "War, Liberty, and Enemy Aliens," 1424, for a discussion of how the Alien Enemy Act applied to persons who were natives of an enemy country and had become citizens of a nation friendly to the United States. Sidak cites Ex parte Gregoire, 61 F. Supp. 92, 93 (N.D. Cal. 1945) where the court's distinction between nativity and citizenship resulted in the internment of a German native who had obtained French citizenship before World War II. Note that the Alien Enemy Act applies to "all natives, citizens, denizens, or subjects of the hostile nation or government," 50 U.S.C. § 21 (2012).

47. PMG Records of Italian Civilian Internees, NACP.

48. Weglyn, *Years of Infamy*, 58–60.

49. Gardiner, *Pawns in a Triangle of Hate*, 17–18.

50. Ibid., 12–13.

51. Fox, *Fear Itself*, 227, 230. See also Fox, "The Deportation of Latin American Germans, 1941–47," 117, 121; Fox, *America's Invisible Gulag*, 89; Fox, *Homeland Insecurity*, 128–31, 143–45.

52. Friedman, *Nazis and Good Neighbors*, 4. This process violated the principles of Roosevelt's Good Neighbor policy under which the United States was not to interfere in the internal affairs of Latin American countries (ibid., 3).

53. Gardiner, *Pawns in a Triangle of Hate*, 25.

54. Weglyn, *Years of Infamy*, 62–63.

55. Gardiner, *Pawns in a Triangle of Hate*, 29.

56. See, generally, Saito, "Crossing the Border," 66–76.

57. Mangione, "Concentration Camps—American Style," 119. He also stated that camp commanders believed impoverished peasants were paid to act as substitutes for

"potentially dangerous" Germans and Japanese. Just as Mangione could not find any official verification of this, my review of the government files did not turn up any evidence of this.

58. Since the State Department wanted to bring the Latin Americans into the United States in an expedient way because of the national security situation, they did not undergo a process to obtain visas or passports beforehand. The INS had to take these individuals into custody even though they had not entered the United States under the ordinary terms of immigration law. Since these individuals had no visas or passports, it was very difficult for the commissioner of immigration to figure out a way to get them out of the country once the war was over. The intermediate solution before they could repatriate was to create a special category for them called "internees-at-large." Many former internees were placed into the custody of Deerfield Farms in southern New Jersey. Telephone Conference with Marian Smith, chief, Historical Research Branch, U.S. Citizenship & Immigration Services, October 25, 2013 (notes on file with author).

59. Gardiner, *Pawns in a Triangle of Hate*, 70.

60. Weglyn, *Years of Infamy*, 63.

61. Ibid., 29.

62. *Administrative History of the INS*, 300. Crystal City housed approximately 1,293 internees from Latin America and the West Indies (ibid., 304).

63. Ibid., 412.

64. Zachary A. Wilske, historian, Historical Research Branch, U.S. Citizenship & Immigration Services, e-mail message to author, December 4, 2012. Wilske explained that since these individuals had to officially remain "internees-at-large," even though they posed no threat to the United States, they were subjected to restrictions similar to those imposed on internee parolees (enemy aliens whose "loyalty was in doubt").

65. Gardiner, *Pawns in a Triangle of Hate*, 116, Table 8. Note that thirty-seven Italians remained in U.S. custody as of January 31, 1946 (ibid., 134, Table 9).

66. Executive Order No. 9066. The designation of the military areas was to "supercede the responsibilities and authority of the Attorney General under the said Proclamations in respect of such prohibited and restricted areas."

67. Ibid.

68. U.S. Congressional Research Service, *The Internment of German and Italian Aliens Compared with the Internment of Japanese Aliens in the United States during World War II*, by Peter B. Sheridan (hereafter cited as *Sheridan Report*), CRS-8.

69. Fox, "General John DeWitt and the Proposed Internment of German and Italian Aliens during World War II," 419.

70. U.S., Congress, House Select Committee Investigating National Defense Migration, *Preliminary Report and Recommendations on Problems of Evacuation of Citizens and Aliens From Military Areas* (hereafter cited as House Select Committee, *Preliminary Report*), 22.

71. Ibid., 24. Presumably the Tolan Committee was contemplating that "immediate families" would necessarily include American citizens, both naturalized and native born.

72. Ibid., 25.

73. See Fox, *Uncivil Liberties*, 227–28. The halting of Asian immigration, beginning with the Chinese Exclusion Act of 1882, had limited the number of Japanese in the United States at this time.

74. See Boston Public Library Interstate Migration/National Defense Migration Online Collections, http://www.bpl.org/online/govdocs/interstate_migration.htm (site discontinued), accessed on January 22, 2015.

75. Fox, *Uncivil Liberties*, 134.

76. U.S. Congress, House Select Committee Investigating National Defense Migration, *Hearings*, Part 29, 77th Cong., 2nd sess., http://archive.org/details/national defensem29unit, accessed on May 5, 2017 (hereafter cited as National Defense Migration, *Hearings*), 10966.

77. Testimony of Angelo J. Rossi, San Francisco, California, February 21, 1942, National Defense Migration, *Hearings*, Part 29, 77th Cong., 2nd sess., 10967, 10968, 10969.

78. Testimony of Ottorino Ronchi, San Francisco, California, February 21, 1942, National Defense Migration *Hearings*, Part 29, 77th Cong., 2nd sess., 11057.

79. Corsi, "Italian Immigrants and Their Children," 105.

80. Diggins, *Mussolini and Fascism*, 400n4.

81. Testimony of Mr. Tramutolo, San Francisco, California, February 23, 1942, National Defense Migration, *Hearings*, Part 29, 77th Cong., 2nd sess., 11128.

82. Fox, *Uncivil Liberties*, 85.

83. An Appeal in Behalf of Anti-Fascist Aliens by Charles H. Tutt, Secretary, San Francisco Chapter, Mazzini Society, San Francisco, California, February 23, 1942, National Defense Migration, *Hearings*, Part 29, 77th Cong., 2nd sess., 11267–68. The aims of the Mazzini Society were identified as follows: "To spread democratic education among the population of Italians and those of Italian origin in the United States; cooperate with the nations fighting for the victory of the democratic ideals in the struggle against naziism and fascism; to keep the American public informed about the true conditions in Italy; to strengthen the faith of the American people in the future of a free Italy." Testimony of Attilio Boffa, of the Mazzini Society, Los Angeles, California, March 6, 7, and 12, 1942, National Defense Migration, *Hearings*, Part 31, 77th Cong., 2nd sess., http://archive.org/details/nationaldefensem31unit, accessed on May 5, 2017, 11759–60. But see Issel, *For Both Cross and Flag*, 147, for evidence that the Mazzini Society in San Francisco was mostly anti-clerical and Communist.

84. Testimony of Charles H. Tutt, San Francisco, California, February 23, 1942, National Defense Migration *Hearings*, Part 29, 77th Cong., 2nd sess., 11267–68.

85. Ibid., 11268.

86. Testimony of Luciano Maniscalo, San Francisco, California, February 23, 1942, National Defense Migration *Hearings*, Part 29, 77th Cong., 2nd sess., 11121–23.

87. Testimony of Paul Armstrong, Assistant District Director, Immigration and Naturalization Service, United States Department of Justice, San Francisco, California, March 12, 1942, National Defense Migration *Hearings*, Part 31, 77th Cong., 2nd sess., 11901.

88. House Select Committee, *Preliminary Report*, 22.

89. Memorandum of Conversation between Alfred Jaretzki Jr., and Captains J. Perry, J. Lansdale, and N. Stepanovich, April 8, 1942, in Daniels, *American Concentration Camps*, vol. 4. Assistant Secretary of War John McCloy had brought Jaretzki in to help with the situation of the German and Italian aliens. U.S. Commission on Wartime Relocation and Internment of Civilians, *Personal Justice Denied*, 287.

90. Memorandum of Interview of Carmelo Zito, taken by Alfred Jaretzki Jr., April 10, 1942, in Daniels, *American Concentration Camps*, vol. 4.

91. Memorandum of Conversation between Alfred Jaretzki Jr., and General De-Witt, Col. McGill, and Capt. Moffitt, April 11, 1942, in Daniels, *American Concentration Camps*, vol. 4.

92. See Goldstein, *Political Repression in Modern America*, 256. The committee was tasked with investigating the Communist Party, fascist organizations, the Nazi bund, and any other organization that it believed might affect California's defense effort or state agencies.

93. Testimony of Carmelo Zito before Assembly Fact Finding Committee on Un-American Activities in California: Investigation into Matters Pertaining to Un-American and Subversive Activities, May 25, 1942 (hereafter cited as Testimony of Carmelo Zito before California Assembly Fact Finding Committee), 3347, http://www.internmentarchives.com/showdoc.php?docid=00406&search_id=77939&pagenum=6, accessed May 5, 2017.

94. Ibid., 3344–77, http://www.internmentarchives.com/showdoc.php?docid=00406&search_id=77939&pagenum=3, accessed May 5, 2017.

95. Testimony of Angelo Rossi before California Assembly Fact Finding Committee, 3455, generally 3451–71, http://www.internmentarchives.com/showdoc.php?docid=00407&search_id=77940&pagenum=2, accessed on May 3, 2017. See Issel, *For Both Cross and Flag*, for a discussion of the political rivalries between Rossi, Sylvester Andriano (San Francisco attorney, supervisor, and police commissioner under Rossi who also testified before the Tenney Committee) and Carmelo Zito, a socialist. Issel writes that media coverage of the hearings "dramatized . . . the long-time political and religious rivalries between Catholics and anti-Catholics in the Italian American community and between Catholic anti-Communists and their Communist Party competitors" (ibid., 146).

96. Testimony of Gilbert Tuoni before Assembly Fact Finding Committee on Un-American Activities in California: Investigation into Matters Pertaining to Un-American and Subversive Activities, May 26–27, 1942, 3662–71, http://www.internmentarchives.com/showdoc.php?docid=00408&search_id=77941&pagenum=2, accessed May 5, 2017.

97. Testimony of Angelo Rossi before California Assembly Fact Finding Committee, 3468. In response to a question as to whether he "ever made a specific direct denunciation against Mussolini," Rossi responded: "I couldn't recall if I did or not, but I consider him an enemy of this country," http://www.internmentarchives.com/showdoc.php?docid=00407&search_id=77940&pagenum=19, accessed May 3, 2017.

98. See Testimony of Carmelo Zito before California Assembly Fact Finding Committee, 3372, http://www.internmentarchives.com/showdoc.php?docid=00406&search_id=77942&pagenum=31, accessed May 5, 2017.

99. House Select Committee, *Fourth Interim Report*, 31, citing its *Preliminary Report*, 24.

100. Memorandum, President Franklin D. Roosevelt to Secretary of War, May 5, 1942, in Daniels, *American Concentration Camps*, vol. 5.

101. Memorandum, Francis Biddle to the President, April 9, 1942, in Daniels, *American Concentration Camps*, vol. 4.

102. Memorandum, President Franklin D. Roosevelt to Secretary of War, May 5, 1942, in Daniels, *American Concentration Camps*, vol. 5.

103. Ibid.

104. Stimson Diaries, reel 7, vol. 39, p. 17. May 15, 1942.

105. Conn, Engelman, and Fairchild, *Guarding the United States and its Outposts*, 146.

106. Stimson Diaries, reel 7, vol. 39, p. 17. May 15, 1942.

107. Ngai, *Impossible Subjects*, 175–76.

108. Grodzins, *Americans Betrayed*, 170–71.

109. Robinson, *A Tragedy of Democracy*, 72.

110. U.S. Commission on Wartime Relocation and Internment of Civilians, *Personal Justice Denied*, 287. Note, however, that the government was cognizant that if Germans and Italians were relocated en masse, they would have to be in relocation camps since residents of the heartland would not tolerate the aliens' integration into Midwest communities. See page 286, citing telephone conversation, Jaretzki to Bendetsen, April 27, 1942, National Archives and Records Service, RG 338 (CWRIC 5226–32).

111. Grodzins, *Americans Betrayed*, 172–73.

112. Persico, *Roosevelt's Secret War*, 169.

113. Memorandum, D. R. VanSickler, Adjutant General, December 11, 1941, to the Commanding General, Western Defense Command, "Supplementary Directions for Western Defense Command," Records of the Office of the Provost Marshal General, Subject Correspondence, Executive Division, Legal Office, 1942–1945, Folder "Executive Order 9066," Box 10, Record Group 389; National Archives at College Park (hereafter cited as PMG Legal Correspondence, NACP).

114. Memorandum, Mark W. Clark, Brigadier General, G.S.C., Deputy Chief of Staff, to the Adjutant General (Thru Secretary, General Staff), "Eastern and Western Defense Commands," January 29, 1942, 2, PMG Legal Correspondence, NACP (hereafter cited as Eastern and Western Defense Commands Memo). Note that on December 24, 1941, the defense of the Gulf Coast from Florida westward came under the direction of the Southern Defense Command, with its own small, separate defense command staff. Conn, Engelman, and Fairchild, *Guarding the United States and its Outposts*, 95.

115. Conn, Engelman, and Fairchild, *Guarding the United States and its Outposts*, 101.

116. Eastern and Western Defense Commands Memo, 2.

117. Conn, Engelman, and Fairchild, *Guarding the United States and its Outposts*, 82.

118. Stimson Diaries, reel 7, vol. 37, p. 85. February 3, 1942.

119. Four defense commands were established in the United States prior to America's entry into World War II: Western, Eastern, Central, and Southern. It is significant to note that the commanders of the Eastern and Southern Defense Commands

were not given the authority to protect against sabotage or other internal threats in their respective regions, but were expected to rely upon troops assigned by the War Department. Draft Memorandum, Maj. J. W. Brabner-Smith to the Provost Marshal General, "Prescribing military areas under Executive Order 9066 for the purpose of protection against sabotage and internal threats," 12–26–42, 2, PMG Legal Correspondence, NACP (hereafter cited as Draft Memorandum Prescribing Military Areas). The commander of the Central Defense Command had authority for the security of the Sault Sainte Marie Locks and Canal. Draft Memorandum Prescribing Military Areas, citing Instructions of March 18, 1942, "Defense of Continental United States," par. 8.

120. *DOJ Report*, 18–19.

121. Grodzins, *Americans Betrayed*, 241, referring to Department of Justice, press releases, January 29, 31, and February 2, 4, and 7, 1942. Grodzins explained that most areas were circles of 1,000-feet radii or rectangles of several city blocks.

122. See *DOJ Report*, 25.

123. See Muller, "*Hirabayashi* and the Invasion Evasion," 1337. Muller presents archival evidence that top army and navy officials neither anticipated nor prepared for a Japanese invasion of California, Oregon, or Washington during the crucial early months of 1942.

124. *DOJ Report*, 9.

125. Telephone conference between Gen. John DeWitt and Maj. Bendetson, Jan. 31, 1942 (transcribed by Daisy B. Gallagher), in Daniels, *American Concentration Camps*, vol. 2.

126. Ibid.

127. See *DOJ Report*, v, 19, 26.

128. See Persico, *Roosevelt's Secret War*, 169, who says that "over 11,000 American residents of German ancestry were held in custody or moved inland during the war." The Germans aliens relocated were on the West Coast. Fox, *Uncivil Liberties*, xiii-xvii.

129. Telephone conference between Major Bendetson and General DeWitt, February 3, 1942 (transcribed by H. Pohlman), in Daniels, *American Concentration Camps*, vol. 2.

130. *DOJ Report*, 9–10, 13, 26, and footnote 88.

131. U.S. Commission on Wartime Relocation and Internment of Civilians, *Personal Justice Denied*, 103–4, citing J. L. DeWitt, *Final Report, Japanese Evacuation from the West Coast, 1942* (Washington, DC: U.S. Government Printing Office, 1943), 107–9.

132. *DOJ Report*, 10.

133. Press release, March 2, 1942, in Daniels, *American Concentration Camps*, vol. 3.

134. *DOJ Report*, 10, citing John McCloy, Assistant Secretary of War, to Lt. General DeWitt, July 20, 1942, in "Individual Exclusion Order Procedure Correspondence."

135. *DOJ Report*, 10–11, citing Western Defense Command, "Individual Exclusion Program of Non-Japanese," *Supplemental Report on Civilian Controls Exercised by Western Defense Command*, January 1947, 839–41.

136. *DOJ Report*, 11, citing Headquarters Western Defense Command and Fourth Army, Individual Exclusion Hearing Board, Notification of Hearing, Form Letter.

137. de Guttadauro, Angelo, U.S. Army Retired Colonel Angelo, to author, July 16, 2008, in the author's possession.

138. *DOJ Report*, 11–12; Colonel Angelo de Guttadauro, "Exclusion Is a Four-Letter Word."

139. See, for example, Ochikubo v. Bonesteel et al., Yamamoto et al. v. SAME, 60 F. Supp. 916 (S.D. Cal. 1945) (Japanese Americans could not successfully challenge exclusion order from Military Area No. 1 and the California portion of Military Area No. 2 since the court found that the commanding officer of the Western Defense Command had power only to create military areas and to make exclusion orders based on military necessity, and that enforcement of orders had to be through criminal prosecution); Schueller v. Drum, 51 F. Supp. 383 (E.D. Pa. 1943) (German restaurant proprietress and naturalized U.S. citizen successfully challenged individual exclusion order from Eastern Military Area where court found that in place where no emergency existed since people pursued normal activities of civilian life, her involvement in German clubs did not warrant denial of right to due process of law); Ebel v. Drum, 53 F. Supp. 189 (D. Mass. 1943) (in considering time and place of exclusion order issued to German cabinetmaker, a naturalized U.S. citizen, on basis that he was "dangerous to the national defense," court determined that exclusion from Eastern Military Area was "an excessive exercise of authority and invalid" since there was no degree of danger necessitating "drastic restriction" of plaintiff's individual liberty).

140. See *Ochikubo*, 60 F. Supp. at 921, where the court said that as of late 1944, "between 9,000 and 10,000 individual exclusion orders had been issued by the Western Defense Command of which something less than a thousand applied to non-Japanese." Footnote 16 explains: "General Wilbur desired not to be exact in his figures for obvious security reasons."

141. *DOJ Report*, 12, citing Western Defense Command, "Individual Exclusion Program of Non-Japanese," *Supplemental Report on Civilian Controls Exercised by Western Defense Command*.

142. *DOJ Report*, see Appendix E.1.

143. *Sheridan Report*, CRS-9; see also U.S. Commission on Wartime Relocation and Internment of Civilians, *Personal Justice Denied*, 288.

144. *DOJ Report*, 13, citing Alien Enemy Control Unit, *Preliminary Report on Study of Individual Exclusion Order Cases*, August, 1943, 2–3.

145. Fox, *Uncivil Liberties*, "Foreword to the Revised Edition," June 2002.

146. Stimson Diaries, reel 8, vol. 43, p. 41. May 13, 1943. The case of San Francisco lawyer Sylvester Andriano is an instance where the Justice Department decided not to prosecute. See Issel, "'Still Potentially Dangerous in Some Quarters,'" 265; see also DiStasi, *Branded*, 214–22, for a discussion of the Andriano case.

147. Compare *Ochikubo*, 60 F. Supp. 916 (S.D. CA 1945); Schueller v. Drum, 51 F. Supp. 383 (E.D. Penn. 1943); Ebel v. Drum, 53 F. Supp. 189 (D. Mass. 1943).

148. Telephone conference between Gen. DeWitt and Asst. Sec. of War McCloy, Feb. 3, 1942, in which DeWitt read a memorandum regarding a meeting at California Governor Culbert Olson's office that he had with the following: Thomas G. Clark of the Office of the Attorney General; G. Murray Thompson of the Department of Agriculture from Washington; William Cecil, the Director of Agriculture of the State of California; Col. Donald A. Stroh, General Staff Corps Assistant G-2, and Col. J. F. Watson, Judge Advocate, in Daniels, *American Concentration Camps*, vol. 2.

149. Letter, Sec. of War Henry Stimson to Gen. John DeWitt, February 20, 1942, enclosing Executive Order 9066, in Daniels, *American Concentration Camps*, vol. 3.

150. Press release regarding General DeWitt's plans for evacuation, March 2, 1942, in Daniels, *American Concentration Camps*, vol. 3.

151. *Sheridan Report*, CRS-4. An exemption was carved out for those who had begun the naturalization process because West Coast officials of the INS testified that many offices were over a year behind in processing applications. House Select Committee, *Preliminary Report*, 22.

152. Telephone conference between Gen. DeWitt and Asst. Sec. of War McCloy, Feb. 3, 1942 (transcribed by Helen Pohlman), in Daniels, *American Concentration Camps*, vol. 2.

153. Memorandum from Meeting of Joint Evacuation Board, February 25, 1942, in Daniels, *American Concentration Camps*, vol. 3. The Joint Evacuation Board had representatives from the following organizations: War Department, Navy Department, American Red Cross, U.S. Office of Education, Office of Civilian Defense, U.S. Public Health Service, U.S. Department of Labor, Federal Security Agency, and Division of Defense Housing Coordination, Executive Office of the President.

154. Starr, *Embattled Dreams*, 92. Starr refers to the "official history of the evacuation" issued by the Center of Military History of the United States Army portraying DeWitt as influenced by the following political leaders in his decision to intern Japanese and Japanese Americans: Governor Culbert Olson, Attorney General Earl Warren, San Francisco Mayor Angelo Rossi, Los Angeles Mayor Fletcher Bowron, Senators Hiram Johnson and Sheridan Downey, and the California House of Representatives. On a national level, the opinion of the California politicians was seconded by Secretary of War Henry Stimson, the columnists Walter Lippmann and Westbrook Pegler, as well as New York Mayor Fiorello La Guardia.

155. Radio address by Governor Culbert L. Olson, Feb. 4, 1942, in Daniels, *American Concentration Camps*, vol. 2.

156. Grodzins, *Americans Betrayed*, 96, citing "Minutes," Meeting of California Joint Immigration Committee, February 7, 1942, 37–38.

157. Sec. of War Henry Stimson to Gen. John DeWitt, February 20, 1942, enclosing Executive Order 9066, in Daniels, *American Concentration Camps*, vol. 3.

158. Telephone conversation between Gen. DeWitt and Col. Bendetson, February 20, 1942, in Daniels, *American Concentration Camps*, vol. 3; see also Address by Tom C. Clark, Chief, Wartime Civilian Control Administration Western Defense Command, Before the Los Angeles Advertising Club, Biltmore Hotel, March 17, 1942, in Daniels, *American Concentration Camps*, vol. 3. The "A strip" of Military Area No. 1, from which DeWitt indicated he would order the removal of all German and Italian aliens and all Japanese and Japanese Americans, extended from Canada to San Diego and was some fifty miles wide in parts (Address by Tom C. Clark).

159. Memorandum from Meeting of Joint Evacuation Board, February 25, 1942, in Daniels, *American Concentration Camps*, vol. 3.

160. W. J. Cecil, Director of State of California Department of Agriculture, to Lieutenant-Colonel William A. Boekel, Office of the Provost Marshall [*sic*], Head-

quarters Western Defense Command and Fourth Army, March 18, 1942, in Daniels, *American Concentration Camps*, vol. 3.

161. John Molinari, interview by Stephen Fox, San Francisco, California, February 6, 1987, in Fox, *Uncivil Liberties*, 142. Molinari said that this group would have supported aliens as well as citizens "because the aliens—so many of them never got around to getting citizenship—had been here for thirty, forty, fifty years" (ibid., 17).

162. See *DOJ Report*, v.

163. Dunn, "Mala Notte," 103–4.

164. Nida Vanni, interview by Stephen Fox, Arcata, California, July 7, 1986, in Fox, *Uncivil Liberties*, 79.

165. Frank Buccellato, interview by Stephen Fox, Pittsburg, California, February 3, 1987, in Fox, *Uncivil Liberties*, 135–36.

166. Memorandum For The President (Draft), Subject: East Coast Military Areas, April 14, 1942, in Daniels, *American Concentration Camps*, vol. 4; see Text of General Drum's Statement, April 27, 1942, in House Select Committee, *Fourth Interim Report*, 35–36.

167. Memorandum of Conversation at Fort Jay among General Drum, General Ward, Colonel Howz, and Colonel (?) of G-2, April 20, 1942, in Daniels, *American Concentration Camps*, vol. 4.

168. Text of General Drum's Statement, April 27, 1942, in House Select Committee, *Fourth Interim Report*, 36.

169. U.S. Commission on Wartime Relocation and Internment of Civilians, *Personal Justice Denied*, 288.

170. Memorandum of Conversation at Fort Jay among General Drum, General Ward, Colonel Howz, and Colonel (?) of G-2, April 20, 1942, in Daniels, *American Concentration Camps*, vol. 4.

171. Stimson Diaries, reel 7, vol. 38, pp. 116–17. April 15, 1942. Stimson told Roosevelt that "Drum couldn't do anything of that sort without my authority and I couldn't authorize him to do it without telling the President." Stimson Diaries, reel 7, vol. 39, p. 17. May 15, 1942.

172. *DOJ Report*, v, 25. One was a large area that spanned the entire coastline of California from the Oregon border south to fifty miles north of Los Angeles, extending inland from thirty to 150 miles. Other restricted areas surrounded hydroelectric generating plants. *DOJ Report*, 19–20.

173. *DOJ Report*, 23. The confiscation of such contraband, authorized by Proclamation 2527, included firearms, weapons, ammunition, bombs, explosives, short-wave radio receiving sets, transmitting sets, signal devices, codes or ciphers, cameras, and documents of military facilities, and other things. See Presidential Proclamation No. 2527, incorporating provisions from Presidential Proclamation No. 2525 (pertaining to Japanese).

174. *DOJ Report*, 24. The Report states that 1,907 searches in these four states resulted in 1,077 confiscations of contraband.

175. See "U.S. Not Inclined to Return Contraband to Enemy Aliens," 5.

176. Benito Vanni, interview by Stephen Fox, Daly City, California, June 24, 1987, in Fox, *Uncivil Liberties*, 74–75.

177. Harry Massagli, interview by Stephen Fox, Eureka, California, July 13, 1987, in Fox, *Uncivil Liberties*, 75–76.

178. Interview of Angela Carroccia Basile, Bristol, Connecticut, December 28, 2012 (notes on file with author). Basile explained that her father, Joseph Carroccia, may have come to the government's attention because he made nine trips back and forth to Italy and even served briefly in the Italian army on one of his return trips.

179. DiStasi, "A Fish Story," 68; DiStasi, *Branded*, 254–59.

180. John Molinari, interview by Stephen Fox, San Francisco, California, February 6, 1987, in Fox, *Uncivil Liberties*, 17.

181. DiStasi, "A Fish Story," 65.

182. *DOJ Report*, 27–28.

183. *DOJ Report*, 34.

184. Salvatore Ferrante, interview by Stephen Fox, Monterey, California, May 14, 1987, in Fox, *Uncivil Liberties*, 101.

185. Giuseppe Spadaro, interview by Stephen Fox, Monterey, California, January 9, 1988, in Fox, *Uncivil Liberties*, 102–3.

186. DiStasi, "A Fish Story," 83.

187. "Explains Benefits to Italian Aliens," 27. According to my data set, 231 had received internment orders by this date.

188. Diggins, *Mussolini and Fascism*, 400.

189. Scherini, "When Italian Americans Were 'Enemy Aliens,'" 21.

190. Annual Report of the Attorney General of the United States for the Fiscal Year Ended June 30, 1943, 10. The report stated that of a total of 599,111 Italian aliens, excluding seamen, 653 had undergone a hearing before alien enemy hearing boards, of which 232 had received internment orders and 265 were placed on parole.

191. Biddle, *In Brief Authority*, 229.

192. See Tintori, "New Discoveries, Old Prejudices," 245–50, for an account of the influence of Joseph Facci, an Italian advisor to the Office of Facts and Figures, in bringing about this policy.

193. Biddle, *In Brief Authority*, 229. Although I could find no evidence of it in my research, another trusted Italian American in a strategic position, whom Biddle mentions in his biography, and who might have had influence over members of Roosevelt's administration with respect to the treatment of Italians, was Ernest Cuneo, a liaison officer with the Office of Strategic Services in Italy (ibid., 228).

194. Francis Biddle quoted in transcript of NBC radio show "Fighting America," October 24, 1942, 2, Material on Attorney General Biddle's Announcement re. Italians in U.S., October 19, 1942, Box 1, Series I, Ugo Carusi Papers; Franklin D. Roosevelt Presidential Library.

195. Ibid., 3.

196. Ibid.

Chapter Three

1. Before I relate the stories of individuals who underwent alien enemy hearings in this chapter and the experiences of internees in the camps in the next chapter, I would like to explain my reason for using the actual names of the individuals whose cases I examine. I weighed the benefits of alternative editorial approaches of replacing the names with pseudonyms or abbreviations out of consideration for the bewilderment and shame that families felt during and after the events I describe. It is my desire not to tarnish anyone's family history with stories of suspicions of disloyalty from over seventy-five years ago, even though they are recorded in publicly accessible archives. But since my analysis shows that in most instances the government was chasing unreliable evidence about the Fascist leanings of individuals, and that flaws in the legal process, as acknowledged by the Justice Department, resulted in the internment of many people who were not harmful to the United States, I decided to use the internees' real names. I believe that concealing the identity of these individuals might only serve to perpetuate the mystery surrounding the process of selective internment. By providing as complete a story as I could uncover of the process and the experiences of the internees who were not given the opportunity to defend against baseless suspicions, my hope is to dispel the mystery and to erase whatever shameful mark internment has left on the memories of the internees' descendants.

2. See, for example, Allesandro Fabbri to Mr. Matthias Correa, U.S. District Attorney, August 26, 1942, in which he wrote: "Since I was never told the reason of my present internment, I can only guess at its causes. It is, at all times, difficult to fence against the unknown." Folder of Allesandro Fabbri, Box 8, PMG Records of Italian Civilian Internees, NACP. See also Mario Ricciardelli to Hon. Edward J. Ennis, September 14, 1942, stating: "Since my apprehension as an alien of enemy nationality nine months ago, I have honestly surveyed my past life during my long residence in this Country, in order to find out what activity or action of mine could have been the cause of my internment here." Folder of Mario Ricciardelli, Box 17, PMG Records of Italian Civilian Internees, NACP.

3. See, for example, File of Augusto Charles Mauro, File No. 146–13–2–52–476, Box 495, DOJ Litigation Files, NACP, where a special hearing board recommended release after about a year because Mauro had become "entirely sympathetic with the United States." The attorney general decided to parole him instead and released him eight months later after he stated in an interview that he hoped the United States would win the war by defeating the Axis powers.

4. See *Senate Intelligence Report*, 419–20. Other statutory tools were the Foreign Agents Registration Act, Pub. L. No. 75–583, 52 Stat. 631 (1938) and the Voorhis Act of 1940, Pub. L. No. 76–870, 54 Stat. 1201 (1940), requiring organizations with foreign ties advocating the violent overthrow of the government to formally register.

5. *Administrative History of the INS*, 382.

6. See Convention relative to the Treatment of Prisoners of War, Geneva, July 27, 1929 (hereafter cited as 1929 Geneva Convention), chapter 3, part 3. Article 62 of the 1929 Geneva Convention provides the right to an attorney and Article 64 the right of appeal, http://www.icrc.org/ihl.nsf/INTRO/305?OpenDocument, accessed on April 17, 2017.

7. See International Committee of the Red Cross, *Report on Its Activities During the Second World War*, 574–75.

8. Moloney, *National Insecurities*, 10.

9. Ibid., 199. Prior to 1940, the Department of Labor housed the Board of Review for deportation hearings and the agency for regulating immigration. The assignment of the INS to the Justice Department in 1940 indicates increasing security concerns surrounding illegal immigration (ibid., 16).

10. U.S. Department of Labor, Secretary of Labor's Committee on Administrative Procedure, *The Immigration and Naturalization Service* (hereafter cited as *Labor Committee Report*), 26. The purpose of the report was to explain the present state of exclusion and deportation hearings and to suggest methods for improving the fairness of such hearings.

11. Ibid.

12. Ibid., 27; Moloney, *National Insecurities*, 199.

13. *Labor Committee Report*, 27.

14. U.S. Commission on Wartime Relocation and Internment of Civilians, *Personal Justice Denied*, 285.

15. See *Labor Committee Report*, 26–27. For an interpretation of how courts should draw the line between regulatory deportation procedures and punitive ones requiring constitutional protections like those afforded alleged criminals, see Kanstroom, *Deportation Nation*.

16. FBI Reports re. Biagio Farese, with aliases Biagio Faresa and Blaise Farese, 1–14–42 and 1–16–42, Farese's A-File.

17. Telegram, U.S. Congressman Thomas A. Flaherty to Edward J. Shaughnessey, Deputy Assistant, Department of Immigration and Naturalization, August 28, 1940, Farese's A-File.

18. FBI Report re. Biagio Farese, 1–14–42, Farese's A-File.

19. Transcript of Deportation Hearing in the case of Biagio Farese, May 14, 1941, Farese's A-File.

20. Ibid., and FBI Report re. Biagio Farese, 1–14–42, Farese's A-File. See FBI Report re. Biagio Farese, 2–20–42, Farese's A-File, citing Immigration Act and Regulations, issued June 1937 by the Minister of Mines and Resources, Ottawa, Canada, confirming that Canadian domicile was lost in Farese's situation: "When any citizen of Canada who is a British subject by naturalization or any British subject not born in Canada having a Canadian domicile shall have resided for one year outside of Canada, he shall be presumed to have lost Canadian domicile and shall cease to be a Canadian citizen."

21. Transcript of Deportation Hearing in the case of Biagio Farese, October 22, 1941, Farese's A-File.

22. FBI Report re. Biagio Farese, 1–14–42, Farese's A-File.

23. Folder of Biagio Farese, Box 8, PMG Records of Italian Civilian Internees, NACP.

24. FBI Report, 1–14–42 re. Biagio Farese, Farese's A-File.

25. FBI Report, 1–16–42 re. Biagio Farese, Farese's A-File; see Transcript of Deportation Hearing in the case of Biagio Farese, May 14, 1941, and Transcript of Deportation Hearing in the case of Biagio Farese, October 22, 1941, Farese's A-File.

26. Opinion of U.S. Department of Justice Board of Immigration Appeals in re. Biagio Farese, August 28, 1943, Farese's A-File.

27. Handwritten notation of attorney general's agreement on Memorandum, Thomas G. Finucane, Chairman, U.S. Department of Justice Board of Immigration Appeals, to the Attorney General, April 15, 1944, Farese's A-File.

28. See A. E. Hanney, Acting Chief, Detention and Deportation Section, Ellis Island, to Mr. Edward J. Ennis, May 25, 1944, Farese's A-File.

29. Memorandum, Edward J. Ennis to Mr. W. F. Kelly, Assistant Commissioner for Alien Control, August 26, 1944, Farese's A-File; Parolee Report of George S. Ader, District Parole Officer, December 1, 1944, Farese's A-File.

30. Folder of Biagio Farese, Box 8, PMG Records of Italian Civilian Internees, NACP.

31. Opinion of the Presiding Inspector in re. Biagio Farese, July 22, 1947, Farese's A-File.

32. Marian Smith, chief, Historical Research Branch, U.S. Citizenship and Immigration Services, e-mail message to author, June 7, 2013, citing Certificate No. 6957742 and Ancestry.com, *Social Security Death Index*.

33. Francis Biddle, Attorney General, Department of Justice "Instructions To Alien Enemy Hearing Boards," December 13, 1941, 1, Griswold Papers, Box 73, Folder 8. Note that some districts, such as the Southern District Court of New York, had more than one hearing board due to the large numbers of aliens in the district. "Rulings on Aliens Speeded by Biddle." See also Annual Report of the Attorney General of the United States for the Fiscal Year Ended June 30, 1941, 14–15. The report states that there were 100 alien enemy hearing boards.

34. Francis Biddle, "Instructions To Alien Enemy Hearing Boards," December 13, 1941, 1, Griswold Papers, Box 73, Folder 8. Note that it was more common to see Assistant U.S. Attorneys than U.S. Attorneys in the transcripts of the hearings that I viewed.

35. "Corsi Heads Board on Enemy Aliens," 11. For example, in the Federal District of Connecticut, the hearing board members were James L. McConnaughy, president of Wesleyan University; Harry Shulman, professor at Yale Law School; Francis S. Murphy, publisher of The *Hartford Times*; and George C. Long Jr., president of the Phoenix Fire Insurance Company of Hartford.

36. U.S. Commission on Wartime Relocation and Internment of Civilians, *Personal Justice Denied*, 285.

37. Telegram, Francis Biddle to Erwin Griswold, Harvard Law School, December 17, 1941, Griswold Papers, Box 73, Folder 8.

38. "General Instructions in re: Alien Enemy Cases" to United States Attorneys, December 15, 1941, Corsi Papers, Box 33, Folder "ACTIVITIES Alien Enemy Hearing Board Correspondence to cases 7 May 1941 to 11 Feb. 1944."

39. Francis Biddle, "Instructions To Alien Enemy Hearing Boards," Griswold Papers, Box 73, Folder 8.

40. Ibid.

41. Biddle, *In Brief Authority*, 208.

42. Francis Biddle, "Instructions To Alien Enemy Hearing Boards," December 13, 1941, 2, Griswold Papers, Box 73, Folder 8. Note that a person on parole had to sever

ties with any organizations that fostered the "spirit, culture, political or social ideas of any nation other than the United States" and could not communicate with any person in a foreign country. U.S. Attorney file No. M 68, Recommendation of Conditions of Parole by Alien Enemy Hearing Board, Kelley Papers, Box 140, Folder 140.2.

43. See U.S. Commission on Wartime Relocation and Internment of Civilians, *Personal Justice Denied*, 285.

44. Department of Justice Release to Morning Papers, June 3, 1942, American Committee for Protection of Foreign Born Records, Box 17, Folder 2 ("Enemy Aliens, 1942–1945"). The statistics for parole and release were approximately 33 percent and 23 percent respectively.

45. Testimony of Dr. W. G. Everson, Portland, Oregon, February 26, 1942, National Defense Migration, *Hearings*, Part 30, 77th Cong., 2nd sess., http://archive.org/details /nationaldefensem30unit, accessed on May 1, 2017, 11378–79.

46. House Select Committee, *Preliminary Report*, 14.

47. Francis Biddle, Attorney General, Department of Justice, "Circular 3616, Supplement No. 1, Instructions To Alien Enemy Hearing Boards," January 7, 1942, Griswold Papers, Box 73, Folder 8 (hereafter cited as Francis Biddle, Circular 3616, Supplement No. 1); see Hoover, "Alien Enemy Control," 398, stating that an alien enemy arrested under 50 U.S.C. § 21 cannot defend himself on the ground that he was deprived of liberty without due process of law, citing Minotto v. Bradley, 252 F. 600 (D.C. Ill. 1918).

48. Cole, "The New McCarthyism," 15. Cole says: "It represents the ultimate form of administrative control over potential threats" (ibid.).

49. Francis Biddle, "Circular 3616, Supplement No. 1.

50. *DOJ Report*, 7, citing Thomas D. McDermott, "Aliens of Enemy Nationality," INS Training Lecture (May 13, 1943), 28–29.

51. Sidak, "War, Liberty, and Enemy Aliens," 1402. Sidak explains that "the president is authorized by statute to arrest, detain, and deport enemy aliens according to rules of his own making—subject . . . to virtually no check from the courts through judicial review" (ibid., 1408).

52. Chae Chan Ping v. United States, 130 U.S. 581 (1889) (upholding the validity of the Chinese Exclusion Act of 1888, prohibiting Chinese laborers who had departed before the passage of the act from entering the United States, as falling within Congress's power to exclude foreigners if deemed within the interests of security and protection of the country).

53. Parker, *The Constitution*, 27–28. For a comprehensive study of changing conceptions of citizenship and alienage from the colonial period to the end of the twentieth century, see Parker, *Making Foreigners*.

54. Yick Wo v. Hopkins, 118 U.S. 356 (1886) (law concerning laundry businesses that was facially race-neutral but administered in a prejudicial manner found to violate the Equal Protection Clause of the Fourteenth Amendment, as equally applied to aliens); United States v. Wong Kim Ark, 169 U.S. 649 (1898) (holding that all native-born Chinese would be U.S. citizens under the Fourteenth Amendment's birthright clause).

55. See Fong Yue Ting v. United States, 149 U.S. 698 (1893). In this case, involving the validity of summary procedure before judicial officers for aliens with an established domicile, the Supreme Court indicated that such aliens are not entitled to a judicial hearing on an issue of exclusion or expulsion. Compare Wong Wing v. United States, 163 U.S. 228 (1896), finding that "imprisonment at hard labor" of Chinese national illegally in the United States could not be imposed without a judicial trial.

56. The Japanese Immigrant Case, Yamataya v. Fisher, 189 U.S. 86 (1903) (finding due process required in the context of deportation, though procedural defects, such as the fact that the investigation was conducted in English, which alien did not understand, and she was not represented by counsel, did not make the hearing constitutionally deficient).

57. Parker, *The Constitution*, 29.

58. *Labor Committee Report*, 46.

59. *Labor Committee Report*, 45. The Committee on Administrative Procedure pointed to Lloyd Sabaudo Societa v. Elting, 287 U.S. 329 (1932), as signaling a change in judicial doctrine from earlier cases. In that case, the Supreme Court held that courts may determine whether administrative action of the Secretary of Labor is within statutory authority, whether there is evidence to support the determination, and whether the procedure satisfies standards of fairness and reasonableness.

60. Francis Biddle, Attorney General, "Circular 3616, Supplement No. 2, Instructions To Alien Enemy Hearing Boards," January 9, 1942, 1, Griswold Papers, Box 73, Folder 8 (hereafter cited as Francis Biddle, Circular 3616, Supplement No. 2).

61. Compare Muller, *American Inquisition*, 39–40, in which Muller discusses the attitudes and agency pressures that came to bear upon the approaches of various hearing boards adjudicating the loyalty of Japanese Americans.

62. My research of the papers of hearing board members in regions of the country outside the Northeast uncovered very little information from which to draw conclusions. The alien enemy board minutes relating to one Italian alien who went before the Alien Enemy Hearing Board for the Northern District of California contain testimony from an FBI special agent, a U.S. Attorney, an INS Bureau representative, and the alien himself. The board unanimously recommended internment "because of his previous associations and his desperate financial condition." Alien Enemy Board minutes, 1942 January 2, Marshall Dill papers and scrapbooks, MS 3357, California Historical Society. In an effort to get a wider sampling of hearing boards, I researched the John C. Fitzgerald Papers in University Archives and Special Collections at Loyola University Chicago concerning Fitzgerald's service on the Alien Enemy Hearing Board in Chicago when that university's law school, where he was dean, closed during World War II. I also researched the Frank E. Holman Papers at the University of Washington Libraries Special Collections concerning Holman's service as chairman of the Alien Enemy Hearing Board for the Western District of Washington and as a member of the National Panel of Alien Enemy Hearing Boards. Unfortunately, I discovered that these archival sources do not contain any transcripts of hearings or reports pertaining to Italian aliens indicating the kinds of questions posed by the board or impressions formed.

63. Scherini, "When Italian Americans Were 'Enemy Aliens,'" 25–26. Scherini did not cite the army report that she referenced, but it is likely that of the Western Defense Command. See U.S. Commission on Wartime Relocation and Internment of Civilians, *Personal Justice Denied*, 286–87, citing Western Defense Command, *Supplemental Report on Civil Controls Exercised by the Western Defense Command*, January 1947, p. 859, NARS, RG 338, stating that there was "not available anywhere prior to Pearl Harbor, a record of German, Italian and Japanese organizations in the United States, with some knowledge of their structure, purposes, and connections with their homelands."

64. Francis Biddle, Circular 3616, Supplement No. 2, 2; see also Edward J. Ennis, "Circular No. 3616, Supplement No. 4, Instructions to Hearing Boards," April 3, 1942, Griswold Papers, Box 73, Folder 7, stating "every effort should be made to prove the alien enemy's personal character and activities, especially in cases where membership in the organization appears to be based upon a single contribution and no activity."

65. Attorney General Biddle appointed the following four others to the Boston hearing board: retired Federal Judge Hugh D. McLellan, who served as chairman; Right Rev. Augustine F. Hickey of St. Paul's Church in Cambridge; Joseph N. Welch, a lawyer at Hale and Dorr; and Bartholomew A. Brickley, a Boston lawyer. "Five Greater Boston Men on State Alien Enemy Hearing Board," 5.

66. Statement by Mr. Griswold, Alien Enemy Hearing Board for Massachusetts, Case of Albert Matthew Di Cillis, January 6, 1942, Griswold Papers, Box 73, Folder 8.

67. Ibid.

68. Statement by Mr. Griswold, Alien Enemy Hearing Board For Massachusetts, Case of Anton-Herman Chroust, January 6, 1942, Griswold Papers, Box 73, Folder 8.

69. File of Ubaldo Guidi-Buttrini (with aliases Ubaldo Guidi, Ubaldo Buttrini, Ubaldi Guidi, Ubaldo Bianco), File No. 146–13-2-36–24, Box 293, DOJ Litigation Files, NACP. A summary of allegations and the hearing board decisions are contained in Memorandum to the Chief of the Review Section, May 6, 1945 (hereafter cited as Memorandum to the Chief of the Review Section). See also Folder of Ubaldo Guidi-Buttrini, Box 11, PMG Records of Italian Civilian Internees, NACP.

70. Memorandum to the Chief of the Review Section, 13; see reference to Judge Forte in Stenographic Report of Rehearing before Alien Enemy Hearing Board in re. Ubaldo Guidi-Buttrini, Boston, December 14, 1942, 35, File of Ubaldo Guidi-Buttrini, File No. 146–13-2-36–24, Box 293, DOJ Litigation Files, NACP; see "Judge Forte Says Italian Aliens Loyal," 9.

71. See Memorandum to the Chief of the Review Section; File of Ubaldo Guidi-Buttrini, File No. 146–13-2-36–24, Box 293, DOJ Litigation Files, NACP.

72. Stenographic Report of Rehearing before Alien Enemy Hearing Board in re. Ubaldo Guidi-Buttrini, Boston, December 14, 1942, 34–37, File of Ubaldo Guidi-Buttrini, File No. 146–13-2-36–24, Box 293, DOJ Litigation Files, NACP.

73. See Memorandum to the Chief of the Review Section; File of Ubaldo Guidi-Buttrini, File No. 146–13–2-36–24, Box 293, DOJ Litigation Files, NACP.

74. See Bruce Mohler, Director, NCWC Bureau of Immigration, to Edward J. Ennis, May 29, 1944; Honorable Edmund E. Capodilupo, Representative, 3rd Suffolk District, Commonwealth of Massachusetts House of Representatives, to Hon. Ugo Carusi, U.S. Attorney General's Office, June 5, 1944; P. F. C. Albert L. Guidi, to President Roosevelt, February 17, 1945, File of Ubaldo Guidi-Buttrini, File No. 146–13–2-36–24, Box 293, DOJ Litigation Files, NACP.

75. Erwin Griswold to Thomas M. Cooley, Esq., Alien Enemy Control Unit, Department of Justice, February 2, 1942, Griswold Papers, Box 73, Folder 8.

76. Corsi, "Italian Immigrants and their Children," 106. Until 1940 Corsi held the position of deputy commissioner of the Department of Public Welfare in New York City, where he had also served as director of a settlement house and of the Emergency Home Relief Bureau. Corsi had also previously been commissioner of immigration and naturalization at Ellis Island.

77. Transcript In the Matter of the Detention of Riccardo Martinolich [Martinoli], Alien Enemy File No. M-68–252, January 26, 1942, 19, Corsi Papers, Box 33, Folder "ACTIVITIES Alien Enemy Hearing Board Correspondence to cases 7 May 1941 to 11 Feb. 1944." The board's more open-ended questions to the alien followed leading questions from the Assistant U.S. Attorney designed to efficiently present all background information on the alien before the board.

78. Ibid., 20–21.

79. Robert M. Benjamin, Alien Enemy Hearing Board member, to Thomas M. Cooley, II, Esq., Alien Enemy Control Unit, May 17, 1943, 4, Corsi Papers, Box 33, Folder "ACTIVITIES Alien Enemy Hearing Board Correspondence to cases 7 May 1941 to 11 Feb. 1944."

80. Hearing Board Correspondence to cases, 7 May 1941–11 February 1944, Corsi Papers, Box 33. The approaches of both Edward Corsi and Erwin Griswold with respect to German aliens, as evident from their hearing board files, stand in stark contrast with Stephen Fox's accounts of internment decisions. Fox describes decisions as guided by "the personalities and characters of German Americans . . . even the authorities' jealousy of them and frustration with their attitudes," which he concludes was essentially racism. Fox, *America's Invisible Gulag*, 293. See also Fox, *Fear Itself*, 380, where he finds that "in the post-arrest setting, racism—ethnocentrism, xenophobia, or plain incomprehension, if you prefer—profoundly affected the German-American experience."

81. See Summary and Recommendation in re. Francesco Scarfi, in re. Romeo Bisson, Kelley Papers, Box 140, Folder 140.5.

82. See Summary and Recommendation in re. Giuseppe Mario Brancucci, in re. Romeo Bisson, in re. Francesco Scarfi, Kelley Papers, Box 140, Folder 140.5.

83. See Summary and Recommendation in re. Francesco Scarfi, in re. Romeo Bisson, Kelley Papers, Box 140, Folder 140.5.

84. Edward J. Ennis, Director, Alien Enemy Control Unit, Department of Justice "Circular 3616, Supplement No. 3, Instructions To Alien Enemy Hearing Boards," February 16, 1942, 1, Griswold Papers, Box 73, Folder 7.

85. U.S. Commission on Wartime Relocation and Internment of Civilians, *Personal Justice Denied*, 285.

86. Edward J. Ennis, Director, Alien Enemy Control Unit, Department of Justice, "Circular No. 3589, Supplement No. 12, To United States Attorneys and Alien Enemy Hearing Boards Re: Rehearing of Alien Enemy Cases," August 21, 1942, Griswold Papers, Box 73, Folder 7.

87. Edward J. Ennis, Director, Alien Enemy Control Unit, Department of Justice, "Circular No. 3589, Supplement No. 14, To All Alien Enemy Hearing Boards," March 8, 1943, Kelley Papers, Box 140, Folder 140.1.

88. Francis Biddle, Attorney General, "Circular No. 3589, Supplement No. 15, To United States Attorneys and Alien Enemy Hearing Boards Re: Rehearing of Alien Enemy Cases," August 10, 1943, Griswold Papers, Box 73, Folder 7 (hereafter cited as Circular No. 3589, Supplement No. 15). The Special Alien Enemy Hearing Board had twenty-two members who sat in panels of four to eight. "Panel of 22 Set Up for Alien Hearings," 36.

89. Circular No. 3589, Supplement No. 15.

90. Memorandum, Edward J. Ennis to All United States Attorneys and Alien Enemy Hearing Board Members Re. Special Alien Enemy Hearing Board, December 18, 1943, Kelley Papers, Box 140, Folder 140.1.

91. Hon. James B. McNally to J. W. B., February 11, 1944, Kelley Papers, Box 140, Folder 140.1.

92. James P. McGranery, Assistant to the Attorney General, "Circular No. 3589, Supplement No. 20, To All United States Attorneys and Alien Enemy Hearing Board Members Re: Special Alien Enemy Hearing Board," March 25, 1944, Griswold Papers, Box 73, Folder 7.

93. Edward Corsi to Honorable Ugo Carusi, Department of Justice, February 11, 1944, Corsi Papers, Box 33, Folder "ACTIVITIES Alien Enemy Hearing Board Correspondence to cases 7 May 1941 to 11 Feb. 1944."

94. Folder of Angelo Gloria, Box 10, PMG Records of Italian Civilian Internees, NACP. Gloria was paroled on February 16, 1944.

95. File of Pericle Adriano Carlo Chieri, Naturalization Certificate File C-7185491, U.S. Citizenship & Immigration Services (hereafter cited as Chieri's C-File).

96. See Testimony of Pericle Adriano Carlo Chieri, "Resumed Hearing" in Deportation case, February 10, 1943, in which he stated "I do not know on what grounds my internment has been ordered." Chieri's C-File.

97. Report in re: Pericle Adriano Carlo Chieri, Petition for Naturalization No. 27886, May 3, 1948, Chieri's C-File. See Exhibit A.

98. Report and Recommendation in re: Pericle Adriano Chieri, January 20, 1943, Chieri's C-File. Note that there is no transcript of the hearings in the file.

99. Statement of Pericle Adriano Carlo Chieri, December 20, 1946, re. naturalization proceedings, Chieri's C-File.

100. Report and Recommendation in re: Pericle Adriano Chieri, June 22, 1943, Chieri's C-File.

101. See Exhibit A to Report in re: Pericle Adriano Carlo Chieri, Petition for Naturalization No. 27886, May 3, 1948, Chieri's C-File, summarizing the proceedings before the alien enemy hearing board.

102. Summary of Facts and Opinions in re: Pericle A. Chieri, September 23, 1943, Chieri's C-File. See also Folder of Pericle A. Chieri, Box 6, PMG Records of Italian Civilian Internees, NACP.

103. Chieri was naturalized on December 29, 1952, at the U.S. District Court in Newark, New Jersey. See Chieri's C-File.

104. File of Aldo Ghirardi, File No. 146–13–2–11–138, Box 39, DOJ Litigation Files, NACP. Unless otherwise indicated, all facts concerning Mr. Ghirardi are derived from his DOJ file.

105. Folder of Aldo Ghirardi, Box 10, PMG Records of Italian Civilian Internees, NACP.

106. File of Mario Giovanni Favoino (also known as Favoino Di Giura, Giovanni Favoino Di Giura, and Giovanni Mario Favoino), File No. 146–13–2–51–81, Box 394, DOJ Litigation Files, NACP. Unless otherwise indicated, all facts concerning Mr. Favoino are derived from his DOJ File.

107. FBI report by R. A. Johnson, 12/15/41.

108. Folder of Giovanni Mario (Mario Giovanni, Favoino, Giovanni Favoino) Favoino (Di Giura), Box 9, PMG Records of Italian Civilian Internees, NACP.

109. Marian Smith, chief, Historical Research Branch, U.S. Citizenship and Immigration Services, e-mail message to author, June 7, 2013, citing Ancestry.com, *Social Security Death Index*.

110. File of Francesco Fragale, File No. 146–13–2–85–30, Box 716, DOJ Litigation Files, NACP. Note that Fragale's file was found with files of German internees in a box labeled "Closed Legal Case Files, 146–13–2–85–19 to 146–13–2–85–47, Alien Enemy World War II, Detention & Internment." See also Folder of Frank Fragale, Box 9, PMG Records of Italian Civilian Internees, NACP.

111. Alien Enemy Hearing Board, Eastern District of Wisconsin, in the Matter of the Detention of Francesco Larencesco Fragale, alias Frank Fragale, "Report and Recommendation," January 13, 1942, File of Francesco Fragale, File No. 146–13–2–85–30, Box 716, DOJ Litigation Files, NACP.

112. Memorandum to Chief of Review Section, Hearing Board's Recommendation re: Francesco Larencesco Fragale, January 30, 1942, 2, File of Francesco Fragale, File No. 146–13–2–85–30, Box 716, DOJ Litigation Files, NACP.

113. McAlester Internment Camp, "Information on Internee Behavior Desired by the Department of Justice" for Frank Fragale, March 5, 1943. The remarks on the back of the report were as follows: "Fragale is outspoken against the United States and for Italy. He associates with the extreme Fascist group." File of Francesco Fragale, File No. 146–13–2–85–30, Box 716, DOJ Litigation Files, NACP.

114. Department of Justice, Immigration and Naturalization Service, Fort Missoula, Montana, "Summary Report on Internee Behavior Desired by Alien Enemy Control Unit" for Frank Fragale, September 1943. On this report, all categories of behavior were noted as "Neutral or Unobserved." File of Francesco Fragale, File No. 146–13–2–85–30, Box 716, DOJ Litigation Files, NACP.

115. Memorandum for the Chief of the Review Section, November 3, 1943; Hubert O. Wolfe, Chairman, Alien Enemy Hearing Board No. 2 to Hon. Edward J. Ennis, Chairman, Alien Enemy Control Unit, Department of Justice, September 24,

1943, File of Francesco Fragale, File No. 146–13–2-85–30, Box 716, DOJ Litigation Files, NACP.

116. Frank Fragale to Hon. Ugo Carusi, Assistant U.S. Attorney General, Department of Justice, October 21, 1943, File of Francesco Fragale, File No. 146–13–2-85–30, Box 716, DOJ Litigation Files, NACP.

117. C. E. Lamiell, Major, CAV, Executive Officer, Headquarters, Aliceville Internment Camp, Aliceville, Alabama, To Whom It May Concern, July 9, 1943; J. T. Carlisle, Captain P. A., Intelligence Officer, Headquarters, McAlester Internment Camp, McAlester, Oklahoma, To Whom It May Concern, May 19, 1943; Rev. John J. Foley, S. J., Principal, Marquette University High School, To Whom It May Concern, July 22, 1943; August D. Leo and Amelia Leo, To Whom It May Concern, July 22, 1943; Rev. Mark S. Gross, S. J., Regis College, To Whom It May Concern, July 8, 1943; A. I. Rickel, Shop Superintendent, United States Department of Agriculture, Forest Service, September 3, 1943. File of Francesco Fragale, File No. 146–13–2-85–30, Box 716, DOJ Litigation Files, NACP.

118. William F. Howard, Parole Inspector, Fort Missoula, Montana, to Mr. Edward J. Ennis, Director, Alien Enemy Control Unit, Department of Justice, May 2, 1944; Report of Maurice Ross, Immigrant Inspector, January 30, 1945; C. E. Rhetts, Acting Assistant Attorney General, to Honorable Timothy T. Cronin, United States Attorney, Eastern District of Wisconsin, December 2, 1944. File of Francesco Fragale, File No. 146–13–2-85–30, Box 716, DOJ Litigation Files, NACP.

119. Order of the Attorney General, Tom C. Clark, in the Matter of Francesco Larencesco Fragale, July 3, 1945, File of Francesco Fragale, File No. 146–13–2-85–30, Box 716, DOJ Litigation Files, NACP.

120. Marian Smith, chief, Historical Research Branch, U.S. Citizenship and Immigration Services, e-mail message to author, June 7, 2013, citing U.S. Department of Veterans Affairs BIRLS Death File, 1850–2010. Fragale's was an "administrative naturalization" since it was based on his service in the U.S. armed forces. The Second War Powers Act of 1942 exempted noncitizen service members from naturalization requirements.

121. See Alien Enemy Hearing Board, Eastern District of Wisconsin, in the Matter of the Detention of Francesco Larencesco Fragale, alias Frank Fragale, "Report and Recommendation," January 13, 1942. File of Francesco Fragale, File No. 146–13–2-85–30, Box 716, DOJ Litigation Files, NACP.

122. Folder of Pauline Tedesco, Boxes 19 and 24, PMG Records of Italian Civilian Internees, NACP. The other woman in my study, who was interned of her own accord, was a housewife/tailor who was apprehended on December 8, 1941, held on Sand Island, Territory of Hawaii, and paroled in October 1942. Folder of Celia Iaculla Ventrella, Box 20, PMG Records of Italian Civilian Internees, NACP.

123. Memorandum for Chief of Review Section, March 9, 1942; Report and Recommendation of the Hearing Board, February 27, 1942; FBI Report of R. J. Huiras, February 24, 1942, File of Pauline Tedesco (aka Pauline Milano, Virginia Tucker, Rose Marino, Rose Marie), File No. 146–13–2-63–33, Carton 567, DOJ Litigation Files, NACP.

124. See Memorandum, W. F. Kelly, Chief Supervisor of Border Control, to Mr. Edward J. Ennis, Director, Alien Enemy Control Unit, September 10, 1942, File of Pauline Tedesco, File No. 146–13–2–63–33, Carton 567, DOJ Litigation Files, NACP.

125. Report of Michael Surgent, Special Inspector, to Acting Inspector in Charge, Immigration and Naturalization Service, October 26, 1943, File of Pauline Tedesco, File No. 146–13–2–63–33, Carton 567, DOJ Litigation Files, NACP.

126. Report of Michael Surgent, Special Inspector, to Officer in Charge, Wilkes-Barre, Penn., September 11, 1944, File of Pauline Tedesco, File No. 146–13–2–63–33, Carton 567, DOJ Litigation Files, NACP.

127. Memorandum to Chief of the Review Section, November 21, 1944, File of Pauline Tedesco, File No. 146–13–2–63–33, Carton 567, DOJ Litigation Files, NACP.

128. Marian Smith, chief, Historical Research Branch, U.S. Citizenship and Immigration Services, e-mail message to author, June 7, 2013, citing Certificate No. 8444981 and Ancestry.com, *Social Security Death Index*.

129. See discussion of the case of the Shitara sisters in Colorado for interesting parallels in Muller, "Betrayal on Trial: Japanese-American 'Treason' in World War II."

130. We do know that Italian women of the first half of the twentieth century were involved in radical political movements. See J. Guglielmo, *Living the Revolution* (portraying women in the needle and textile trades in New York City and Paterson, New Jersey, who helped shape transnational, radical political culture in the United States by drawing on traditions of protest in peasant uprisings in southern Italy). Guglielmo counters the popular notion that women were marginal players in immigrant politics.

131. File of Calogero Carolo (aka Calogero Carollo, Charlie Carolo, Charles Carolo), File No. 146–13–2–51–1361, Box 417, DOJ Litigation Files, NACP. Unless otherwise indicated, all facts concerning Mr. Carolo are derived from his DOJ file as well his folder in Box 5, PMG Records of Italian Civilian Internees, NACP.

132. Summary and Recommendation in re. Calogero Carollo, Kelley Papers, Box 140, Folder 140.5.

133. Marian Smith, chief, Historical Research Branch, U.S. Citizenship and Immigration Services, e-mail message to author, June 7, 2013, citing Ancestry.com, *Social Security Death Index*.

134. Alfonso Zirpoli, interview by Stephen Fox, San Francisco, California, May 13, 1987, in Fox, *Uncivil Liberties*, 201. He said that Italians formed this club in 1929. Its members included professors, bankers, doctors, lawyers, and the mayor (ibid., 201–2).

135. See "John Molinari, 94; Former Justice of State Appellate Court."

136. John Molinari, interview by Stephen Fox, San Francisco, California, February 6, 1987, in Fox, *Uncivil Liberties*, 191.

137. Ibid., 192.

138. Valdastri was not the only naturalized citizen taken from the Territory of Hawaii. Gildo (Tony) Marta, a former waiter in Honolulu and U.S. citizen since 1932, was interned with Valdastri at Camp McCoy in Wisconsin and returned to Hawaii

at the same time. During his internment, Marta wrote to Secretary Stimson stating that he could not understand why he was not released given that his hearing was favorable. Gildo Tony Marta to Henry L. Stimson, Secretary of War, June 1, 1942, Folder of Tony (Gildo, Egildo) Marta, Box 13, PMG Records of Italian Civilian Internees, NACP. In my review of the civilian internee files in the Provost Marshal General records, I have identified four more naturalized U.S. citizens who were interned: Pasquale DeCicco, whose legal status was before a federal district court in 1943; Frank Membrini, whose citizenship was terminated; Arturo Pasquini, who was ordered interned upon release from the Northeastern Penitentiary; and Domenico Trombetta, who was denaturalized in September 1942. Folder of Pasquale DeCicco, Box 7, Folder of Frank Membrini, Box 13, Folder of Arturo Pasquini, Box 15, Folder of Domenico Trombetta, Box 19, PMG Records of Italian Civilian Internees, NACP.

139. Robinson, *A Tragedy of Democracy*, 226.

140. Mario Valdastri to the President of the United States, May 28, 1942, Folder of Mario Valdastri, Box 20, PMG Records of Italian Civilian Internees, NACP.

141. Record of the Hearings of a Board of Officers and Civilians Convened Pursuant To Paragraph 1, Special Orders No. 315, Headquarters, Hawaiian Department, Dated at Fort Shafter T. H., December 14, 1941, Folder of Mario Valdastri, Box 2643, Records of the Office of the Provost Marshal General, Subject File, 1942–1946, Hawaii, Civilian Internees, Record Group 389; NACP.

142. Ibid. Compare this record with the reasons Lawrence DiStasi provides for Valdastri's internment in his book of essays, *Una Storia Segreta*. DiStasi cites to an interview with Valdastri's son, Mario Valdastri Jr., which offers remarks made by his father in a dispute with a powerful businessman on Oahu and mistaken identity when the elder Valdastri first arrived in Hawaii as the most likely reasons for his internment. See DiStasi, "A Tale of Two Citizens," 150. DiStasi suggests all the evidence against Valdastri may have been "tenuous and circumstantial" (ibid., 151). A third reason given by Valdastri's son for his father's detention is his brief presidency of the Italian American Club in Honolulu in 1938, which my findings corroborate. DiStasi, "A Tale of Two Citizens," 152n16.

143. Note that habeas corpus was only suspended within Hawaii and arguably, martial law would not have followed Valdastri to the mainland. See Robinson, *A Tragedy of Democracy*, 232–34, regarding court challenges to the martial law regime by several German Americans arrested in Honolulu, one of whom was also sent to Camp McCoy.

144. Mario Valdastri to American Civil Liberties, New York, New York, May 10, 1942, Folder of Mario Valdastri, Box 20, PMG Records of Italian Civilian Internees, NACP.

145. Mario Valdastri to the President of the United States, May 28, 1942, Folder of Mario Valdastri, Box 20, PMG Records of Italian Civilian Internees, NACP. The letter bears a handwritten note, "no further action necessary," which leads one to conclude that Valdastri's letter went unanswered.

146. Frances Valdastri to Allen W. Gullion, Provost Marshall [sic] General, July 18, 1942; Mario Valdastri to Allen W. Gullion, Provost Marshall [sic] General, June 1, 1942, Folder of Mario Valdastri, Box 20, PMG Records of Italian Civilian Internees, NACP.

147. Major General Allen W. Gullion to Frances Valdastri, July 28, 1942, Folder of Mario Valdastri, Box 20, PMG Records of Italian Civilian Internees, NACP. The label "Aliens Div." which appears in the upper right-hand corner of the letter indicates that Valdastri was categorized as an alien despite his American citizenship.

148. DiStasi, "A Tale of Two Citizens," 151.

149. See DiStasi, "Morto il Camerata," 3–4, discussing the case of Prospero Cecconi, a pasta maker at the Roma macaroni factory in North Beach, San Francisco.

150. Dennis, Letters to *The Times*, "Enemy Aliens Pose Problem," 14.

151. Ibid.

152. Memorandum from Edward J. Ennis, Director, Department of Justice, Alien Enemy Control Unit, to the Attorney General, March 14, 1944, FBI Records, The Vault on Custodial Detention, 121, http://vault.fbi.gov/Custodial%20Detention, accessed on May 1, 2017.

153. See Biddle, *In Brief Authority*, 207–8; see also Mangione, *An Ethnic at Large*, 320, footnote, who reported a larger number of 85,000 German and Austrian Jews interned.

154. See "WW2 People's War: An archive of World War Two memories—written by the public, gathered by the BBC, Fact File: Civilian Internment 1939–1945," http://www.bbc.co.uk/history/ww2peopleswar/timeline/factfiles/nonflash/a6651858.shtml, accessed on May 1, 2017. See Sponza, "The Internment of Italians in Britain," 259 and 276n8, who says there were 18,000 Italian nationals registered with the police, but the Italian community as a whole was about 30,000.

155. See Tom Conti, "My Dad, Sent to a Prison Camp for Being Italian," *BBC News Magazine*. http://www.bbc.co.uk/news/magazine-22278664, accessed on May 1, 2017. Note that 403 Italian internees from Great Britain ended up in Canada in 1940. Sponza, "The Internment of Italians in Britain," 260.

156. Sponza, "The Internment of Italians in Britain," 264.

157. Bosworth, "The Internment of Italians in Australia," 229.

158. See National Archives of Australia, "Wartime Internment Camps in Australia: World War II, http://www.naa.gov.au/collection/snapshots/internment-camps/introduction.aspx, accessed on May 1, 2017. See also Gitano Rando, "Italo-Australians During the Second World War: Some Perceptions of Internment," http://ro.uow.edu.au/cgi/viewcontent.cgi?article=1123&context=artspapers, accessed on May 1, 2017. Rando estimates that 4,700 mainly Italian Australian men (approximately 16 percent) were interned when the Australian government viewed the Italian Australian community of 30,000 as posing a national security threat. The tribunals granted fewer than 150 releases after a year of operation. Citing 4,721 as the number of internees, Bosworth estimates that between 12 and 15 percent of all Italo-Australians were eventually interned, although the national average would rise to 25 percent if children and women in the population were excluded. Bosworth, "The Internment of Italians in Australia," 228, 239.

159. Bosworth, "The Internment of Italians in Australia," 239.

160. See Liberati, "The Internment of Italian Canadians," 89. Compare figures from Government of Canada, "Citizenship and Immigration Canada, Italian-Canadian Community Projects," http://www.cic.gc.ca/english/multiculturalism/programs

/italian.asp, accessed on May 1, 2017. The Government of Canada says that as of September 1939 when war broke out in Europe, 31,000 Italian Canadians were designated "enemy aliens," and 600 were arrested and interned in camps across Canada. Liberati reports that Canadian sources, including a report prepared by Gerald Fauteux who was an examining officer from the Department of Justice, suggest that approximately 600 were detained at the height of internments, but this figure includes 99 seamen from Italian merchant ships in Canadian ports. In Montreal alone, which had a population of about 30,000 residents of Italian descent, there were 198 internees. Liberati, "The Internment of Italian Canadians," 89.

Chapter Four

1. See U.S. Department of Justice Immigration and Naturalization Service, Instruction No. 58 "To The Immigration and Naturalization Service: Subject: Instructions Concerning the Treatment of Alien Enemy Detainees" from Lemuel B. Schofield, special assistant to the attorney general, April 28, 1942, in Tolzmann, *German-Americans in the World Wars*, 1580–89.

2. *Administrative History of the INS*, 280. INS immigration detention centers used to detain enemy aliens were located in Ellis Island, East Boston, Detroit, Seattle, San Francisco, Gloucester City, New Jersey; and San Pedro, California. *Administrative History of the INS*, 284. As the war progressed, the INS set up additional temporary detention facilities in Portland, Salt Lake City, Saint Louis, Saint Paul, Kansas City, Cleveland, Houston, Hartford, Niagara Falls, Chicago, Miami, Pittsburgh, Nanticoke, Pennsylvania; and Fort Howard, Maryland. DiStasi, "Let's Keep Smiling," 215n8; see also *Administrative History of the INS*, 294–96.

3. *Administrative History of the INS*, 283–84. In March 1941, Italian seamen were sent to Fort Missoula, and German seamen went to Fort Stanton and Fort Lincoln (ibid., 288, 297). The war made their deportation at that time too difficult.

4. Ibid., 288–89.

5. Ibid., 298.

6. Ibid., 297, 283–84. Tuna Canyon, outside Los Angeles, and Sharp Park, outside San Francisco, resembled permanent internment camps in their structures, but were under the jurisdiction of the district directors, not the central office. See *Administrative History of the INS*, 285, 294.

7. "All Enemy Alien Internees Now in Custody of Immigration Service," 21.

8. *Administrative History of the INS*, 298–99.

9. Ibid., 304. The twelve included four males, five females, and three female minors.

10. Zachary A. Wilske, historian, U.S. Citizenship and Immigration, Records Division, History Office and Library, e-mail message to author, March 20, 2013.

11. W. de Bourg, Chief of the Department, Legation of Switzerland, to Mrs. Angelina Farese, March 25, 1943, Farese's A-File. In my research, I have not come across any evidence that families residing in the United States were reunited with their husbands and fathers in the internment camps. Presumably these families could visit their family members, while the Italian families from Latin America would have

faced much greater barriers to visitation and therefore opted to be interned to-gether. The only attempt that I saw of a wife trying to join her husband was that of Angelina Farese. The Alien Enemy Control Unit denied Mrs. Farese's request because it reserved the limited space for the most needy families, based on the stud-ies of social workers, and felt that she was adjusting to her community in New York. See W. F. Miller, Acting Assistant Commissioner for Alien Control, to Mrs. Ange-lina Farese, July 13, 1943, and Report, August 20, 1943, Farese's A-File.

12. Mario Valdastri to Mr. Riley H. Allen, Editor of the *Honolulu Star-Bulletin*, Folder of Mario Valdastri, Box 20, PMG Records of Italian Civilian Internees, NARA. This letter is undated, but had to be written between March and June 1942 during his stay at Fort McCoy.

13. There is no record in Valdastri's Provost Marshal General files that the Hono-lulu paper ever received the letter and published it. Lawrence DiStasi says that ac-cording to Valdastri's son, Mario Valdastri Jr., the letter was not published. DiStasi surmises that martial law and restrictions on news may have been the reasons. DiS-tasi, "A Tale of Two Citizens," 152n14.

14. See *Administrative History of the INS*, 320–27.

15. See ibid., 326.

16. Mangione, "Concentration Camps—American Style," 121.

17. Gardiner, *Pawns in a Triangle of Hate*, 36.

18. Mangione, "Concentration Camps—American Style," 123; see also 121–23. Man-gione said that Seagoville, unlike the other internment camps, had a trained dietician on staff who planned healthy meals that conformed to each ethnic group's tastes. See also *Administrative History of the INS*, 301–2.

19. *Administrative History of the INS*, 300.

20. Gardiner, *Pawns in a Triangle of Hate*, 30.

21. Mangione, *An Ethnic at Large*, 328.

22. 1929 Geneva Convention, Part I, Art. 4 (regarding maintenance of internees) and Part III, Sec. II, ch. 2, Arts. 11 and 12.

23. 1929 Geneva Convention, Part III, Sec. II, ch. 2, Art. 12.

24. Gardiner, *Pawns in a Triangle of Hate*, 32.

25. Mangione, *An Ethnic at Large*, 329.

26. *Administrative History of the INS*, 366, 372. Border Patrol officers or guards from the camps intercepted all persons who attempted escape.

27. Mangione, *An Ethnic at Large*, 328.

28. *Administrative History of the INS*, 302–5; Gardiner, *Pawns in a Triangle of Hate*, 59–60.

29. Mangione, *An Ethnic at Large*, 330.

30. Ibid., 330–31.

31. Van Valkenburg, *An Alien Place*, 15–16; Lothrop, "Unwelcome in Freedom's Land," 170.

32. Van Valkenburg, *An Alien Place*, citing Internment Camp Operation Memo, 5.

33. See Van Valkenburg, *An Alien Place*, 28.

34. See ibid., 27, citing "News From Montana," *Time*, August 18, 1941, 24. The Italian media also reported positive conditions. See, for example, *Corriere D'America-Domenica*,

New York, August 17, 1941, reporting "no spirit of a concentration camp or prison camp," cited in Van Valkenburg, *An Alien Place*, 27.

35. Alfredo Cipolato, interview by Stephen Fox, Missoula, Montana, April 17, 1989, in Fox, *Uncivil Liberties*, 202–3.

36. Mangione, "Concentration Camps—American Style," 127; see also 127–28.

37. Van Valkenburg, *An Alien Place*, 55, reprinted in Sigrid Aren, "Italian, Japanese Internees Won't Eat Together," *Wide World*, August 8, 1942.

38. Ibid., 56; Mangione, *An Ethnic at Large*, 347.

39. Mangione, *An Ethnic at Large*, 347.

40. Mangione, "Concentration Camps—American Style," 127.

41. See, for example, Summary Report on Internee Behavior Desired by the Enemy Alien Control Unit and Memorandum for Chief of the Review Section, October 27, 1944, 3, File of Francesco Fragale, File No. 146–13–2–85–30, Box 716, DOJ Litigation Files, NACP.

42. Memorandum to the Chief of the Review Board (Reconsideration), May 6, 1945, 14, File of Ubaldo Guidi-Buttrini, File No. 146–13–2–36–24, Box 293, DOJ Litigation Files, NACP.

43. Sylvernale, "Alien in Texas," 197.

44. DiStasi, "Let's Keep Smiling," 203–4, regarding Fort Meade; see also Sylvernale, "Alien in Texas," 197, regarding Fort Sam Houston.

45. Scherini, "Letters to 3024 Pierce," 229, showing correspondence with Carmelo Ilacqua.

46. Mario Valdastri to Mr. Riley H. Allen, Editor of the *Honolulu Star-Bulletin*, Folder of Mario Valdastri, Box 20, PMG Records of Italian Civilian Internees, NACP. Note that Valdastri's "Basic Personnel Record" indicates that he was held for a few days at Fort McDowell on Angel Island in San Francisco Bay before being transferred to Fort McCoy in Wisconsin. Although Valdastri does not name the camp in his letter, given that his stay at Fort McDowell was so brief, it is more likely that his camp description refers to Fort McCoy.

47. DiStasi, "Let's Keep Smiling," 203, citing evidence from the experiences of Louis Berizzi and Ubaldo Guidi-Buttrini.

48. See Mario Valdastri to Mr. Riley H. Allen, Editor of the *Honolulu Star-Bulletin*, Folder of Mario Valdastri, Box 20, PMG Records of Italian Civilian Internees, NACP.

49. See *Administrative History of the INS*, 349.

50. See Mario Valdastri to Mr. Riley H. Allen, Editor of the *Honolulu Star-Bulletin*, Folder of Mario Valdastri, Box 20, PMG Records of Italian Civilian Internees, NACP.

51. Van Valkenburg, *An Alien Place*, 19–23.

52. Ibid., 28.

53. 1929 Geneva Convention, Part III, Sec. II, ch. 4, Art. 16.

54. Mario Valdastri to Mr. Riley H. Allen, Editor of the *Honolulu Star-Bulletin*, Folder of Mario Valdastri, Box 20, PMG Records of Italian Civilian Internees, NACP.

55. See letters in The National Catholic Welfare Conference Papers (hereafter cited as NCWC Papers), Box 123, Folder 6 (NCWC U.S. Government: Relocation of Aliens, 1942, January–June).

56. Laurence J. Fitzsimon, Bishop of Amarillo, to Most Rev. Edward Mooney, D. D., Archbishop of Detroit, August 2, 1943, NCWC Papers, Box 58, Folder 5 (Military Affairs: Prisoners of War, 1941–43). Note that issues concerning internees and internment camps appear in the NCWC files labeled "Prisoners of War." Therefore, it is unclear whether these religious provisions were meant only for prisoners of war or civilian internees as well. However, by this date, most of the civilian internees had been transferred back to the INS.

57. Allen W. Gullion, Major General, The Provost Marshal General, to Most Reverend Edward Mooney, Chairman, Administrative Board, National Catholic Welfare Conference, September 2, 1943, NCWC Papers, Box 58, Folder 5 (Military Affairs: Prisoners of War, 1941–43).

58. See 1929 Geneva Convention, Part III, Sec. II, ch. 2, Art. 11.

59. See Van Valkenburg, *An Alien Place*, 27. The internees at Fort Missoula got sugar, oil, and coffee when they requested it, and even enjoyed round steak, which caused resentment among Missoulians (ibid., 32).

60. See *Administrative History of the INS*, 353.

61. 1929 Geneva Convention, Part III, Sec. III, ch. 1, Art. 27 and ch. 2, Art. 29.

62. 1929 Geneva Convention, Part III, Sec. III, ch. 2, Art. 28.

63. B. M. Bryan, Colonel F. A., Chief, Aliens Division, to Mrs. Anthony Pidala, undated, Folder of Anthony Pidala, Box 16, PMG Records of Italian Civilian Internees, NACP. See 1929 Geneva Convention, Part III, Sec. III, ch. 5, Art. 34.

64. See Mrs. Anthony Pidala to Dept. of Justice, September 23, 1942, Folder of Anthony Pidala, Box 16, PMG Records of Italian Civilian Internees, NACP.

65. *Administrative History of the INS*, 354.

66. Lothrop, "Unwelcome in Freedom's Land," 171.

67. *Administrative History of the INS*, 351–54.

68. Ibid., 352–55.

69. Alfredo Cipolato, interview by Stephen Fox, Missoula, Montana, April 17, 1989, in Fox, *Uncivil Liberties*, 203. Cipolato said that instead of receiving cash for their work, they were issued requisitions for purchases at clothing stores and other places.

70. Gardiner, *Pawns in a Triangle of Hate*, 60.

71. Memorandum for the Chief of the Review Section, October 27, 1944, 4, File of Francesco Fragale, File No. 146–13–2–85–30, Box 716, DOJ Litigation Files, NACP.

72. See Mangione, *An Ethnic at Large*, 328.

73. Mario Valdastri to Mr. Riley H. Allen, Editor of the *Honolulu Star-Bulletin*, Folder of Mario Valdastri, Box 20, PMG Records of Italian Civilian Internees, NACP.

74. See *Administrative History of the INS*, 361; see also Van Valkenburg, *An Alien Place*, 16–17.

75. *Administrative History of the INS*, 362; see also Van Valkenburg, *An Alien Place*, 33–35.

76. See *Administrative History of the INS*, 360.

77. Mario Valdastri to Mr. Riley H. Allen, Editor of the *Honolulu Star-Bulletin*, Folder of Mario Valdastri, Box 20, PMG Records of Italian Civilian Internees, NACP.

78. See *Administrative History of the INS*, 361.

79. Mario Valdastri to Mr. Riley H. Allen, Editor of the *Honolulu Star-Bulletin*, Folder of Mario Valdastri, Box 20, PMG Records of Italian Civilian Internees, NACP; see *Administrative History of the INS*, 361.

80. *Administrative History of the INS*, 363.

81. Mario Valdastri to Mr. Riley H. Allen, Editor of the *Honolulu Star-Bulletin*, Folder of Mario Valdastri, Box 20, PMG Records of Italian Civilian Internees, NACP.

82. See Miscellaneous Documents on Italian Internment, the Historical Museum at Fort Missoula.

83. See Van Valkenburg, *An Alien Place*, 59, 62. Internees at INS camps could also buy clothes from mail-order catalogs from Montgomery Ward and Sears, Roebuck. See Gardiner, *Pawns in a Triangle of Hate*, 37.

84. DiStasi, "Let's Keep Smiling," 208.

85. Drypolcher, "Orders to Take Him Away," 220–21.

86. See Van Valkenburg, *An Alien Place*, 56, reprinted in Sigrid Aren, "Italian, Japanese Internees Won't Eat Together," *Wide World*, August 8, 1942. Aren reported that "prisoners" had to speak in English or "in the presence of an interpreter."

87. DiStasi, "Let's Keep Smiling," 205. This conversation was not only observed but also recorded in a report.

88. Mario Valdastri to American Civil Liberties, New York, New York, May 10, 1942, Folder of Mario Valdastri, Box 20, PMG Records of Italian Civilian Internees, NACP.

89. Valdastri Jr., "Two Men in Suits," 154; see also DiStasi, "A Tale of Two Citizens," 151.

90. *Administrative History of the INS*, 395.

91. Ibid., 395–96.

92. Leroy Kostenbauder, Captain, F. A. Adjutant, to Subscription Department, *Washington Star*, August 18, 1942, and Mario Ricciardelli, to Hon. Edward J. Ennis, Sept. 14, 1942, Folder of Mario Ricciardelli, Box 17, PMG Records of Italian Civilian Internees, NACP.

93. Mario Valdastri to Mr. Riley H. Allen, Editor of the *Honolulu Star-Bulletin*, Folder of Mario Valdastri, Box 20, PMG Records of Italian Civilian Internees, NACP.

94. Scherini, "Letters to 3024 Pierce," 224, 228, 231.

95. See 1929 Geneva Convention, Part III, Sec. IV, ch. 5 ("Relations of Prisoners of War with the Exterior"), Arts. 35–41. Article 40 mandates: "The censoring of correspondence shall be accomplished as quickly as possible."

96. *Administrative History of the INS*, 396.

97. Ibid., 398.

98. Idiomatic Translation of an Italian letter from Mario Ricciardelli, to H. E. N. D. Borgus, Swiss Minister, Folder of Mario Ricciardelli, December 9, 1942, Box 17, PMG Records of Italian Civilian Internees, NACP.

99. DiStasi, "Let's Keep Smiling," 200.

100. Folder of Mario Ricciardelli, Box 17, PMG Records of Italian Civilian Internees, NACP.

101. Note by camp official that passage was deleted from a letter from "Angelo B. Tribuiani" to Mrs. Adele Tribuiani, Wilmington, Delaware. I believe this is a mistake

since there was only an Alfredo Tribuiani among the civilian internees. Official's translation of *di Gloucester, ma pur tutto . . . la mancanza della LIBERTÀ opprime l'anima e il cuore.* Folder of Alfredo B. Tribuiani (Tribuani), Box 19, PMG Records of Italian Civilian Internees, NACP.

102. Notes by camp official that passages were deleted from letters from Filippo Cipri-Romano [*sic*] to Mrs. Maria Cipri-Romano [*sic*] Philadelphia, Pennsylvania, July 6, 1942 and 4–27–42. A camp officer translated the letter of 4–27–42. The original letter in Italian was missing from the file. Folder of Filippo Cippri Romano, Box 17, PMG Records of Italian Civilian Internees, NACP.

103. See DiStasi, "Let's Keep Smiling," 208, citing Velleda Guidi, Letter to Her Father, May 7, 1942, Guidi-Buttrini file, RG 389, NARA II.

104. See the Verse "Let's Keep Smiling" in a letter written to Tribuiani from Ralph Ottaviano on or about August 10, 1942, and analysis in DiStasi, "Let's Keep Smiling," 209, citing Deletion, Alfredo Tribuani file, RG 389, NARA II. [Note alternate spellings of the internee's last name in his files.]

105. Folder of Alessandro Fabbri, Box 8, PMG Records of Italian Civilian Internees, NACP. See discussion about the deletion of Mariana Fabbri's drawings in DiStasi, "Let's Keep Smiling," 212–14.

106. See Mangione, "Concentration Camps—American Style," 123.

107. Carmelo Ilacqua from Fort Missoula to Bruna Ilacqua, March 6, 1942, cited in Scherini, "Letters to 3024 Pierce," 228. Ilacqua reports of a snowstorm in Missoula and being "in another storm," implying internment.

108. Raymond W. Hall, Vice President and General Counsel, Federal Reserve Bank of Kansas City, to First National Bank, McAlester, Oklahoma, February 3, 1943, File of Giovanni Maiorana, Box 12, PMG Records of Italian Civilian Internees, NACP. Restrictions on access to one's property and the conduct of one's business could occur if an internee were subject to the Freezing Order (Executive Order No. 8389) or Trading with the Enemy Act prohibiting certain transactions on behalf of nationals of certain foreign countries. See U.S. Department of Justice, "Questions and Answers on Regulations Concerning Aliens of Enemy Nationalities," American Committee for Protection of Foreign Born Records, Box 17, Folder 2 ("Enemy Aliens, 1942–1945").

109. U.S. Office of War Information, Division of Public Inquiries, *United States Government Manual: 1945*, 456.

110. Scherini, "Letters to 3024 Pierce," 226. Scherini reported that Bruna Ilacqua, internee Carmelo's wife, sought relief from these agencies but was turned away, requiring her to share her flat with her sister and brother-in-law to help out with household expenses. In her July 20, 1942, letter to Carmelo, Bruna said that the Federal Emergency Board denied her assistance and suggested that she work. Scherini, "Letters to 3024 Pierce," 231.

111. Fox, *Uncivil Liberties*, 184–85. To give an idea of the extent of assistance, Fox's research of ten California counties indicated that the amount of money involved in the program from November 1, 1942, to May 30, 1943, was only $7,589.72. The number of individual cases ranged from twenty-nine during the peak month of January 1943 to six in May 1943 (ibid., 184).

112. B. M. Bryan, Colonel F. A., Chief, Aliens Division, to Mrs. Anthony Pidala, undated, Folder of Anthony Pidala, Box 16, PMG Records of Italian Civilian Internees, NACP.

113. See Bert H. Fraser, Officer in Charge, Fort Missoula, Montana, to Mrs. Angelina Farese, November 20, 1943, Farese's A-File.

114. See Edward J. Ennis to Abner Green, Secretary, American Committee for Protection of Foreign Born, March 4, 1943 regarding release of an Italian alien seaman, and Abner Green, Secretary, American Committee for Protection of Foreign Born, to W. F. Kelly, Ass't Commissioner for Alien Control, April 8, 1943, regarding status of aliens from Hungary, Rumania, and Bulgaria, American Committee for Protection of Foreign Born Records, Box 17, Folder 1 ("Enemy Aliens, 1942–1945").

115. Memorandum, Bruce Mohler, Director, Bureau of Immigration, to Monsignor Ready, January 11, 1943, and Memorandum, Bruce Mohler, Director, Bureau of Immigration, to Monsignor Ready, April 28, 1943, NCWC Papers, Box 127, Folder 27 (201 Church: Apostolic Delegation).

116. Bruce Mohler, Director, NCWC Bureau of Immigration to Edward J. Ennis, May 29, 1944, File of Ubaldo Guidi-Buttrini, File No. 146–13–2–36–24, Box 293, DOJ Litigation Files, NACP.

117. Memorandum, Bruce Mohler, Director, Bureau of Immigration, to Monsignor Ready, September 1, 1943, and Letter, A. G. Cicognani, Archbishop of Laodicea, Apostolic Delegate, to Right Reverend Msgr. Michael J. Ready, August 20, 1943, NCWC Papers, Box 58, Folder 5 (Military Affairs: Prisoners of War, 1941–43).

118. H. J. C. to the Most Rev. William T. McCarty, January 15, 1945 [i.e., 1946], NCWC Papers, Box 58, Folder 7 (Military Affairs: Prisoners of War, 1945).

119. Diego N. Riggio to the Department of Justice, Enemy Aliens Division (undated), Folder of Diego Nando Riggio, Box 17, PMG Records of Italian Civilian Internees, NACP.

120. See Folder of Diego Nando Riggio, Box 17, PMG Records of Italian Civilian Internees, NACP.

121. Domenico Rosati to Alien Division, P. M. G. Office, War Department, January 14, 1943, Folder of Domenico N. Rosati, Box 17, PMG Records of Italian Civilian Internees, NACP.

122. See Memorandum, Brief Resume of the Case of Dr. Domenico Rosati of Pittsburgh, Penn., Folder of Domenico N. Rosati, Box 17, PMG Records of Italian Civilian Internees, NACP.

123. See Folder of Domenico N. Rosati, Box 17, PMG Records of Italian Civilian Internees, NACP.

124. Michelangelo Scicchitani, to the Hon. George L. Grobe, U.S. District Attorney, June 9, 1942, Folder of Michael Angelo Scicchitani, Box 18, PMG Records of Italian Civilian Internees, NACP.

125. See George L. Grobe, United States Attorney, to Michael Angelo Scicchitano (*sic*), May 26, 1942, Folder of Michael Angelo Scicchitani, Box 18, PMG Records of Italian Civilian Internees, NACP.

126. See, for example, Gardiner, *Pawns in a Triangle of Hate*, 61, describing the sparse local press coverage of the launching of Crystal City Internment Camp. Neither the number of internees nor their nationality was made public.

127. Mangione, "Concentration Camps—American Style," 119–20.

128. *Administrative History of the INS*, 391–92.

129. See Van Valkenburg, *An Alien Place*, 24.

130. Price, "Harbor Camp for Enemy Aliens," SM29.

131. "Legion Head Hits U.S. Treatment of Italian Prisoners," 13. Although the terms "prisoner of war" and "internees" are used interchangeably, the intended reference appears to be the subjects of internment.

132. International Committee of the Red Cross, *Report on Its Activities During the Second World War*, 611. Note that Ellis Island qualified under the Geneva Convention for long-term internment and that many internees requested this location to be closer to family members. *Administrative History of the INS*, 307.

133. Inspection Report of Ellis Island Camp, Dec. 3, 1943, in Tolzmann, *German-Americans in the World Wars*, 2078–79. The report indicates that the last inspection was performed on April 12, 1943.

134. See "Legion Head Hits U.S. Treatment of Italian Prisoners," 13.

135. 1929 Geneva Convention, Part III, Sec. V, ch. 3, Art. 45; see also International Committee of the Red Cross, *Report on Its Activities during the Second World War*, 574–75.

136. Mangione, "Concentration Camps—American Style," 126.

137. See Van Valkenburg, *An Alien Place*, 107.

138. Benedetti, *Italian Boys at Fort Missoula, Montana 1941–1943*, 1.

139. 1929 Geneva Convention, Part III, Sec. V, ch. 1, Art. 42.

140. Van Valkenburg, *An Alien Place*, 30.

141. Francesco Panciatichi to Hon. Francis Biddle, Attorney General, December 25, 1942, Folder of Francesco Panciatichi, Box 15, PMG Records of Italian Civilian Internees, NACP.

142. Edward J. Ennis, Director, to Brig. Gen. B. M. Bryan Jr., Chief, Aliens Division, War Department, January 1, 1943, Folder of Francesco Panciatichi, Box 15, PMG Records of Italian Civilian Internees, NACP.

143. Gardiner, *Pawns in a Triangle of Hate*, 37–38.

144. Frank Caracciolo to Hon. Francis Biddle, July 11, 1942, Folder of Francesco Caracciolo, Box 5, PMG Records of Italian Civilian Internees, NACP.

145. Illidio Di Bugnara to Hon. Edward J. Ennis, January 5, 1943, and Ilidio Di Bugnara to Hon. J. Sexton Daniel, U.S. District Attorney, January 30, 1943, Folder of Illidio Di Bugnara, Box 7, PMG Records of Italian Civilian Internees, NACP. Di Bugnara had served fifteen months in the U.S. Army but refused to go to the front lines against Italian soldiers, which he believed was the reason he was interned. He had two brothers in the Italian army.

146. Complaint of Vincenzo Beltrone, Spartaco Bonomi, Frank Fragale, Angelo Gloria, Frank Membrini, Italo Silvestrini, Enrico Torino, Biagio Farese, Fort Missoula, Montana, to Hon. Ugo Carusi, Department of Justice, December 9, 1943, File of Francesco Fragale, File No. 146–13–2–85–30, Box 716, DOJ Litigation Files, NACP.

147. See Mangione, "Concentration Camps—American Style," 129–30.

Conclusion

1. House Select Committee, *Fourth Interim Report*, 25.

2. Mangione, *An Ethnic at Large*, 287.

3. Biddle, *In Brief Authority*, 229.

4. *DOJ Report*, 8, citing Memorandum, Attorney General Francis Biddle to Hugh B. Cox and J. Edgar Hoover, July 16, 1943.

5. Scherini, "When Italian Americans Were 'Enemy Aliens,'" 26. Scherini relies upon Yale Law School Professor Eugene Rostow for the proposition that in court "exclusion can be sustained only on a showing of 'clear and present danger' of an imminent threat to public safety, or of aid to the enemy." This is admittedly a high standard.

6. Memorandum of Conversation between Alfred Jaretzki Jr., and Captains J. Perry, J. Lansdale, and N. Stepanovich, April 8, 1942, in Daniels, *American Concentration Camps*, vol. 4.

7. See, for example, FBI Report re. Biagio Farese, 1–16–42, 17, Farese's A-File.

8. See Howard Williams (pseudonym), interview by Stephen Fox, Arcata, California, February 6, 1986, in Fox, *Uncivil Liberties*, 45.

9. "The World War 2 Diaries, Biography of John Basilone," http://www.world-war -2-diaries.com/john-basilone-biography.html, accessed on May 6, 2017. Preferring the battlefield to celebrity tours, Basilone returned to the Pacific theater and lost his life at the Battle of Iwo Jima.

10. Thomas La Costa, oral history interview by G. Kurt Piehler and Grant Dietrich, 12–13, November 1, 1994, Rutgers Oral History Archives, http://oralhistory.rutgers .edu/alphabetical-index/31-interviewees/1052-la-costa-thomas, accessed on May 6, 2017. Mr. La Costa served in the army's Counter Intelligence Corps and fought espionage in the United States during World War II.

11. Interviews of Italian American Veterans of World War II, Rutgers Oral History Archives, http://oralhistory.rutgers.edu/military-history, accessed on May 6, 2017. I read all the interviews of World War II veterans of Italian descent in this collection. For the most part, these men grew up in ethnically diverse neighborhoods in New York and New Jersey.

12. Victor J. Campi, oral history interview by G. Kurt Piehler and Brett Marin, 6, March 27, 1995, Rutgers Oral History Archives, http://oralhistory.rutgers.edu /alphabetical-index/31-interviewees/1446-campi-victor-j, accessed on May 6, 2017. Mr. Campi served as an artillery officer in the U.S. Marine Corps during World War II.

13. Edward G. Scagliotta, oral history interview by Sandra Stewart Holyoak and John Ench, 9, October 29, 2003, Rutgers Oral History Archives, http://oralhistory .rutgers.edu/alphabetical-index/31-interviewees/1226-scagliotta-edward-g, accessed on May 6, 2017. Dr. Scagliotta served onboard a light cruiser in the Caribbean during World War II. He recalled that Italian prisoners of war who were working on the chicken farms in South Jersey were entertained in the homes of Italian families on the weekends.

14. Diggins, *Mussolini and Fascism*, 418.

15. T. Guglielmo, *White on Arrival*, 172–73.

16. Ibid., 173.

17. Vecoli, "The Search for an Italian American Identity: Continuity and Change," 98.

18. See Lothrop, "A Shadow on the Land," 343. Lothrop argues that while the Italian American community in Los Angeles in the 1920s and 1930s had a strong sense of ethnic pride, facilitated by newspapers and radio programs, "all these elements were subservient to the fact that Italo-Americans had entrusted themselves and their futures to their newly adopted country."

19. V. A. Lapenta to Captain, March 31, 1942, Folder of Vincent Anthony Lapenta, Box 11, PMG Records of Italian Civilian Internees, NACP.

20. "Alien Hatred Issue Expected to Stir Row at Legion Meet Today," 1, 3.

21. Ibid., 3.

22. Scherini, "Letters to 3024 Pierce," 235.

23. DiStasi, "A Tale of Two Citizens," 151.

24. Parolee Report of George S. Ader, District Parole Officer, December 1, 1944, Farese's A-File.

25. DiStasi, "Morto il Camerata," 8; see also Folder of Prospero Cecconi, Box 6, PMG Records of Italian Civilian Internees, NACP.

26. See DiStasi, "A Tale of Two Citizens," 151. At least two other internees retired in Italy. See File of Mario Giovanni Favoino File No. 146–13–2–51–81, Box 394, DOJ Litigation Files, NACP; and File of Calogero Carolo (aka Calogero Carollo, Charlie Carolo, Charles Carolo), File No. 146–13–2–51–1361, Box 417, DOJ Litigation Files, NACP.

27. de Guttadauro, "Exclusion Is a Four-Letter Word," 160.

28. *DOJ Report*, 13.

29. *DOJ Report*, 13–14; Issel, " 'Still Potentially Dangerous in Some Quarters,' " 265. Issel discusses an anti-Catholic campaign against Andriano led by Communist Party activists, Masonic anti-Catholics in the Italian community, and Italian anti-Fascist exiles.

30. Fox, *Uncivil Liberties*, 205–6. This group included Ettore Patrizi, the publisher of the Italian daily *L'Italia* who went to Reno, and Luigi Vinci, employed at the Bank of America, who went to Montana.

31. John Molinari, interview by Stephen Fox, San Francisco, California, February 6, 1987, in Fox, *Uncivil Liberties*, 226.

32. Lawrence DiStasi reflects on the aftermath of wartime restrictions. He says that they "accelerated the Americanization process that replaced a cohesive population clustered in Little Italys rife with ancient and well-tried modes of behavior, with modern consumers dispersed to suburbs and congratulating themselves on having 'made it' into full Americanism." *Branded*, 289.

33. DiStasi, "Morto il Camerata," 8.

Afterword

1. Korematsu v. United States, 323 U.S. 214 (1944); Glaberson, "War on Terrorism Stirs Memory of Internment," A18.

2. Comment of Peter N. Kirsanow, cited in Clemetson, "Civil Rights Commissioner under Fire for Comments on Arabs," A14. In response to those who interpreted his

comments about the potential loss of civil liberties as condoning detention camps, Kirsanow stated his opposition to internment camps and insisted that "the war on terrorism and the protection of civil rights are not mutually exclusive."

3. Muller, "Inference or Impact?," 108. Muller argues that *Korematsu* has been used as a rhetorical weapon for criticizing race consciousness in law enforcement. He instructs that among the inferences at the core of Japanese American internment was that "a person's mixed, confused, or lapsed loyalty to the United States would make that person more likely to engage in subversive conduct that would threaten national security" (ibid., 115).

4. See ibid., 123–24.

5. Volpp, "The Citizen and the Terrorist," 1577–78. See also Harnden, "Muslims Detained in U.S., Mostly on Immigration Charges," A18, stating that the detention of 1,147 Muslims "has angered civil liberties groups and yielded few concrete leads," which Bush administration officials conceded.

6. Akram and Johnson, "Race, Civil Rights, and Immigration Law after September 11, 2001," 341.

7. See Motomura, "Immigration and We the People after September 11," 424.

8. See Byron York, "Fight on the Right: 'Muslim Outreach' and a Feud between Activists," *National Review Online*, March 19, 2003, http://old.nationalreview.com /york/york031903.asp (site discontinued), accessed on November 5, 2013.

9. See Muller, "Inference or Impact?," 122.

10. Baker, "Obama's War over Terror," 37. Baker explains: "Obama left the surveillance program intact, embraced the Patriot Act, retained the authority to use renditions and embraced some of Bush's claims to state secrets. He preserved the military commissions and national security letters he criticized during the campaign, albeit with more due-process safeguards."

11. "Fact Sheet: The White House Summit on Countering Violent Extremism," https://www.whitehouse.gov/the-press-office/2015/02/18/fact-sheet-white-house -summit-countering-violent-extremism, accessed on May 3, 2017. The policy of "Countering Violent Extremism" has been tested in federal pilot programs in Boston, Los Angeles, and Minneapolis–Saint Paul aimed at young people susceptible to extremist messages circulated on social media. See also Davis, "Against Radicals," A1.

12. See Davis, "Against Radicals," A1. For a report on a nationwide survey of efforts to prevent homegrown violent extremism, see Triangle Center on Terrorism and Homeland Security (David Schanzer and Joe Eyerman), "United States Attorneys' Community Outreach and Engagement Efforts to Counter Violent Extremism: Results from a Nationwide Survey."

13. Uniting and Strengthening America by Providing Appropriate Tools Required to Intercept and Obstruct Terrorism Act of 2001 (USA PATRIOT Act), Pub. L. No. 107-56, 115 Stat. 272 (2001) (codified as amended in scattered titles of U.S.C.). For a discussion of the growth of the U.S. intelligence system since 9/11, see Dunlap, "Responses To The Five Questions," 1565–70.

14. See Muller, "Inference or Impact?," 116–17.

15. See Cole, "Are Foreign Nationals Entitled to the Same Constitutional Rights As Citizens?," 384. With respect to what rights to afford them, Professor Cole argues

that the significance of the citizen/noncitizen distinction should not be presumed. "Upon examination, there is far less to the distinction than commonly thought. In particular, foreign nationals are generally entitled to the equal protection of the laws, to political freedoms of speech and association, and to due process requirements of fair procedure where their lives, liberty, or property are at stake" (ibid., 369). See generally chapter 14, "The Bill of Rights as Human Rights" in Cole, *Enemy Aliens*.

16. See Cole, *Enemy Aliens*, 12, explaining that the "'enemy alien' rule applies only in a time of *declared war* and only to *citizens of the country with which we are at war*." He recognizes that there is an argument that the "enemy alien" concept should be "updated and expanded to justify differential treatment of foreign nationals associated with Al Qaeda or terrorism," but the "enemy alien" authority has not been invoked since World War II, which raises questions about the viability of that authority.

17. Davis, "Against Radicals," A1. Consider Dzhokhar Tsarnaev, who is of Chechen and Avar descent and became a naturalized U.S. citizen just seven months before his involvement in the twin bombings at the finish line of the Boston Marathon on April 15, 2013, resulting in the deaths of three people and injuries to more than 260 people. The jury found him guilty of all thirty counts. He was also found guilty in the related killing of a Massachusetts Institute of Technology police officer. "The Boston Marathon Bombing Verdict," *CNN Online*, April 8, 2015, http://www.cnn.com /2015/04/08/us/boston-marathon-bombing-verdict-list/index.html, accessed on April 17, 2017.

18. Bergen, "Can We Stop Homegrown Terrorists?," C1.

19. Bernabei and Cole, "Stereotyping Hurts the War—Little Cooperation in Finger-Pointing," A23. Bernabei and Cole argue that by accusing major Islamic charities, such as Al Haramain (Oregon), as "terrorist," without a fair hearing, the U.S. government "further alienates Muslims, and provides fertile recruiting ground for al Qaeda and other terrorist groups."

20. Cole, *Enemy Aliens*, 77. Cole explains how the International Emergency Economic Powers Act "allows the president to blacklist any group he chooses without substantive standards or meaningful procedural safeguards." By means of President Bush's executive order, the Secretary of the Treasury could extend sanctions to persons associated with these groups "regardless of the character of those associations."

21. See Cole, *Enemy Aliens*, 169–79, for a discussion of immigration cases in which the government has relied on secret evidence so as not to jeopardize national security. Cole shows how the evidence is often unreliable.

22. See generally chapter 3, "Rights Against Detention," in R. Posner, *Not a Suicide Pact*.

23. Issacharoff and Pildes, "Between Civil Libertarianism and Executive Unilateralism," 181.

24. See Hamdi v. Rumsfeld, 542 U.S. 507 (2004). Hamdi, a U.S. citizen allegedly taken from the battlefield in Afghanistan, was deemed an enemy combatant but had the right to notice and to challenge this status before a neutral decision-maker. Compare Rumsfeld v. Padilla, 542 U.S. 426 (2004) involving a U.S. citizen, allegedly once on the battlefield with Al Qaeda and Taliban fighters captured in Chicago. In this case, the Supreme Court held that Padilla's habeas corpus petition had been improperly

filed, never reaching the principal issue of whether, under the Authorization for Use of Military Force post September 11, the president could detain a U.S. citizen, captured within the United States, under military custody by classifying him as an enemy combatant. Once the case was in the Fourth Circuit, the Supreme Court never had the opportunity to resolve this conflict because the government transferred Padilla back to the custody of law enforcement for criminal prosecution on the eve of the Court's consideration of whether to grant Padilla's petition for certiorari. See Dycus, et al., *National Security Law*, 916. Compare Boumediene v. Bush, 553 U.S. 723 (2008), in which the Supreme Court held that the right of habeas corpus review applies to persons held in Guantánamo, including those designated as enemy combatants. However, the D.C. Circuit Court of Appeals has been deemed to subvert the *Boumediene* decision by adopting holdings in cases that seem at least to undermine the 2008 decision. See Vladeck, "The D.C. Circuit After *Boumediene*."

25. See Issacharoff and Pildes, "Between Civil Libertarianism and Executive Unilateralism," 181–82. For a history of military tribunals and a discussion of enemy combatant cases, see chapter 6, "Military Tribunals and Detentions," in Fisher, *The Constitution and 9/11*.

26. See Tushnet, *The Constitution in Wartime*, 1–7. See also Dudziak, *War Time*, 17. Dudziak explores how wartime and peacetime might be understood "as cultural features, as self-made categories, as constructs." See Dudziak, "Bush administration lawyers and policymakers looked to the past for examples, setting their own time within the context of past wartimes. In so doing they could see themselves as part of an inevitable pattern" (107).

27. Graber, "Counter-Stories: Maintaining and Expanding Civil Liberties in Wartime," 97–98. See also Polenberg, "World War II and the Bill of Rights," arguing that during World War II, the U.S. Supreme Court protected the First Amendment rights of naturalized citizens, political extremists, and religious dissenters. Polenberg discusses the following key cases protecting naturalized citizens: Schneiderman v. United States, 320 U.S. 118 (1943); Baumgartner v. United States, 322 U.S. 665 (1944); and Hartzel v. United States, 322 U.S. 680 (1944).

28. Tushnet, *The Constitution in Wartime*, 5.

29. Tushnet argues that through the "process of social learning," we are "increasingly skeptical" about government claims of threats to national security since we know that in the past threats have been exaggerated and measures taken that were ineffective, thus reducing the scope of government responses to threats. Tushnet, "Defending *Korematsu?*," 125. Compare E. Posner and Vermeule, *Terror in the Balance*, 85–86, arguing "it may well be rational for governments to react harshly at the start of an emergency, and then to adjust policies as time reveals whether the original reactions were warranted." The authors assert that lawyers are limited in their ability to contribute value to governmental decision-making during emergencies, and that policies should be left to national security experts and the political process (273–75).

30. See Executive Order No. 13769, revoked and replaced by Executive Order 13780. The "travel ban" in the original order gave rise to numerous lawsuits. Most relevant to the purposes of this discussion, the Court of Appeals for the Ninth Circuit held that the federal government failed to show a likelihood of success on its claim that Ex-

ecutive Order 13769 did not violate various aliens' due process rights, namely notice and a hearing prior to restricting an individual's right to travel. The Ninth Circuit denied an appeal of the temporary restraining order entered by a federal district court in the state of Washington, preventing enforcement of the executive order. See Washington v. Trump, 847 F.3d 1151 (9th Cir. 2017). The second order, Executive Order 13780, which alters the scope of the suspension of entry to certain foreign nationals from countries where terrorist groups such as ISIS have a presence, has likewise met with numerous constitutional challenges in federal courts across the country.

31. See American Immigration Council Doc. No. 17012775, "Summary and Analysis of Executive Order."

32. See Galston, "Nothing Redeems Trump's Travel Ban."

Bibliography

Primary Sources

Archival Material

Ann Arbor, Michigan
    University of Michigan Library (Special Collections Library)
        Joseph A. Labadie Collection, American Committee for Protection of
            Foreign Born Records
Cambridge, Massachusetts
    Historical & Special Collections, Harvard Law School Library
        Erwin Griswold Papers
College Park, Maryland
    National Archives at College Park
        Records of the Department of Justice, Record Group 60
            WWII Alien Enemy Internment Case Files, 1941–1951
        Records of the Office of the Provost Marshal General, Record Group 389
            Alien Enemy Information Bureau, Records Relating to Italian Civilian
                Internees during World War II, 1941–1946
            Subject Correspondence, Executive Division, Legal Office, 1942–1945
            Subject File, 1942–1946, Hawaii, Civilian Internees
Fort Missoula, Montana
    The Historical Museum at Fort Missoula
        Miscellaneous Documents on Italian Internment
Hyde Park, New York
    Franklin D. Roosevelt Presidential Library
        Franklin D. Roosevelt Collections
        Grace Tully Collection
        Ugo Carusi Papers
Minneapolis, Minnesota
    University of Minnesota, Immigration History Research Center Archives 1496
        The Dominic R. Massaro Collection (Order Sons of Italy in America)
New Haven, Connecticut
    Manuscripts and Archives, Yale University Library
        Henry Lewis Stimson Papers (MS 465)
            Henry Lewis Stimson Diaries (microfilm edition)
New York, New York
    The New York Public Library, Manuscripts and Archives, Astor, Lennox, and
        Tilden Foundations

Fiorello H. La Guardia Papers
Gino Speranza Papers
Nicholas Kelley Papers
Vito Marcantonio Papers
San Francisco, California
California Historical Society
Marshall Dill Papers
Syracuse, New York
Syracuse University Libraries, Special Collections Research Center
Edward Corsi Papers
Washington, DC
The American Catholic History Research Center and University Archives, The Catholic University of America
The National Catholic Welfare Conference Papers
Department of Homeland Security, U.S. Citizenship & Immigration Services, National Security & Records Verification Directorate, Genealogy Section
Biagio Farese, Alien Registration File A-3442924
Pericle Adriano Carlo Chieri, Naturalization Certificate File C-7185491
National Archives Building
Records of the Immigration and Naturalization Service, Record Group 85
World War II Internment Files, Fort Missoula, Montana

Presidential Materials

Executive Order No. 9066, *Federal Register* 7 (February 25, 1942): 1407.
Executive Order No. 13769, *Federal Register* 82 (February 1, 2017): 8977.
Executive Order No. 13780, *Federal Register* 82 (March 9, 2017): 13209.
Presidential Proclamation No. 2525, *Federal Register* 6 (December 7, 1941): 6321.
Presidential Proclamation No. 2527, *Federal Register* 6 (December 8, 1941): 6324.

Published Government Documents

U.S. Commission on Wartime Relocation and Internment of Civilians. *Personal Justice Denied: Report of the Commission on Wartime Relocation and Internment of Civilians.* Washington, DC: U.S. Government Printing Office, 1982.
U.S. Congress. House. Committee on the Judiciary, Subcommittee on the Constitution. *Wartime Violation of Italian American Civil Liberties Act: Hearing before the Subcommittee on the Constitution of the Committee on the Judiciary*, 106th Cong., 1st sess. H. REP. NO. 2442, October 26, 1999. Washington, DC: U.S. Government Printing Office, 1999.
———. *Fourth Interim Report: Findings and Recommendations on Evacuation of Enemy Aliens and Others From Prohibited Military Zones*, 77th Cong., 2nd sess., H. REP. NO. 2124, May, 1942. Washington, DC: U.S. Government Printing Office, 1942.

———. *Final Report of the Select Committee Investigating National Defense Migration*, 77th Cong., 2nd sess., H. REP. NO. 3, January, 1943. Washington, DC: U.S. Government Printing Office, 1943.

———. Select Committee Investigating National Defense Migration. *Preliminary Report and Recommendations on Problems of Evacuation of Citizens and Aliens From Military Areas*, 77th Cong., 2nd sess., H. REP. NO. 1911, March 19, 1942. Washington, DC: U.S. Government Printing Office, 1942.

U.S. Congress. Senate. *Final Report of the Select Committee to Study Governmental Operations with respect to Intelligence Activities. Supplementary Detailed Staff Reports of Intelligence Activities and the Rights of Americans*, Book 3, 94th Cong., 2nd sess., Report 94–755, April 23, 1976. Washington, DC: U.S. Government Printing Office, 1976.

U.S. Congressional Research Service. *The Internment of German and Italian Aliens Compared with the Internment of Japanese Aliens in the United States during World War II: A Brief History and Analysis*, by Peter B. Sheridan, November 24, 1980. In Boehm, *Papers of the U.S. Commission on Wartime Relocation and Internment of Civilians*, 25886–25904.

U.S. Department of Commerce, Bureau of the Census. *Sixteenth Census of the United States: 1940*, "Population," Vol. 2, "Characteristics of the Population." Washington, DC: U.S. Government Printing Office, 1943.

U.S. Department of Justice. *Annual Report of the Attorney General of the United States for the Fiscal Year Ended June 30, 1941*. Washington, DC: U.S. Government Printing Office, 1942.

———. *Annual Report of the Attorney General of the United States for the Fiscal Year Ended June 30, 1943*. Washington, DC: U.S. Government Printing Office, 1943.

———. *Questions and Answers on Regulations Concerning Aliens of Enemy Nationalities*. Washington, DC: U.S. Government Printing Office, 1942.

U.S. Department of Labor, Secretary of Labor's Committee on Administrative Procedure. *The Immigration and Naturalization Service*. Washington, DC: U.S. Government Printing Office, 1940.

U.S. Office of War Information, Division of Public Inquiries. *United States Government Manual: 1945*. Washington, DC: U.S. Government Printing Office, 1945.

Western Defense Command, "Individual Exclusion Program of Non-Japanese." *Supplemental Report on Civilian Controls Exercised by Western Defense Command*, January, 1947. In Boehm, *Papers of the U.S. Commission on Wartime Relocation and Internment of Civilians*, 1608–1622, 2220–2321.

Reports and Manuscripts

American Immigration Council, Doc. No. 17012775, "Summary and Analysis of Executive Order 'Protecting the Nation from Foreign Terrorist Entry into the United States,'" January 27, 2017.

Triangle Center on Terrorism and Homeland Security (David Schanzer and Joe Eyerman), "United States Attorneys' Community Outreach and Engagement Efforts to Counter Violent Extremism: Results from a Nationwide Survey," December 2016.

U.S. Department of Justice, Immigration and Naturalization Service, Office of Research and Educational Services, General Research Unit. *Administrative History of the Immigration and Naturalization Service during World War II*. Unpublished manuscript in U.S. Citizenship & Immigration Services History Office & Library, Washington, DC, August 19, 1946.

Secondary Sources

Akram, Susan M., and Kevin R. Johnson. "Race, Civil Rights, and Immigration Law after September 11, 2001: The Targeting of Arabs and Muslims." *New York University Annual Survey of American Law* 58 (2002): 295–355.

"Alien Curbs Aimed Only at Disloyal." *New York Times*, December 14, 1941.

"Alien Hatred Issue Expected To Stir Row at Legion Meet Today." *Boston Daily Globe*, August 12, 1944.

"All Enemy Alien Internees Now in Custody of Immigration Service." *Department of Justice Immigration and Naturalization Service Monthly Review* 1, no. 1 (July 1943): 21.

"The Attorney General Warns Against Race Prejudice and Discrimination," excerpts from speech given November 11, 1943, reprinted in *Department of Justice Immigration and Naturalization Service Monthly Review* 1, no. 6 (December 1943): 8–9.

Baker, Peter. "Obama's War over Terror." *New York Times Magazine*, January 17, 2010, 30–39, 46–47.

Bayor, Ronald H. "Comments on the Papers by Philip V. Cannistraro, George W. Carey and Miriam Cohen." In Lydio F. Tomasi, *Italian Americans*, 289–301.

Benedetti, Umberto. *Italian Boys at Fort Missoula, Montana 1941–1943*. Missoula, Montana: Pictorial Histories, 1991.

Bergen, Peter. "Can We Stop Homegrown Terrorists?" *Wall Street Journal*, Saturday/ Sunday, January 23–24, 2016.

Bernabei, Lynne, and David Cole. "Stereotyping Hurts the War—Little Cooperation in Finger-Pointing." *Washington Times*, November 24, 2003.

Biddle, Francis. *In Brief Authority*. Garden City, New York: Doubleday, 1962.

Boehm, Randolph, ed., guide compiled by Robert Lester. *Papers of the U.S. Commission on Wartime Relocation and Internment of Civilians*, Part 1, Numerical File Archive. Frederick, MD: University Publications of America, 1983.

Bosworth, R. J. B. "The Internment of Italians in Australia." In Iacovetta et al., *Enemies Within*, 227–55.

Brinkley, Alan. *Franklin Delano Roosevelt*. New York: Oxford University Press, 2010.

———. *Voices of Protest: Huey Long, Father Coughlin, and the Great Depression*. New York: Knopf, 1982.

Bruner, Jerome S., and Jeanette Sayre. "Shortwave Listening in an Italian Community." *Public Opinion Quarterly* (Winter 1941): 640–56.

Cannato, Vincent J. *American Passage: The History of Ellis Island*. New York: Harper Perennial, 2010.

Cannistraro, Philip V. "Generoso Pope and The Rise of Italian American Politics, 1925–1936." In Lydio F. Tomasi, *Italian Americans*, 264–88.

Cannistraro, Philip V., and Gerald Meyer, eds. *The Lost World of Italian American Radicalism: Politics, Labor, and Culture.* Westport, CT: Praeger, 2003.

Clemetson, Lynette. "Civil Rights Commissioner under Fire for Comments on Arabs." *New York Times*, July 23, 2002.

Cole, David. "Are Foreign Nationals Entitled to the Same Constitutional Rights As Citizens?" *Thomas Jefferson Law Review* 25 (2003): 367–88.

———. *Enemy Aliens: Double Standards and Constitutional Freedoms in the War on Terrorism.* New York: New Press, 2003.

———. "The New McCarthyism: Repeating History in the War on Terrorism." *Harvard Civil Rights-Civil Liberties Law Review* 38 (2003): 1–30.

Conn, Stetson, Rose C. Engelman, and Byron Fairchild, eds. *Guarding the United States and its Outposts.* Washington, DC: Center of Military History, United States Army, 2000.

Corsi, Edward. "Italian Immigrants and Their Children." *The Annals of the American Academy of Political and Social Science* 223 (September 1942): 100–106.

"Corsi Heads Board on Enemy Aliens." *New York Times*, December 23, 1941.

Culp, Eugene M. "Alien Enemy Paroles." *Department of Justice Immigration and Naturalization Service Monthly Review* 3, no. 4 (October 1945): 204–8.

Daniels, Roger, ed. *American Concentration Camps: A Documentary History of the Relocation and Incarceration of Japanese Americans, 1942–1945.* 9 vols. New York: Garland, 1989.

Davis, Julie Hirschfield. "Against Radicals, Obama Urges Global United Front." *New York Times*, February 19, 2015, late edition (East Coast).

de Guttadauro, Angelo. "Exclusion Is a Four-Letter Word." In DiStasi, *Una Storia Segreta*, 156–60.

Dennis, William C., Letters to *The Times*, "Enemy Aliens Pose Problem," *New York Times*, April 13, 1942.

Dies, Martin. *The Trojan Horse in America.* New York: Dodd, Mead, 1940.

Diggins, John P. *Mussolini and Fascism: The View from America.* Princeton, NJ: Princeton University Press, 1972.

DiStasi, Lawrence, *Branded: How Italian Immigrants Became 'Enemies' During World War II.* Bolinas: Sanniti, 2016.

———. "A Fish Story." In DiStasi, *Una Storia Segreta*, 63–96.

———. "Let's Keep Smiling." In DiStasi, *Una Storia Segreta*, 198–216.

———. "Morto il Camerata." In DiStasi, *Una Storia Segreta*, 1–9.

———. "A Tale of Two Citizens." In DiStasi, *Una Storia Segreta*, 137–52.

———, ed. *Una Storia Segreta: The Secret History of Italian American Evacuation and Internment during World War II.* Berkeley: Heyday Books, 2001.

Drypolcher, Lucetta Berizzi. "Orders to Take Him Away." In DiStasi, *Una Storia Segreta*, 217–22.

Dudziak, Mary L. *War Time: An Idea, Its History, Its Consequences.* New York: Oxford University Press, 2012.

Dunlap, Charles J. Jr. "Responses to the Five Questions." *William Mitchell Law Review* 38.5 (2012): 1564–86.

Dunn, Geoffrey. "Mala Notte: The Relocation Story in Santa Cruz." In DiStasi, *Una Storia Segreta*, 103–14.

Dycus, Stephen, Arthur L. Berney, William C. Banks, Peter Raven-Hansen, and Stephen I. Vladeck. *National Security Law*. 6th ed. New York: Wolters Kluwer, 2016.

"The 'Enemy Alien.'" *Herald Tribune*, March 23, 1942.

"Explains Benefits to Italian Aliens." *New York Times*, October 14, 1942.

"Ezio Pinza Seized as Enemy Alien; FBI Takes Singer to Ellis Island." *New York Times*, March 13, 1942.

Ferraro, Thomas J. *Feeling Italian: The Art of Ethnicity in America*. New York: New York University Press, 2005.

Fisher, Louis. *The Constitution and 9/11: Recurring Threats to America's Freedoms*. Lawrence, KS: University Press of Kansas, 2008.

"Five Greater Boston Men on State Alien Enemy Board." *Boston Daily Globe*, December 23, 1941.

Fox, Stephen. *America's Invisible Gulag: A Biography of German American Internment & Exclusion in World War II*. New York: Peter Lang, 2000.

———. "The Deportation of Latin American Germans, 1941–47: Fresh Legs for Mr. Monroe's Doctrine." *Yearbook of German-American Studies* 32 (1997): 117–42.

———. *Fear Itself: Inside the FBI Roundup of German Americans during World War II: The Past as Prologue*. New York: iUniverse, 2005.

———. "General John DeWitt and the Proposed Internment of German and Italian Aliens during World War II." *Pacific Historical Review* 57, no. 4 (November 1988): 407–38.

———. *Homeland Insecurity: Aliens, Citizens, and the Challenge to American Civil Liberties in World War II*. New York: iUniverse, 2009.

———. *Uncivil Liberties: Italian Americans under Siege during World War II*. Rev. ed. Boca Raton: Universal Publishers, 2002.

———. *The Unknown Internment: An Oral History of the Relocation of Italian Americans during World War II*. Boston: Twayne, 1990.

Friedman, Max Paul. *Nazis and Good Neighbors: The United States Campaign against the Germans of Latin America in World War II*. New York: Cambridge University Press, 2003.

Gage, Beverly. *The Day Wall Street Exploded: A Story of America in Its First Age of Terror*. New York: Oxford University Press, 2009.

Gallagher, Dorothy. *All the Right Enemies: The Life and Murder of Carlo Tresca*. New Brunswick, NJ: Rutgers University Press, 1988.

Galston, William A. "Nothing Redeems Trump's Travel Ban." *Wall Street Journal*, February 1, 2017.

Gardiner, C. Harvey. *Pawns in a Triangle of Hate: The Peruvian Japanese and the United States*. Seattle: University of Washington Press, 1981.

Glaberson, William. "War on Terrorism Stirs Memory of Internment." *New York Times*, September 24, 2001.

Goldstein, Richard. "Charles Poletti Dies at 99; Aided War-Ravaged Italy." *New York Times*, August 10, 2002.

———. "John Pastore, Prominent Figure in Rhode Island Politics for Three Decades, Dies at 93." *New York Times*, July 17, 2000.

Goldstein, Robert Justin. *Political Repression in Modern America: From 1870 to 1976.* Chicago and Urbana: University of Illinois Press, 2001.

Graber, Mark A. "Counter-Stories: Maintaining and Expanding Civil Liberties in Wartime." In Tushnet, *The Constitution in Wartime*, 95–123.

Grodzins, Morton. *Americans Betrayed: Politics and the Japanese Evacuation.* Chicago: University of Chicago Press, 1949.

Guglielmo, Jennifer. *Living the Revolution: Italian Women's Resistance and Radicalism in New York City, 1880–1945.* Chapel Hill: University of North Carolina Press, 2010.

Guglielmo, Thomas A. " 'No Color Barrier': Italians, Race, and Power in the United States." In *Are Italians White? How Race Is Made in America*, edited by Jennifer Guglielmo and Salvatore Salerno, 29–43. New York: Routledge, 2003.

———. *White on Arrival: Italians, Race, Color, and Power in Chicago, 1890–1945.* Oxford: Oxford University Press, 2003.

Handlin, Oscar. *The Uprooted: The Epic Story of the Great Migration that Made the American People.* Philadelphia: University of Pennsylvania Press, 2002.

Harnden, Toby. "Muslims Detained in U.S., Mostly on Immigration Charges." *Gazette*, November 6, 2001.

Heckscher, August. *When LaGuardia Was Mayor: New York's Legendary Years.* With Phyllis Robinson. New York: W. W. Norton, 1978.

Hoover, J. Edgar. "Alien Enemy Control." *Iowa Law Review* 29 (1943–44): 396–408.

Hull, Cordell. *The Memoirs of Cordell Hull in Two Volumes.* Vol. 2. New York: Macmillan, 1948.

Iacovetta, Franca, Roberto Perin, and Angelo Principe, eds. *Enemies Within: Italian and Other Internees in Canada and Abroad.* Toronto: University of Toronto Press, 2000.

Ianni, Francis A. J. "Familialism in the South of Italy and in the United States." In S.M. Tomasi, *Perspectives in Italian Immigration and Ethnicity*, 103–7.

International Committee of the Red Cross. *Report of the International Committee of the Red Cross on Its Activities during the Second World War.* Vol. 1 (September 1, 1939–June 30, 1947). Geneva, May 1948.

Issacharoff, Samuel, and Richard H. Pildes. "Between Civil Libertarianism and Executive Unilateralism: An Institutional Process Approach to Rights during Wartime." In Tushnet, *The Constitution in Wartime*, 161–97.

Issel, William. *For Both Cross and Flag: Catholic Action, Anti-Catholicism, and National Security Politics in World War II San Francisco.* Philadelphia: Temple University Press, 2010.

———. " 'Still Potentially Dangerous in Some Quarters': Sylvester Andriano, Catholic Action, and Un-American Activities in California." *Pacific Historical Review* 75 (2006): 231–70.

Jacobson, Matthew Frye. *Whiteness of a Different Color: European Immigrants and the Alchemy of Race.* Cambridge: Harvard University Press, 1998.

"John Molinari, 94: Former Justice of State Appellate Court." *Los Angeles Times*, September 16, 1994.

"Judge Forte Says Italian Aliens Loyal." *Boston Daily Globe*, March 16, 1942.

Kanstroom, Daniel. *Aftermath: Deportation Law and the New American Diaspora.* New York: Oxford University Press, 2012.

———. *Deportation Nation: Outsiders in American History.* Cambridge, MA: Harvard University Press, 2010.

Kashima, Tetsuden. *Judgment without Trial: Japanese American Imprisonment during World War II.* Seattle: University of Washington Press, 2003.

Kohler, Max J. *Immigration and Aliens in the United States: Studies of American Immigration Laws and the Legal Status of Aliens in the United States.* New York: Bloch, 1936.

Kohn, Richard. *Eagle and Sword: The Beginnings of the Military Establishment in America.* New York: Free Press, 1975.

Krase, Jerome. "Ironies of Icons: The Slings and Arrows of Outrageous Multiculturalists." In *Italian Americans in a Multicultural Society: Proceedings of the Symposium of the American Italian Historical Association*, edited by Jerome Krase and Judith N. DeSena, 1–18. Stony Brook: Forum Italicum, 1994.

LaGumina, Salvatore J. "American Political Process and Italian Participation in New York State." In S. M. Tomasi, *Perspectives in Italian Immigration and Ethnicity*, 85–97.

"Legion Head Hits U.S. Treatment of Italian Prisoners." *Boston Daily Globe*, July 26, 1944.

Liberati, Luigi Bruti. "The Internment of Italian Canadians." Translated by Gabriele Scardellato. In Iacovetta et al., *Enemies Within*, 76–98.

Liebmann, George W. *Diplomacy between the Wars: Five Diplomats and the Shaping of the Modern World.* London: I. B. Tauris, 2008.

Lothrop, Gloria Ricci. "A Shadow on the Land: The Impact of Fascism on Los Angeles Italians," *California History* 75, no. 4 (Winter 1996–1997): 338–53.

———. "Unwelcome in Freedom's Land: The Impact of World War II on Italian Aliens in Southern California." In DiStasi, *Una Storia Segreta*, 161–94.

Mangione, Jerre. "Concentration Camps—American Style." In DiStasi, *Una Storia Segreta*, 117–31.

———. *An Ethnic at Large: A Memoir of America in the Thirties and Forties.* New York: G. P. Putnam's Sons, 1978.

McGirr, Lisa. "The Passion of Sacco and Vanzetti: A Global History." *The Journal of American History* 93 (2007): 1085–115.

Meyer, Gerald. *Vito Marcantonio: Radical Politician 1902–1954.* Albany: State University of New York Press, 1989.

Moloney, Deirdre M. *National Insecurities: Immigrants and U.S. Deportation Policy Since 1882.* Chapel Hill: University of North Carolina Press, 2012.

Motomura, Hiroshi. "Immigration and We the People after September 11." *Albany Law Review* 66 (2003): 413–29.

Muller, Eric L. *American Inquisition: The Hunt for Japanese American Disloyalty in World War II.* Chapel Hill: University of North Carolina Press, 2007.

———. "Betrayal on Trial: Japanese-American 'Treason' in World War II." *North Carolina Law Review* 82 (2004): 1759–98.

———. "*Hirabayashi* and the Invasion Evasion." *North Carolina Law Review* 88 (2010): 1333–88.

———. "Inference or Impact? Racial Profiling and the Internment's True Legacy." *Ohio State Journal of Criminal Law* 1 (2003–2004): 103–31.

Nelli, Humbert S. *From Immigrants to Ethnics: The Italian Americans*. New York: Oxford University Press, 1983.

———. *Italians in Chicago 1880–1930: A Study in Ethnic Mobility*. New York: Oxford University Press, 1970.

Ngai, Mae M. *Impossible Subjects: Illegal Aliens and the Making of Modern America*. Princeton, NJ: Princeton University Press, 2004.

"Panel of 22 Set Up for Alien Hearings." *New York Times*, August 22, 1943.

Panunzio, Constantine. "Italian Americans, Fascism, and the War." *Yale Review* 31 (June 1942): 771–82.

Parker, Kunal M. *The Constitution, Citizenship, and Immigration in American History, 1790–2000*. Washington, DC: American Historical Association, 2013.

———. *Making Foreigners: Immigration and Citizenship Law in America, 1600–2000*. New York: Cambridge University Press, 2015.

Pernicone, Nunzio. *Carlo Tresca: Portrait of a Rebel*. New York: Palgrave Macmillan, 2005.

Persico, Joseph E. *Roosevelt's Secret War: FDR and World War II Espionage*. New York: Random House, 2001.

Polenberg, Richard. "World War II and the Bill of Rights." In *The Home-Front War: World War II and American Society*, edited by Kenneth O'Brien and Lynn Parsons, 11–24. Westport, CT: Greenwood, 1995.

Posner, Eric A., and Adrian Vermeule. *Terror in the Balance: Security, Liberty, and the Courts*. New York: Oxford University Press, 2007.

Posner, Richard A. *Not a Suicide Pact: The Constitution in a Time of National Emergency*. New York: Oxford University Press, 2006.

Powers, Richard Gid. *Secrecy and Power: The Life of J. Edgar Hoover*. New York: Free Press, 1987.

Preston, William, Jr. *Aliens and Dissenters: Federal Suppression of Radicals, 1903–1933*. 2nd ed. Urbana: University of Illinois Press, 1994.

Price, Clair. "Harbor Camp for Enemy Aliens." *New York Times*, January 25, 1942.

"Report on Progress: Naturalization Delays Decreasing," *Department of Justice Immigration and Naturalization Service Monthly Review* 1, no. 2 (August 1943): 20.

Ribuffo, Leo P. "Religion in the History of U.S. Foreign Policy." In *The Influence of Faith: Religious Groups and U.S. Foreign Policy*, edited by Elliott Abrams, 1–32. Lanham: Rowman & Littlefield, 2001.

Richards, David A. J. *Italian American: The Racializing of an Ethnic Identity*. New York: New York University Press, 1999.

Robinson, Greg. *A Tragedy of Democracy: Japanese Confinement in North America*. New York: Columbia University Press, 2009.

"Roundup of Axis Aliens: Germans, Italians Taken by Federal Agents Here." *Boston Daily Globe*, December 10, 1941.

"Rulings on Aliens Speeded by Biddle." *New York Times*, December 21, 1941.

Saito, Natsu Taylor. "Crossing the Border: The Interdependence of Foreign Policy and Racial Justice in the United States." *Yale Human Rights & Development Law Journal* 1 (1998): 53–84.

Salvemini, Gaetano. *Italian Fascist Activities in the United States*. Edited with introduction by Philip V. Cannistraro. New York: Center for Migration Studies, 1977.

Scherini, Rose D. "Letters to 3024 Pierce." In DiStasi, *Una Storia Segreta*, 223–35.

———. "When Italian Americans Were 'Enemy Aliens.'" In DiStasi, *Una Storia Segreta*, 10–31.

Sexton, Patricia Cayo. *The War on Labor and the Left: Understanding America's Unique Conservatism*. Boulder: Westview, 1991.

Sidak, J. Gregory. "War, Liberty, and Enemy Aliens." *New York University Law Review* 67 (1992): 1402–32.

Smith, James Morton. *Freedom's Fetters: The Alien and Sedition Laws and American Civil Liberties*. Vol. 1. Ithaca: Cornell University Press, 1956.

Sponza, Lucio. "The Internment of Italians in Britain." In Iacovetta et al., *Enemies Within*, 256–79.

Starr, Kevin. *Embattled Dreams: California in War and Peace, 1940–1950*. New York: Oxford University Press, 2002.

Stone, Geoffrey. *Perilous Times: Free Speech in Wartime*. New York: W. W. Norton, 2004.

Sylvernale, Gloria Micheletti. "Alien in Texas." In DiStasi, *Una Storia Segreta*, 196–97.

Taubman, Howard. *The Maestro: The Life of Arturo Toscanini*. New York: Simon and Schuster, 1951.

Temkin, Moshik. *The Sacco-Vanzetti Affair: America on Trial*. New Haven: Yale University Press, 2009.

Tintori, Guido. "New Discoveries, Old Prejudices: The Internment of Italian Americans during World War II." In DiStasi, *Una Storia Segreta*, 236–54.

"Tolerance Toward Aliens Urged at Annual Dinner." *Boston Daily Globe*, March 20, 1942.

Tolzmann, Don Heinrich, ed. *German-Americans in the World Wars*. Vol. 4, *The World War Two Experience: The Internment of German-Americans, Parts One and Two*. Munich: K. G. Saur, 1995.

Tomasi, Lydio F., ed. *Italian Americans: New Perspectives in Italian Immigration and Ethnicity*. Staten Island: Center for Migration Studies of New York, 1985.

Tomasi, S. M., ed. *Perspectives in Italian Immigration and Ethnicity: Proceedings of the Symposium Held at Casa Italiana, Columbia University May 21–23, 1976*. New York: Center for Migration Studies, 1977.

Tushnet, Mark. "Defending *Korematsu*? Reflections on Civil Liberties in Wartime." In Tushnet, *The Constitution in Wartime*, 124–140.

———, ed. *The Constitution in Wartime: Beyond Alarmism and Complacency*. Durham, NC: Duke University Press, 2005.

"U.S. Not Inclined to Return Contraband to Enemy Aliens." *Boston Daily Globe*, October 26, 1943.

Valdastri, Mario Jr. "Two Men in Suits." In DiStasi, *Una Storia Segreta*, 153–55.

Van Valkenburg, Carol Bulger. *An Alien Place: The Fort Missoula, Montana, Detention Camp, 1941–1944*. Missoula: Pictorial Histories, 1995.

Vargas, Zaragosa. *Labor Rights Are Civil Rights: Mexican American Workers in Twentieth-Century America*. Princeton, NJ: Princeton University Press, 2005.

Vecoli, Rudolph J. "The Search for an Italian American Identity: Continuity and Change." In Lydio F. Tomasi, *Italian Americans*, 88–112.

Vladeck, Stephen I. "The D.C. Circuit After *Boumediene*." *Seton Hall Law Review* 41 (2011): Article 12.

Volpp, Leti. "The Citizen and the Terrorist," *University of California at Los Angeles Law Review* 49 (2001–2002): 1575–1600.

Wechman, Robert J. *The Economic Development of the Italian-American*. Champaign, IL: Stipes, 1983.

Weglyn, Michi. *Years of Infamy: The Untold Story of America's Concentration Camps*. New York: William Morrow, 1976.

Whitehead, Don. *The FBI Story: A Report to the People*. Foreword by J. Edgar Hoover. New York: Random House, 1956.

Zelizer, Julian E. *Arsenal of Democracy: The Politics of National Security—from World War II to the War on Terrorism*. New York: Basic Books, 2010.

Index

public policy and, 147; significance of, 147; Tolan Committee and, 133

Civil Affairs Division of the army, 62

Civilian Conservation Corps, 110

Civil liberties, 3, 12, 36, 45, 134, 136, 143, 158n10

Civil War, 12

Cold War, 12

Colombia, 50

Columbus Day, 71, 135

Combattenti, 32

Communism, 30, 35. *See also* House Un-American Activities Committee (HUAC)

Conference of Foreign Ministers of the American Republics, 50

Consolidated (aircraft company), 60

Constitutional rights, 3, 9, 75, 82, 95, 149

Conte Biancamano (ship), 37, 118, 129, 168–69n188

Contraband items, 69

Cooley, Thomas M., *88*

Corriere D'America, 34

Corriere del Popolo, 56

Corsi, Edward, 87, 90–91, 137

Costa Rica, 50

Costello, Frank, 18

Coughlin, Father, 25

Council of Marconi, 32

Counsel, right to, 76, 80

Counter violent extremism (CVE), 146

Criminality, 26, 49, 82, 98, 148–49

Crystal City, Texas, 52, 108–11, 117

Cuba, 77

Cuneo, Ernest, 182n193

Curfews, 3, 6, 44, 54, 69

Custodial detention list, 30

Custodial Detention Program, 31, 41, 135

D'Amato, Alfonse, 3

d'Amico, Guglielmo, 125

Dante Alighieri Society, 32

Defense Commands, 177n119

de Guttadauro, Angelo, 62–63

Democratic National Committee, 34

Denaturalization, 46, 74

Deportation: after internment, 79–80; due process and, 12, 82; hearings, 75–76

Deportation-Internment Program, 51

Detaining Power, 38, 116, 129

Detention facilities, 50, 83, 94, 107, 123, 196n2. *See also* Internment camps

Detroit, 25, 93–94, 137

DeWitt, John, 44, 56, 60–68, 134

Di Bugnara, Ilidio, 131

Dies, Martin, 23–24, 56

Dies Committee, 18, 86. *See also* House Un-American Activities Committee (HUAC)

Diggins, John, 21, 55

DiMaggio, Dominic, 55

DiMaggio, Giuseppe, 55, 61

DiMaggio, Joe, 55

DiMaggio, Vincent, 55

Discrimination: employment, 26–27; internment and, 31; against Italians, 16; against Japanese, 134; against Mexicans, 25; protection from, 43

Disloyalty. *See* Loyalty

DiStasi, Lawrence, 5, 122, 143

Douglas (aircraft company), 60

Drum, Hugh, 44, 58, 60, 68, 134

Drypolcher, Lucetta Berizzi, 120

Dual citizenship, 61

Due process, 148–49; aliens and, 82–83; alien enemy hearings and, 7, 74, 85; deportation and, 12, 14, 75–76; exclusion hearings and, 62–63; internment and, 45, 127, 136–37; Tolan Committee and, 81–82

East Coast, 46–47, 58, 134

Eastern Defense Command, 6, 9, 44, 60, 63, 69

Eastern Military Area, 68

Ecuador, 50

Einstein, Albert, 44

Ellis Island, New York, 78–79, 95, 108, 128

French Revolution, 12
Friedman, Max, 50–51

Galleanists, 14
General Intelligence Division, 14, 30
Geneva Convention of 1929, 38, 75, 106, 110, 115–17, 122, 130
Germans: in alien enemy hearings, 84–85; internment of, 2, 5, 13, 44; in Latin America, 51–52; loyalty of, 5; and prohibited zones, 61, 65; race and, 65–66, 133–34; relocation of, 178n128
Ghirardi, Aldo, 94
Gloria, Angelo, 90–91
Gloucester City Detention Center, New Jersey, 98, 108, 123
Great Britain, 3, 44, 77; internment of Italians in, 104, 195n154
Great Depression, 21, 25
Green, William, *140*
Gregory, Thomas, 13
Griswold, Erwin, 84–87, *88*
Grodzins, Martin, 59
Group relations, in internment camps, 112–13
Grudges, 49
Guadalcanal, 139
Guatemala, 50
Guidi, Velleda, 123
Guidi-Buttrini, Ubaldo, 85–86, 92, 113–14, 123, 125, 137
Guilt, presumptive, 7, 12
Gullion, Allen, 102–3
Guttadauro, Nino, 62–63, 142

Hague Convention X of 1907, 38
Handlin, Oscar, 21
Harlem Italian Defense League, 19
Hawaii, 60–61, 157–58n7
Health care, in internment camps, 114–15
Hearings, alien enemy, 74–77, 80–105
Hearsay evidence, 48, 76
Hemispheric security measures, 50

Hitler, Adolf, 23
Hobbs Bill, 26
Home visits, 120
Honduras, 50
Honolulu Immigration Station, 102
Honolulu Star Bulletin, 109
Hoover, J. Edgar, 14, 29, 41, 100
House of Representatives Select Committee Investigating National Defense Migration, 53–54
House Un-American Activities Committee (HUAC), 24–25, 47, 56
Hull, Cordell, 2, 29, 38, 51–52
Hungarian aliens, 155n1, 157n6
Husbands, wives and, in internment camps, 108

Ickes, Harold, 33
Ickes, Raymond W., 52
Ilacqua, Bruna, seeking financial assistance, 201n110
Ilacqua, Carmelo, 43, 114, 141–42
Il Cenacolo, 100. *See also* Cenacalo Club
Il Cittadino, 77
Il Corriere Italiano, 96
Il Grido della Stirpe (The Cry of the Ancestry), 32, 99, 121
Illinois, 47. *See also* Chicago
Illiteracy, 32, 56, 70, 133, 136
Il Progresso, 33, 85
Immigration Act of 1917, 161n22
Immigration Act of 1918, 13
Immigration Act of 1924, 15, 93, 161n26
Immigration and Naturalization Service (INS), 8, 42, 45, 52, 75, 107–9
Individual exclusion, 3, 44, 58, 62–64, 133
Individual Exclusion Program of Non-Japanese, 62
Instructions (remedial), 7, 74, 91
Intelligence, military, 30
International Committee of the Red Cross, 38, 106, 129
International Workers Order, 35

H. Eugene and Lillian Youngs Lehman Series

LAMAR CECIL, *Wilhelm II: Prince and Emperor, 1859–1900* (1989).

CAROLYN MERCHANT, *Ecological Revolutions: Nature, Gender, and Science in New England* (1989).

GLADYS ENGEL LANG AND KURT LANG, *Etched in Memory: The Building and Survival of Artistic Reputation* (1990).

HOWARD JONES, *Union in Peril: The Crisis over British Intervention in the Civil War* (1992).

ROBERT L. DORMAN, *Revolt of the Provinces: The Regionalist Movement in America* (1993).

PETER N. STEARNS, *Meaning Over Memory: Recasting the Teaching of Culture and History* (1993).

THOMAS WOLFE, *The Good Child's River*, edited with an introduction by Suzanne Stutman (1994).

WARREN A. NORD, *Religion and American Education: Rethinking a National Dilemma* (1995).

DAVID E. WHISNANT, *Rascally Signs in Sacred Places: The Politics of Culture in Nicaragua* (1995).

LAMAR CECIL, *Wilhelm II: Emperor and Exile, 1900–1941* (1996).

JONATHAN HARTLYN, *The Struggle for Democratic Politics in the Dominican Republic* (1998).

LOUIS A. PÉREZ JR., *On Becoming Cuban: Identity, Nationality, and Culture* (1999).

YAAKOV ARIEL, *Evangelizing the Chosen People: Missions to the Jews in America, 1880–2000* (2000).

PHILIP F. GURA, *C. F. Martin and His Guitars, 1796–1873* (2003).

LOUIS A. PÉREZ JR., *To Die in Cuba: Suicide and Society* (2005).

PETER FILENE, *The Joy of Teaching: A Practical Guide for New College Instructors* (2005).

JOHN CHARLES BOGER AND GARY ORFIELD, eds., *School Resegregation: Must the South Turn Back?* (2005).

JOCK LAUTERER, *Community Journalism: Relentlessly Local* (2006).

MICHAEL H. HUNT, *The American Ascendancy: How the United States Gained and Wielded Global Dominance* (2007).

MICHAEL LIENESCH, *In the Beginning: Fundamentalism, the Scopes Trial, and the Making of the Antievolution Movement* (2007).

ERIC L. MULLER, *American Inquisition: The Hunt for Japanese American Disloyalty in World War II* (2007).

JOHN MCGOWAN, *American Liberalism: An Interpretation for Our Time* (2007).

NORTIN M. HADLER, M.D., *Worried Sick: A Prescription for Health in an Overtreated America* (2008).

WILLIAM FERRIS, *Give My Poor Heart Ease: Voices of the Mississippi Blues* (2009).

COLIN A. PALMER, *Cheddi Jagan and the Politics of Power: British Guiana's Struggle for Independence* (2010).

W. FITZHUGH BRUNDAGE, *Beyond Blackface: African Americans and the Creation of American Mass Culture, 1890–1930* (2011).

MICHAEL H. HUNT AND STEVEN I. LEVINE, *Arc of Empire: America's Wars in Asia from the Philippines to Vietnam* (2012).

NORTIN M. HADLER, M.D., *The Citizen Patient: Reforming Health Care for the Sake of the Patient, Not the System* (2013).

LOUIS A. PÉREZ JR., *The Structure of Cuban History: Meanings and Purpose of the Past* (2013).

JENNIFER THIGPEN, *Island Queens and Mission Wives: How Gender and Empire Remade Hawai'i's Pacific World* (2014).

GEORGE W. HOUSTON, *Inside Roman Libraries: Book Collections and Their Management in Antiquity* (2014).

PHILIP F. GURA, *The Life of William Apess, Pequot* (2015).

DANIEL M. COBB, ed., *Say We Are Nations: Documents of Politics and Protest in Indigenous America since 1887* (2015).

DANIEL MAUDLIN AND BERNARD L. HERMAN, eds., *Building the British Atlantic World: Spaces, Places, and Material Culture, 1600–1850* (2016).

WILLIAM FERRIS, *The South in Color: A Visual Journal* (2016).

LISA A. LINDSAY, *Atlantic Bonds: A Nineteenth-Century Odyssey from America to Africa* (2017).

MARY ELIZABETH BASILE CHOPAS, *Searching for Subversives: The Story of Italian Internment in Wartime America* (2017).